SMOKE IN THE LANES

"The life of travellers . . . is a communal life lived to its fullest extent."

SMOKE
IN THE LANES

by

DOMINIC REEVE

Illustrated by Beshlie

UNIVERSITY OF HERTFORDSHIRE PRESS

First published by Constable & Co, Ltd, in 1958

This edition published in Great Britain in 2003 by
University of Hertfordshire Press
Learning and Information Services
University of Hertfordshire
College Lane
Hatfield,
Hertfordshire AL10 9AB

ISBN 1 902806 24 7 paper back

British Library Cataloguing in Publication Data
A catalogue record for this book is available from the British Library.

Cover design based on a painting by Beshlie

Printed in Great Britain by
Antony Rowe Ltd, Chippenham SN14 6LH

CONTENTS

ILLUSTRATIONS

TO BESHLIE

"When we stop travelling, the first thing in mind
It's tent-rods and ridge-poles we now got to find.
We tied the old pony's legs, and away he did go.
Where shall we find him? The Lord only knows.
We got up next morning, and sarched all around.
Where did we find him? We found him in pound.
We *jalled* to the old *rai*, and what did he say?
Pack up your old trap, and clear right away!"

FOREWORD

I am neither an academic nor a man of letters but I
do possess a lifetime's knowledge and experience
of the 'Affairs of Little Egypt' and it gives me
great pleasure to have been asked to write this
forward. I have known Dominic and his wife Beshlie
(who has provided the evocative illustrations to the
books) for well over thirty years and since that first
meeting of like minds beside a yog on a bitterly cold
January afternoon I have always held a great respect
and admiration for them both.

Those who have read Dominic's books will know
that he is no ordinary writer. His keen observation,
wit and dedication to a unique way of life make those
books an unrivalled account of the period—the
tail-end of wagon time. Dominic Reeve, like myself,
learnt early on that the Romany way of life is
frequently a far from romantic one and Dominic
writes his books with no holds barred. No other
person has written about Gypsy life in quite the same
way because, unlike Dominic, no other writer has
spent a lifetime living it. Even the most renowned
Romany Rais merely dipped in and out of the
lifestyle. Dominic writes from personal, first-hand
experience—unlike many of today's armchair 'gypsy
scholars'. These gypsiologists, though they may think
they know about Gypsy people don't, for how many

of these people are invited, like Dominic, to Gypsy weddings, christening and funerals, and have had children named after them? Mention practically any Gypsy family living in Great Britain today and Dominic's knowledge of the family tree goes back several generations. Dominic Reeve is the Romany Rai of all Rais and has always been looked upon with great respect by travelling people for his ability to better himself and his possessions and to change with the times.

There are many who still hold an unrealistic view of the Traveller lifestyle and Dominic has always shown how erroneous the romantic notion of a free-living colourful people is; yet what shines through in his books is the winning spirit of an outcast race of people, subjected to the constant harassment and persecution of the house-dweller and officialdom. Some have questioned the veracity of Dominic's books. I have before me a Gypsy Lore Society review of Dominic's last book which ludicrously states that the people portrayed within its pages 'were not real Romanies...' and the '...conversation loaded with expletives and indecent allusions to their own grandmothers [which he records] is not part of their ordinary peaceful conversation'. All unschooled nomadic peoples have a somewhat truncated but 'poetic' vocabulary where feelings, thoughts and emotions are expressed simply and succinctly. I too travelled with the same verbally exuberant families in the lanes of Dorset, Wiltshire and Somerset in the mid 1960s. If these people were not real Gypsies, then the Pope is not and has never been Catholic!

Today any of the old travelling families, to survive and prosper, have become rather like an iceberg, a little of the Gypsiness showing (to those in the know), the rest residing beneath the surface. Travelling people still maintain a love of the open fire and the kettle prop, of a good horse and the drama of life, but these days the only people with horses and caravans—with a few exceptions—are new-agers aping the Gypsy lifestyle, few of whom would be able to recognise a Gypsy face if they saw one. "What a shame Gypsies don't still live in horse-drawn caravans," people often say to me. Well, they no longer live in a house with an outside loo or have to draw and carry home water from the village pump anymore, native American Indians don't live permanently in teepees, and the only stagecoach we ever see these days is on television. Travellers have progressed just as the rest of society has progressed, and their lives have improved immeasurably as a consequence.

Dominic has been documenting a way of life that has now all but vanished—the like of which will never be seen again—and he has stayed the course, still chopping and changing motors every year as is his want. Now, progressing into his youthful autumn years, he still spins a good yarn with that same twinkle in the eye and he has kept me laughing with his quick wit, enviable powers of mimicry and uncanny perception throughout the years that I have had the luck to know him. He is still independently earning a living day-by-day, travelling and living the life that he loves—a brave thing to do in an age when the pressures to conform have become stronger than ever.

Smoke in the Lanes, originally published in 1958, set out to show the travelling life as it was then; *No Place Like Home*, with a forward by Augustus John, followed in 1960 and concentrated upon one winter's travel while *Whichever Way We Turn*, published four years later, portrayed the move from the horse-drawn to the horse-powered way of life.

Dominic Reeve's incredibly important books are a history of *our* times; describing a way of life that is as much a part of this country's heritage as the age of steam or sail.

Peter Ingram
Founder of the Romany Folklore Museum
Selborne, 2002

INTRODUCTION

Few Open Roads

Few Open Roads

TO the Romani, depending upon his own geographical location, England is divided into two parts: 'up the country' and 'down the country'. The inhabitants he divides even more sharply as between Romanies or 'travellers' (who may even lead a sedentary life, the blood being the deciding factor) and the rest: non-Romanies or 'non-travellers'—the *gaujes*.

The world of the travelling people is, to a very large extent, a secret world of well-defined habits and traditions. It is built up on intricate patterns of family relationships, and so conservative is it that the majority of travellers move about only over their own territories, scarcely covering any 'strange country' in the course of a lifetime. Yet such travellers often go unrecognised by the *gaujes* in whose districts they have spent all their lives. This is due in part to constant changes of wagons and horses, and in part to strong 'family resemblances', for to a greater or lesser extent most Romanies are in-bred, first cousins often 'going together' for several generations. Different members of each family usually have the same roads and their routes stretch from place to place like rabbit runs, crossing here and there on to other travellers' territories. There are, of course, a few exceptions— travellers who have longer and more varied routes which

13

sometimes stretch over three and four counties, but this is comparatively rare and only happens when they have travelled with families other than their own. But should a well-meaning *gaujo* inquire of a traveller where his paths lie he will almost invariably be met with the vastly exaggerated reply: "Why, sir, I gits about all over the country, sir. From one end to t'other, sir."

As a part-Romani only—taken away from the roads in childhood, drawn back in early manhood—my life is perhaps more fundamentally complex than that of most other travellers, the majority of whom have known only one form of existence. And so, for good or bad, I am able to appreciate—if not approve of—the distaste felt and expressed by so many *gaujes* for our people's rough wagons and for the straggling, noisy, litter-strewn encampments on the roadsides or in their lanes. But though our presence may breed a feeling of dislike, suspicion and unease, such feelings are more than returned by both the adults and the children of our camps. For whilst the *gaujes* sit in the safety and comfort of their homes, plotting ways to see that we are moved on again, we *wait*, living always on our nerves, waiting for the arrival of the inevitable policeman or farmer to force our departure—sometimes from two or even three places in one day. It is then that the traveller's life is hard and unenviable. The *gavmush may* not arrive for two or three days, but his *eventual* appearance is inevitable, and it is the uncertainty which preys on us all, causing us to be always on the alert, aware that by our very way of living we are almost certainly breaking some small by-law or rule. We have, it is true, few responsibilities, but the popular conception of the carefree quality of the 'open road' is not for us.

Innocent but well-meaning souls periodically inquire whether we travel during the winter months as well as in the summer. That is a sad question; sad because, as every traveller is only too well aware, stopping-places where one may remain unmolested for even a week or two are hard enough to find; and it is virtually impossible to find a permanent resting-place for the whole winter. There are places of which Romanies optimistically and with misplaced confidence say, 'You can bide there till you'm grey-headed,' but even these rarely allow of a stay of more than three weeks at the outside. Except when snow is falling we continue moving all through the year. The most depressing of climatic conditions, without doubt, are the winter spells of rain. Then mud is our enemy. Once it gets on the boots it is caught by the trouser leg or skirt hem and, like a foul disease, it spreads, gradually working its way all over one's body. It finds its way into anything that is put down on the ground: into the water-carriers, the kettles, into the food-hamper, and all over the harness. It covers the coats of the dogs, matting and discolouring them, cakes itself on the feathers of the bantams, and causes a great melancholy to descend upon all livestock except pigs! It seeps up into the wagon, and even on to the bedding, driving the oldest and hardiest travellers into a mood of profanity and great sorrow. Beshlie, with whom I travel the roads of the south counties of England and who is a non-Romani and possesses a great love of prettiness and colour, finds it more distressing than do most of our people.

During wet spells a move may be an act of escape rather than an act of necessity. On some such wretched occasions as these our wagon may have sunk almost to the axles when we have been stopping on soft spongy ground, and then our horse has had to heave and strain to shift the wagon from the clinging grasp of mud and water, hauling us out at last, splashed and cold, on to the hard road. I have known wagon locks to snap under such pressure —the horse and shafts leaping forward, leaving the wagon still firmly embedded in the mud. Travellers *should* learn by such experiences—but few do. Pull-ins are too scarce for one to be over-fastidious about their condition. It is all part of the façade of bravado and boastfulness which most Romanies erect in connection with the staying power of their horses and the solidity of their wagons. Other people's horses may be 'dead-napskins', refusing to pull out of soft places and liable to fall. Other people's wagons may stick fast or break up. But their's—never! It is, of course, a fallacy, and one for which I have fallen as badly as anyone else.

Whether one is travelling in a group with other wagons and families or whether one is on one's own, the problem of living—and of making a living—is with us all the time. One of the great paradoxes of the life of the traveller is that although he is usually less likely to be moved-on if he can find a remote and isolated stopping-place where his presence may go unnoticed, it is nevertheless essential that he should stop fairly close to other human habitations in order that the women may go out hawking. For this, built-up areas are preferable. Scattered houses are of little use for 'calling', as for every one householder who likes, or may buy from, Romanies, there are ten who hate or distrust us and will turn us away.

I frequently experience considerable rudeness and abuse when calling at houses—very often before I have even been given the opportunity of stating the nature of my visit. Doors have been slammed in my face, dogs set on me, and I have been threatened with the police. It is very depressing. The Romani today is undoubtedly on the lowest rung of society's ladder, and people who have climbed a rung or two higher dislike them intensely. It is these prejudices, and the difficulties they cause, that drive so many Romani men when out 'ragging' or scrap-collecting to avoid the colourful appendages to the traditional traveller's costume. And so the earrings and bright neckerchiefs have now largely disappeared, except round the camp-fire or on Sundays or at fairs. Not all the men, of course, have given up wearing these things—I have not myself—but the exceptions are *usually* those who do not engage in any 'calling' themselves, leaving such occupations to their sons or wives.

Life for us passes swiftly; evenly in its manner, un-evenly in its surroundings. Our wagon and our animals are all that stand for home. The stopping-places are transient, to be judged according to their provision of wood or grazing and, for Beshlie and me, who are more fastidious than some, by their degree of privacy and seclusion. Many travellers, however, fear isolation and remoteness; they worry for fear of 'ghosties' and of 'lonely ole places'. Many are the 'children of nature' riddled with superstition and archaic beliefs, who crave a security they will never know. And they stay in groups, for ever fearing loneliness.

As a part-Romani only—and therefore, by rights, assigned to the ignominious ranks of the *diddikais*—I am by

17

instinct and inclination drawn to the ways and to the life of the travelling people. Yet, at the same time, the *gaujo* part of me rebels and discriminates against the raggle-taggle, senselessly unmethodical ways in which the travellers conduct their lives.

One of the commonest accusations levelled against travellers—and one which brings down much un-necessary wrath on their own heads—is that they have a habit of leaving their regular stopping-places littered with every conceivable kind of rubbish—old tins, rags, bottles, old iron, bicycle frames, prams, bits of harness, and even old wagons. But this, I fear, is simply due to a complete lack of æsthetic values, a primitive outlook in fast-moving times, and it is unlikely that it will ever be remedied. It is part of the unseeing, unminding, rough, coarse outlook which must have been evident in London and other large towns at the time of the plague. This is brought into still sharper relief today by the nation's phobia for tidiness and neatness which, if carried to ex-tremes, may prove more depressing than the rougher, less methodical ways of the past. But when we are stopping in company with a lot of other travellers I am forced to admit that a stopping-place fouled with rubbish, decay-ing food and human excreta—always left uncovered behind the nearest hedge or bush—is hardly either romantic or healthy. It is mainly for these reasons, and because large encampments are terribly noisy, that Beshlie and I do not remain at *all* times with other travellers, often preferring to be on our own.

On the other hand, of course, it is the travellers' com-plete inability to absorb change or new ideas in any form that has kept them true to their traditional existence—a life within a life; and it is often their very clinging to the past, and to many of the worst kinds of bygone superstitions and beliefs, that causes them to be so scorned, disliked and even feared today.

Often, when we have been stopping with others, squatting round the fire in the evening half-light with the heavy ominous shapes of the wagons as a backcloth, my glance has passed round my companions, noting their dark seamed faces, their glittering eyes and their mat clothing. With the conversation flying to and fro in guttural spasmodic gusts and with the insanity that is present in so many travellers briefly leaping into view, I have seen the reason for fear. I have listened to tiny children, hand-rolled cigarettes clutched in their fingers, cursing one another roundly or making observations that would be well calculated to shock even a barrackroom audience by its frankness concerning human relationships. I have listened to such talk so long and so often that it now seems quite unremarkable, and I have realised that *basically* it cannot matter. Fear is out of place, and the only way in which the company can affect us personally—and that is true of *any* travellers—is the difficulty which confronts Beshlie when she tries to concentrate on her illustration work.

The life of travellers is *completely* devoid of privacy in any form. It is a communal life lived to its fullest extent. The individualist cannot wholly admire the life as in it no true individuality exists for him to admire. Everyone is part of a larger family pattern. Perhaps it is partly this factor which appears to have discouraged *gaujes* from ever *really* taking to the life. In all my years on the roads I have not once encountered a person without a trace of Romani blood living and *travelling* permanently with a horse-drawn wagon. There are a few romantics who live in Romani caravans, often on sites for which they pay rent, and there are even a few people who go away for brief holidays with horse-drawn vans—but they do not really count. Theirs is the life of the dilettante and it is untrue and false.

Few house-dwellers can comprehend the sacrifices that such an existence entails—particularly to a completely non-Romani like Beshlie. We have not entered a theatre or cinema for eight years. We can very rarely both leave the wagon at the same time, unless we are staying with other travellers. We have no television—and have only recently acquired a wireless, having been without one for two years. As we are constantly moving we are unable to patronise laundries; and we have no amenities at all—no wash-basins, sinks, or running-water. All water has to be carried, sometimes for considerable distances and often from rather dubious cattle-troughs. We can entertain only other travellers or crankish friends of hardy disposition and physique who regard an evening in mid-February spent in the open around a camp-fire as exhilarating—and such are rare! In common with most other travellers I have not had a bath for as many years as I can remember. But the reader need not worry unduly about this: the skin scales off naturally, and this process, combined with fairly frequent changes of clothing, proves entirely adequate. I might also mention the lack of sanitary arrangements which, although no worry, can cause some discomfort in very chilly weather.

The great point is that in a life which might, to the uninitiated, seem boring and slow, the one shortage is *time*. We are for ever fighting time, and even more fiercely during the winter months when so much activity has to be crammed in between the long hours of darkness. The very essentials of living—wooding, water-fetching, harness maintenance, wagon repairs, looking after the horses—demand an enormous amount of time, all these processes take in the aggregate hours from the day. And these chores are secondary to the actual business of travelling about and endeavouring at the same time to earn sufficient money to keep alive. The years spin by with astounding rapidity, our calendar being mainly marked by the gradually-diminishing horse-sales and fairs.

Often, as we survey our few personal possessions—few of necessity thanks to the eternal battle against carrying excess weight in any form lest the wagon should be too great a load for a horse to pull—we realise that, even in our small world, much is set against our way of life and against that of all travelling people. Yet we are the last links with independence and self-sufficiency in an over-organised country. Shuffling along our own courses, we elude to a great extent the tentacles of officialdom which seek to enclose everyone within their grasp, plotting their lives by standards and times and dates. We are free from many futilities, from the 'eleven-plus' examination to National Service and from thence to the Old-Age Pension—tabbed and indexed all the way.

Freedom, we are told, is every man's heritage—yet how few achieve it and how few exploit it.

PART ONE

Roadside Eastertide

'Vizes Fair

PART ONE

Roadside Eastertide

1

BESHLIE and I had been moving steadily for some weeks, savouring with great joy the early spring days; for that is probably the pleasantest period of the year for our people, with new and plentiful grass for the horses and with the chill of winter gradually losing its hold. We were in a corner of Wiltshire hitherto unknown to us and, with the hazards of unknown hills and slippery roads ahead of us, the going was a little difficult, especially as we had met no other travelling-people for over a week from whom to ask directions about roads suitable for our mode of transport. Our plan was to fill in time for a few weeks until Devizes Spring Fair in mid-April. It was, however, unwise to travel too close to the town until immediately before the Fair as the district round Devizes was notoriously inhospitable to Romanies.

It was the Thursday prior to Good Friday and we were nearing the small town of Trowbridge. Suddenly the mare's ears pricked and I saw a tiny governess cart, drawn by a little fast-trotting, odd-coloured pony, approaching us from the opposite direction. As it drew closer we could distinguish two Romani women seated in it; and as it came closer still we saw that they were quite young, one very dark skinned with black hair, the other fairer. Their hair was in braids and bright silver rings flashed on their fingers. Two large hawking baskets filled with pegs were also in the little tub-cart, and they were on their way out to a neighbourhood in which to hawk them. The fairer woman, who was driving, pulled the pony to a halt almost beside our wagon, and I jumped down from the footboard and walked over to speak to them.

"How you gittin' on?" asked the black woman, her eyes scanning our turn-out with interest.

They were strangers to me—as I was to them.

"Ain't too bad," I replied, returning their curious gaze. "What's this country like for *'atchin'tans*?"

" 'Tis terrible country, brother," answered the fairer one, her voice harsh and rough. "The *gavvers*'ll run you to death."

"Is it as bad as it is around 'Vizes?" I inquired.

"Wusser," replied the black woman, smiling.

"These Wiltshire police are bad, they won't let you stop anywhere," I remarked. "Is this your country or are you waiting for the Fair, like us?"

"You'm right—that's wot we'm a-hangin' about fer," agreed the black woman. "Cah! This ain't my country—'tis a terrible ole place to bide in. There ain't no places to stop, man."

"Which part is you from?" asked the fair one.

"Devon, Somerset—down that part mostly," I said.

"I ain't never bin down that country, though I've heerd some of me delations talk of it. Nice ole country, ain't it?"

"Parts of it are," I said. "How many are there of you stopping together now?"

"There's me sister, here," said the black woman,

26

nodding at her companion, "an' there's four other *verdos* along of us besides."

"By the road?" I asked.

"Yeah, just agin the road on a wide green. Why don't you come an' have a day or two 'long wi' us?"

" 'Twould be a bit o' compny fer you, wouldn't it?" murmured the fair one, putting into words the eternal fear of all Romanies—the fear of being left alone.

"Yes, all right, we'll have a day or two with you," I agreed, for we had been alone for a long time. "How do you get to where you're stopping?"

"We'm agin the Bratton wide-roads—anyone'll tell you where we'm to."

"But *you* tell me," I insisted, "then I can't go wrong. This is strange country to me." For I knew from experience how difficult it can be to locate other travellers when one is on strange roads.

" 'Tis easy to foller," said the black one. "Why, you goes on down this road, an' right on through the town till you comes to the stop-an'-go lights. Then you turns right there an' keeps a-goin' till you gits to the cross. An' then you goes straight over the cross an' turns left-handed an' keeps straight the way on till you comes to the public called 'The Black Bull.' Then jest past the public there's a dee-little road wot turns off to the right— an' iffen you follers him on fer 'bout half a mile you'll see the wagons on yer left hand. Why 'tis easy to git there, brother. 'Tain't above three miles away, ain't that the truth, Polly?"

Her sister nodded in agreement, and they ran through the entire directions again lest we had not fixed them firmly in our heads.

"We'll see you later. *Kushti bok!*" called the black one and they drove off.

I re-crossed the road, climbed back on the footboard and we started once more towards Trowbridge. The narrow streets of the little town were packed with traffic, and the pavements were overflowing with people scurrying in and out of the shops, trying to complete their Easter shopping. Luckily it is a flat town and so we were not bothered and hindered by steep gradients or other difficulties unknown to the motorist. I led the mare steadily through the town centre, our presence causing no little astonishment to other road users and to pedestrians—to most of whom the sound of a horse's hooves was but a fading memory. We scraped through between two enormous motor-vans, parked opposite each other in the narrow main street, missing one by perhaps the greater part of an inch. However, unscathed if somewhat shattered in spirit, we gradually emerged from the worst of the town and began to attempt to follow the instructions we had been given. Eventually we neared our destination—or so we thought—and saw a sign-post pointing to Bratton. The post did not coincide exactly with the directions given us by the black woman. Deciding, however, that she had probably made a mistake we determined to follow the direction of the sign-post. All went well for some time. Then, on turning a sharp bend in the road, we suddenly found ourselves at the foot of a steep, glass-surfaced hill, stretching skywards ahead of us.

Beshlie was for retracing our steps to the town's outskirts to take the other road. But it was noon and I had no wish to go back over ground we had already covered.

"We'll get up it," I shouted optimistically.

We dropped the wooden roller down so that it hung, dragging in readiness, behind the outer rear wheel; and then we set off up the incline. The mare climbed willingly until we were about half-way to the crest, though she sweated profusely in the hot sun. Then she slowed, her hooves slipping and slithering in an effort to retain a grip on the smooth surface. I quickly slewed the wagon right across the road and tried zig-zagging back and forth across its full breadth. Once . . . twice . . . then on the third crossing, the gradient increasing, the mare's forefeet slipped in turn and she was only just able to regain her feet. She was almost down on her knees before I managed to jerk her on to her feet and bring her to a standstill.

"We'll never get up—the surface is too bad," I shouted to Beshlie, myself sweating with tension and exertion. Hardly had I spoken when a large furniture removal van came down the hill and stopped beside us. Out jumped five men.

"This is a bad hill, horses never come up here," one of them said.

"We're strangers here," I answered, "and we weren't expecting this one."

"We'll give you a push. Have another try," urged the man.

So the five stationed themselves against the wagon's back and sides, ready to heave. I started the mare forwards and, her eyes rolling slightly, we moved slowly upwards, gradually and steadily, until we had reached the crest. So five strong and generous men had done what a 'sider' pony would have accomplished. A 'sider' pony, as its name implies, is an extra pony which is harnessed alongside the horse in the shafts of a wagon to assist in drawing the load up excessively steep hills. Unfortunately, our own 'sider' had recently been killed, and at this time we had not the money to buy another. Therefore, thanking the five men sincerely, we continued somewhat shakily upon our way—discovering to our chagrin that we could have missed out the bad hill entirely had we followed the original directions given to us by the black woman. Our goal lay about three-quarters of a mile further on.

Suddenly and unexpectedly the greater part of a hunt, both horses and hounds, trotted round a bend towards us and we were engulfed in their midst. Several of the tall graceful hunters reared in fright at the sight of our small equipage, and their immaculate riders had to use all their skill in horsemanship to pass us successfully and without loss of dignity. Some of the hunt members gazed balefully at us, not altogether pleased, we felt, to see anyone else using a horse on the roads.

A short distance further and the road surface changed, and we were able to discern the tell-tale trails left by iron-bonded wheels. The numbers of the trails, crossing and overlapping each other, showed that many vehicles had recently passed that way. The marks made by wheels vary, of course, according to the material of the road and according to the amount of other traffic which uses it. The rubber tyres of motor vehicles act in much the same way as an eraser on paper, and it is not always possible to judge correctly the time that has elapsed since the tracks were made. However, practice in this purely Romani necessity greatly aids one's accuracy.

These tracks, it was clear, were not old and we could follow them easily. Soon we noticed the public-house,

'The Black Bull,' and passing it, we drove on for about fifty yards. We then turned to the right down a narrow, little-used road that appeared to be acting mainly as a short-cut from one hamlet to another. It was bordered by wide grass verges flush with the lane's surface, and it was therefore easy for the wagons to pull off the road. There were tall hedges separating the verges from the fields and the lane wound snakily along. However, our ears were our guides, for we could gradually distinguish spasmodic bursts of singing, shouts, barks, screams from children, and occasionally the faint hollow note of an inferior gramophone. We knew that the travellers were close by.

Rounding the next bend, we came upon the straggling encampment. Along the grass verge were strung out six wagons, three or four trolleys, and three tiny pony traps, while tethered at intervals along the opposite hedgerow were close on a dozen horses and ponies of all shades of colour and varying in size from the tiny to large thick vanner cobs. Several cross-bred dogs chained under the wagons began barking loudly and a swarm of children ran out to greet us—only to draw back in fright as Naylor, our Great Dane, growled and boomed menacingly at them.

"Cah! Ain't he a gurt *jukel!*" shouted a small dark boy with long ragged black hair, adding awestruck: "Do 'e bite, mush?"

"Certainly he does," I replied, and advised them not to come too close to the wagon.

"Cah! He'm an ole beardy mush, like me Uncle 'Lijah," I heard one small girl exclaim on perceiving my stubble-covered features.

31

I pulled the mare to a halt just before we reached the first wagon, which I rightly judged to belong to the black woman and her man. It was a tall lantern-roofed van—of the type that is known to Romanies as a 'skylight *verdo*'—and it had the most intricately carved underworks that I had ever seen in southern England, for it was made up entirely of carved horses' heads, flowers, and horse-shoes; a work which must have cost the woodworker many months of labour. The wheels were yellow-painted, picked out in red; and their appearance was further enhanced by delightful archaic bell-shaped brass hubs—which have mostly, unfortunately, disappeared from the wagons in use today. It had been a fine ornate wagon, made probably during the rococo period of Victorian England—when exotic vans were produced whose over-ornate finish seemed to add so greatly to the romanticism of the 'gypsies.' These wagons, together with the colour of their occupants (who were themselves so often clad in a vivid array of Victorian ladies' cast-off clothing), served to spark off the flame of the super-romantic illusion with which so many artists and writers have since invested the Romanies. Nowadays, when such vehicles are neither made nor obtainable, the poor travelling people in lesser wagons are unendingly and unflatteringly compared with "the gypsies I remember when I was a child." Yet I have never heard any *gauji* woman drawing such comparisons or suggesting that her own or her neighbour's modern home or apparel is unlike that of her grandmother.

Romanies have, for centuries, *monged* most of their clothing; and it is only their *way* of wearing clothes, plus a tendency to be fifty years behind the current fashions by inclination (women, for example, in very long skirts;

men wearing neckerchiefs instead of ties, etc.), that distinguishes them from the *gaujo*. Thus, logically, as current fashions become less exotic so, in consequence, the Romanies receive less interesting garments when *monging*. It would be an error, however, to assume that Romanies do not either appreciate or like *good* clothes and fine materials. Indeed, most men of the race are quite dandified in their own way, and are very proud of their headgear and scarves—or any particularly pleasant garment which comes their way. Only recently I was lucky enough to have a very fine riding jacket presented to me as a gift. When I returned to the encampment it was much admired, and bids of more than five pounds were immediately made for it.

Many of the older men, of course, with more money to spend, frequently have their trousers made in the old-fashioned way, with pipe-stem legs, raised seams, and fall-fronts. Such trousers are much esteemed, and I know from experience that they are very fine. Nowadays I always have my nether garments tailored for me in that manner.

The black woman and her man were sitting by their fire in front of the van. The man, slight, pinch-faced and shifty-eyed, was making pegs.

"You found us out, then," remarked the black woman, smiling. "Why don't you draw-in behind us there?" And she pointed towards the back of her van.

"Yeah, we found you out—but we only just made it," I replied, ignoring the last part of her statement and explaining our difficulties on the hill.

"O my blessed Jesus!" she exclaimed. "You come up Ironmonger's Hill? *Dordi*, you took the wrong road, brother. Why didn't you goo the ways wot we told you?"

33

"Fairish ole pull up that hill," commented the man, rolling a cigarette, his eyes darting about our wagon and horse.

"Ain't a bad sort've an ole mare you've got there," he continued without showing too much approval. "I've a-got one tied up along there," he gestured down the lane, "that I might chop fer her, iffen you've a mind to have a deal."

And he deftly continued drawing lengths of hazel wood up and down against the steadily-held peg-knife supported against his knee, paring off the bark in long clean slithers, preparatory to cutting them into lengths for the actual pegs. This paring of the hazel *koshties* is known as *chinning* and is accomplished with a razor-sharp knife which is generally made from the blade of an old kitchen-knife mounted in a wooden handle. The *koshties* are cut on a tiny block, sunk in the ground, with a knife which is struck by a wooden mallet. Contrary to the belief and knowledge of most *gaujes* a small measuring-stick is held—invisibly—in the hand during the cutting of each peg length—thus the uniformity of size is due to that rather than to the 'hawk-like' eyesight and judgment as has been recorded by certain writers. Peg-making is largely a family business, each member doing his or her part in order to run up sufficient numbers to make the job worth while at all. At least a gross should be made in the hour.

Returning to his question, "She's not for trade," I answered firmly, for she was a mare that we had grown very fond of and she was sound, quiet and willing.

The other wagons were all canvas-topped 'open lots,' one being nothing more than a flat trolley with an old canvas sheet thrown clumsily over long hazel-rod hoops, quite open at the front. Another was long and low, tunnel-like, with a vivid Red Indianish jagged design painted along its sides, the whole being on tiny frail wheels. The rest were more usual and much superior—open lots with wooden fronts and backs, each painted in fairly bright colours which had grown shabby. The general effect, however, was not of colour but rather of shabbiness and neglect—and this equally applied to the wagons' owners, whose smoke-yellowed faces, ragged, grimy clothes and rough unkempt appearance made them brigand-like of aspect and more villainous-looking than any other southern travellers I had ever seen.

I led the mare up on to the verge and placed the wagon about fifteen feet away from the black woman's, with its back to hers. We quickly unhitched the mare, removed her harness and hung it on the side of the wagon. Next I attached the tethering chain round her neck, and hammered in the stake a chain's length from our wagon. The dogs were tied underneath the van. I then began pulling dead sticks from the hedgerow, hastening to light the fire, for we had had nothing to eat that day and it was nearly three o'clock.

A few of the children still stood watching and questioning us a little, but they were mostly called away when it was seen that we were going to have a meal.

"Mush!" called the black woman's husband, whose name was Samson. "Come and take a bit o' fire."

I followed up his suggestion in order to save time and effort, and carried a flaming brand from their fire and placed it amongst some small dry twigs which I had ready. In a few minutes the fire was blazing readily and the kettle was hanging on the crane amidst the leaping flames. We had luckily taken the precaution of filling our water-carrier at a friendly cottager's well that morning, so that I was saved the extra task of having to find water.

Beshlie quickly plucked and cleaned two wood-pigeons that I had shot with a catapult the previous day, and dropped them into the stew-pot, with some rice, potatoes and a few onions. I tossed a lump of bread and some bones under the wagon for the two dogs, who were becoming somewhat restive at the sight and sound of so many other dogs.

I built up a large fire and the stew-pot's contents were soon cooked, and even more quickly eaten. Soon after we had finished and had rubbed over the greasy plates with a rag—water being too scarce—several of the travellers came up to our *yog* and joined us, squatting in a circle round its heat. After some little conversation I discovered that three of the women and at least four of the men were closely related to Romanies whom I knew well, and with whom we had often travelled.

A tiny triangular-faced woman, whose piercing eyes seemed to hang over her cheekbones and whose features were framed in flat braided hair parted in the centre in a wavering line, discovered that her sister Eldorai, whom she had not seen for five years, had often spoken of me when last they met.

"Me sister Eldi, wot I ain't a-seed these last five years, said about yous. An' ain't she got the wagon wot used to be yourn?"

"That's right," I agreed. "I sold it to a *gaujo* for eighty pounds, and then they bought it from him about a year later."

"There now! Weren't it right wot I tole you?" And she thumped her man's arm vehemently. "How *is* me sister, young man?"

"Well, I think," I replied. "But I haven't seen her for about three months. She's got another son, don't you know?"

"Wot?" exclaimed the little woman, Caroline, in great excitement. "I never heerd that. Why 'tis eleven year since she had her last *chavi*."

And she turned to a fair-haired but leathery-skinned woman sitting beside her and began a long discourse on the peculiarities of her sister's erratic child-bearing.

"Will that dog bite?" asked a tall young man in a torn cap with tufts of black hair protruding from it.

I assured him that he would.

"I wouldn't keep a dog like that—no, not fer a hundred pun," advised little Caroline, buttoning her ragged green coat up to her throat with a silver-ringed hand. "Why, mush, iffen he wuz to bite anyone you'd be *lelled* (in this case, fined) fer sure."

"And I wouldn't part with him fer a hundred pun," I rejoined.

Besides our tiny aged Griffon, Mossy, we normally have two or three other larger dogs—either Great Danes, like Naylor, greyhounds, or sometimes Alsatians or Alsatian-cross retrievers or a similar guard-dog. These larger dogs live permanently beneath the wagon as watch-dogs and companions. Once we have trained them to be guards, and to be fully obedient in every way, we allow them their freedom except at nights when they are chained. We have owned many wagon dogs in our time, and we generally like to buy them when they are only

37

about six weeks old. Having them so young, we have found—if they have the right temperament—that they will prove themselves to be good watchdogs by the time they are three months old. Our own experience has generally taught us not to keep a puppy which has shown no signs of pugnacity by that age.

"How long is we gwin bide yere?" Caroline's man, Nelson, asked inconsequentially.

"Well, we ain't had no one come to us yet—an' we'll bide here till they do!" Samson announced firmly.

A very ancient woman shuffled up to us at this point. I was told that she was the mother of the dangerous-looking, badger-like man whom Beshlie and I nick-named Fangs but whose real name was Luke. She was Old Hannah. Her gaunt bent form was swathed in an old-fashioned black 'pinna,' button-boots adorned her feet, and a yellow silk scarf, low over her forehead, almost obscured coils of fine tawny-orange hair, un-greyed despite her age which was generally estimated to be well over eighty. I knew many of her sons and daughters— she had had eighteen children—and also two of her sisters. Her voice, however, had been affected by a stroke some years before, and this caused her utterances to be slurred and indeed often incoherent except to those who knew her well. Frequent mocking at her expense, combined with many requests to repeat most of her remarks more clearly, had caused her temper to become distinctly uncertain.

Her son remarked loudly to me: "She talks like she'm *motto*, so 'tis no good to talk to her, ain't that right, Mother?"

"My bloody God, you poxy bastard!" exclaimed his

mother like one shouting through a blanket. "I'll lay me stick about yer head—you nose-and-a-half!"

And she moved unsteadily and aggressively in his direction to his great mirth.

I hastily intervened and gave her an old tin to sit on, offering her a cup of tea.

"Thank you, young man," she said primly, adding, "I've a-seed you somewheres before—wot family is you?"

I told her my family and inquired whether she knew my parts of country.

"No, young man, I don't know that country," she answered. "But I've a-seed you somewheres. P'raps 'twas up agin Salisbury—do you ever travel that part, my son?"

"Yes I do, about once a year," I confirmed. "Then I always stop in the Green Lane, don't you know?"

"Ar!" shouted Old Hannah indistinctly, spitting nicotine and saliva to one side of her—some of it landing on a small boy's head, to his intense delight. "*That's* where I've a-seed you, my young man. Why, don't you mind the time when you come there fer the Fair—'bout three year ago—an' bid there fer just the one night? I wuz led up into the bed—bad wi' the quinzes! Ole Jimmy an' me dear Amos wuz there wi' their wagons as well—don't you mind the time? You had a nice black horse. . . ."

"O *dordi*, yes!" I recollected suddenly. "Why certainly I do, though I never spoke one word to you—I wuz on my way to Southampton, and in a bit of a hurry. Isn't that right?"

"Sure it is, young man," Old Hannah boomed.

"Did he goo up in the bed 'long wi' you, Mother?" inquired Luke, to an outburst of mirth.

Old Hannah was not amused, or pretended not to be. She struck a small whippet which had come close to the fire a sharp blow across its back with her stick. It squeaked and slunk away. Old Hannah chuckled and rolled herself a thin cigarette, her hands, dirt- and smoke-stained, moving slowly, stiffly and almost automatically at their oft-repeated task.

One of our bantams flew up on to her lap, and sat preening its multi-coloured plumage. The others laughed at its impudence.

"Ain't these birds quiet—how do yet git 'em so tame, gal?" she asked Beshlie, who explained that it was achieved by handling them frequently when very young, and by never chasing them. For, alas, it is for that reason that so few of the travellers' birds are tame, the children being allowed to run about after them for fun.

We demonstrated how *our* bantams would come individually when called with certain sounds, or *en masse* to another call. They were astounded at this.

"My bloody Gawd!" ejaculated one young man, his hat pushed far back on his head and long black mat hair spilling out over his once-white silk neckerchief. His jaw dropped in astonishment, a thin fragment of cigarette adhering to his lower lip. "I never seed sich *kanis* in all me life!"

"O my baby, look at they dee-little banties," murmured his wife, a blue-eyed, fair-haired girl, wearing ear-rings of silver threepenny-pieces.

We had fifteen bantams at that particular moment; and after some energetic haggling and argument we eventually disposed of eight of them to various people, including one which we presented as a gift to Old Hannah, so that she could give it to her favourite grandchild, Nilly-Lizbee.

For utilitarian, traditional and æsthetic reasons we always possess a considerable number of bantams. These pretty, fascinating little fowl—so much more charming than larger poultry—are all, in our case, wagon-bred and sleep in special baskets which are suspended on the rear axles under the van. We have trained them to roost there of their own accord—a difficult feat as by nature they prefer to sleep in high places off the ground. Wherever we stop, even on grass verges by roadsides, they are always free, rarely wandering far from the wagon. Living in such close proximity to us from the time they hatch, our bantams are all hand-tame and quite without the nervous qualities which are usually so evident amongst their kind. Indeed, ours think nothing of snatching food from our very plates when we are eating our meals. We have kept Sea-brights, Duckwings, Japanese-buffs, Plymouth-rocks, Polish, Indian game, and Old English game. These last are a fast-disappearing breed, graceful and possessing beautiful lines. Many people view all poultry with supreme disdain, refusing to believe that any individuality can exist in their ranks. However, we have proved that to be quite false and can truthfully assert that many of our bantams have become characters in their own right.

Gradually the light began to fade, a cold draught of air blew down the lane, and I piled more large lumps of wood on to the fire.

At about six o'clock most of the children over the age of ten set out for the nearest town to go to the cinema, where a Western was showing. Most Romanies, both the adults and children, like Westerns, as the constant action, together with the presence of horses and a usually simple plot, provide them with the spectacle and excitement which they love. However, a somewhat violent argument broke out in one family when it was discovered by the father that one of the young men intended to take his daughter, only just thirteen, to see the film that evening.

"Wot?" he shouted, tugging at his drooping moustache with wrath. "I ain't a-goin' to have my gal go out to the pitchers wi' him alone—she'll have to bide here."

"Why not, man?" returned his wife. "Do you think I cain't trust my gal?"

"My gal ain't a-goin' to no pitchers wi' that young Freddie. . . ."

"Wot's ever the matter wi' you, man?" his wife shouted, much enraged. "Why that gal'll be so safe as iffen she wuz bidin' here along o' we, I tells you."

At this point the girl, Queenie, burst into a storm of frenzied tears and screams of wrath and frustration.

"There now, you goo on, gal—an' here's the money," and her mother pressed a silver coin into the girl's palm. "He'm so full up wi' the beer into him," she explained, "that he don't know wot he'm a-sayin' half his time."

Queenie's face immediately cleared and she quickly jumped up into their wagon, reappearing after a few minutes, her mouth a vivid gash of inexpertly applied lipstick, her hair watered-down and crimped, and wearing a bright red coat several sizes too large.

Before her enraged father had time to speak she was gone, swallowed into the darkness of the lane beyond the fire's feeble glow.

"Wot do ye mean by lettin' her goo wi' . . . ," he began.

"God's cuss the day as ever I did go wi' you," snapped his wife venomously. "God's cuss you, man! Iffen you don't shut yer bloody foxin' mouth I'll shut it fer you, you foxin' bastard! Why you'm wusser'n a poxy German!"

And so saying the woman snatched an enormous burning stick from the fire, and brandished it in front of her husband's face. He relapsed, swearing to himself beside the fire. The whole scene had been watched with great amusement and approval by the rest of their children, who were only sorry that it had not ended in blows.

Left alone by their separate fires, each family muttered together in undertones in their own little groups until it became quite dark. Then the men, after some argument and indecision, decided on the best field in which to *poove* the *grais* that night. Eventually, with the exception of Fangs and myself, they quietly slipped all the horses into one of the fields bordering the lane. Fangs did not do so because, like ours, his horse was quite fat enough and could do well feeding on the grass verge and the hedge-rows. Sonner, Fangs's eldest boy, put *his* pony in the field with those belonging to the others, and took a canvas sheet with him so that he could sleep out on the ground near his pony and thus be sure of waking up early enough to take the pony out of the field before the farmer or his men were abroad. I learned that the others had had their horses impounded on both the previous nights because they had not woken early enough in the mornings—and the farmer had forced them to pay a pound a head before he would allow them to take their horses from his stables where his men had locked them up. This had made their grazing rather expensive, but had not deterred them from still further *pooving*—which is almost a challenge to some Romanies, who do it senselessly and often even needlessly.

At about nine o'clock everyone went to bed. I was

43

woken by the sound of voices and the barking of dogs.
Glancing at my watch, I saw it was nearly midnight. I
quickly put on my boots, hat and coat and jumped down
from the wagon to investigate the cause of the disturbance.
I was somewhat taken aback to discover that a carload of
constables and a sergeant—about eight in all—had arrived,
and that they were working their way up the line of
wagons, questioning the inmates of each of them. It was
apparent that the farmer, tiring of his grass being devoured
by uninvited guests, had telephoned to the County Police
and had asked for official action to be taken promptly.

Some of the men had been alert enough to remove their
animals quickly from the field at the sound of the car's
arrival—instinct warning them in time. Others had not
been so warned and there still remained upwards of half
a dozen horses in the *poove*.

Voices sounded erratically through the darkness, the
constables' torches flashing occasionally over brown faces
in an effort to achieve recognition.

". . . ain't my hoss, policeman—an' that's so true as I'm
here. Why, you can see my ole mare, policeman, tied
agin that hedge. An' that's where she've bid all night,
policeman. . . ."

"Wot? In the field? How ever did she git in there?
Must've broke loose. . . ."

"Mary-Anne, ain't it right I left the horses in this
lane all . . . ?"

"Now then! Now then! Your name and age . . . Liberty
Barney . . . forty-two years. . . ."

After some time one of the constables reached me. A
torch flashed in my face, flickered away, and then rapidly
flashed back into my eyes.

"Your name . . . ? Yes . . . age . . . ?"

I gave my name but declined, as I generally do, to give my age. Unless needed for a specific purpose, I feel it to be of little concern to authority. Such a course of action, of course, hardly endeared me to the policeman.

"Ah well, of course, if you're going to be difficult and take that attitude. . . ."

"I am taking the attitude that I have the right to object to being cross-questioned as though I were a criminal. I have committed no crime. . . ."

"You know, I can make things difficult for you," the constable said. "Now how about that fire by the road-side . . . ?"

I vainly endeavoured to point out that when farmers light fires beside roads nobody makes any trouble, yet our people are quite frequently fined for such an 'offence.'

Ultimately some kind of a truce is usually reached. Sometimes I am taken for a *diddikai*—and treated accordingly; sometimes for a crank; and once I was even given fatherly advice on the unwise course of stopping with my own people! It is harder to be individualistic in the 'gypsy' world than in any other walk of life.

In fairness to the police I should mention that not *all* of them are entirely unreasonable in their treatment of our people. Some have, on rather rare occasions, actually gone so far as to discuss with me their views on the 'problem' of travellers (from the police point of view, that is).

Two or three suggested that all travellers should be provided with huts to live in, and should be banned from the roads; others frankly admitted they had no suggestions to offer but that they 'kicked 'em off' *their* beats as soon as possible; and still others seemed to regard the 'Compounds' of the New Forest as the solution. These last, in my view, provide no real solution. Forcing travellers to live in these small areas of land, in shacks and shanties of their own construction, without floors or windows, has hurled them into a world of their own—half-way between that of the wagon-dwellers and of the 'working man.' An interesting point to note is that most of the compound-dwellers still live in roughly the same manner as if they were in wagons. That is to say they have only wood-burning stoves—often fashioned from old cut-out milk churns or oil-drums—on which they cook. Some still continue to make and hawk pegs and baskets; but most of the men are either in the scrap-metal business or else are on National Assistance. In fact, they are leading an unnatural life to which they have not as yet adjusted themselves, and are in no way superior to their wagon-dwelling counterparts.

My own solution is that councils should provide various official stopping-places, dotted about the country, in which our people should be allowed to pull-in for a limited period so many times each year. A pensioned-off constable or some such reliable person could be installed to supervise such places. If this course was followed, much unnecessary wasting of time by the police in moving-on our people could be avoided. One feels that *something* should be done for travelling people. Constant harrying and badgering by officials does not solve anything.

The police, on this occasion, having at last completed their lists of names and ages—most of them false—proceeded there and then to issue various 'papers' regarding the *pooving* of the horses, tethering them on the highway, lighting fires within forty feet of the centre of the high-way and on almost any pretext they could find. Then, on penalty of further 'papers' being issued, we were all ordered to leave in the morning.

"God's cuss they brazen policemens," Old Hannah's hollow voice carried through the darkness from her wagon. "Comin' a-wakin' all we poor people h'up in the middle o' the night. Why don't you goo on an' kitch all they murderers wots all over the country, 'stead o'wastin' yer time on the likes o' we wot on'y wants to be left alone?"

One or two of the constables shifted a trifle uneasily, but the sergeant remained unmoved except to remind us to be sure to be gone early in the morning. So, packing themselves back into the car, they drove off, the car's headlamps shining far into the darkness ahead of them.

"I never knowed nothin' like it," Samson moaned. "A-bringin' we they papers out in the middle o' the night in a control car. 'Tain't right!"

We were all agreed on that—especially those who had had the misfortune to receive 'papers.' With much cursing and muttering we all dispersed to our own wagons for the remainder of the night.

2

I woke the next morning to the sound of birds singing and to the familiar clinking of the horses' tethering chains. It was only half-past six and a thin mist was rising from the ground, the pink sky showing the promise of a beautiful day ahead. I rose, fully-dressed, and swung quietly down from the wagon. As I had guessed, no one else was yet astir. I splashed a cup full of water over my face, and as I dried it with my handkerchief a layer of dirt detached itself in little black lumps and my skin felt taut and new. After some little searching I managed to pull sufficient wood from the hedges to start the morning's fire.

It was long after we had breakfasted and when I was lying on the ground beside the fire that the first sign of life showed from any of the other wagons' occupants. By then it was nearly nine, and Good Friday. The youth Sonner emerged from the open lot standing next but one to us, his clothes creased from sleeping in them and his mat hair standing tousled and upright. He jumped heavily down to the ground and stretched himself, doubtless stiff from his habit of spending most of the night sleeping out in the fields. He was followed a few seconds later by his father, who pulled on his hat as he leapt awkwardly to the ground.

"Mawnun," they remarked.

"Wot's the time?" inquired Sonner.

"Nine," I replied.

"There's a time to get up," said Fangs grinning unashamedly, and he ordered Sonner to light the fire.

"I'm bad wi' me back," he explained, "or I'd do it meself."

"Can I have a bit o' fire, please?" Sonner asked me.

I pulled out a lump of burning wood and handed it to him. He took it without a word and placed it in the ashes of their previous night's fire, tearing up a cardboard box and then adding a few twigs as it caught alight.

"Sonner! We ain't got no *pani!*" exclaimed Fangs, inspecting an old chipped enamel slop-bucket which was hanging under their wagon.

"Well, I ain't goin' after none—send Daniel!" Sonner said ill-humouredly.

"Here, young man," I shouted, slightly mocking, "you can have a kettleful from our bucket."

"Is you sure you've got 'nuff?" asked Fangs considerately.

I assured them that it could be spared.

Sonner was very like his father: tall for a Romani, with dark complexion and hair. His face was long and hard, the eyes wide-set and expressionless. Fangs, however, was darker than his son, with pitch-black curly hair and a pencil-line moustache above a long mouth devoid of teeth except for two lone fangs an inch or so apart in his upper jaw, and hanging like those of a sabre-toothed tiger. He wore a wide-brimmed, greasy felt hat pulled low over his eyes and, surprisingly, a thick, once-good overcoat. The rather town-like dress, shabby and colourless, made him difficult to place. Out of his setting he might easily have been taken for a very seedy, down-at-heel Spanish business man. But in his drooping, hooded eyes there was more than a hint of insanity: and as I got to know him better and saw his curious smile, his sudden changes of mood and his maniacal temper, I knew that my first impression had not been far astray. In many ways, though, his quick, cunning and even intelligent brain, combined with several very likeable traits, rather appealed to me. We much enjoyed his company and appreciated his 'flyness.'

Before ten o'clock all the other men had got up and had lit their fires, over which they crouched, sleepy and drugged-looking, waiting for their kettles to boil to make the tea. All travelling people—tramps included—are very

49

4

fond of tea. They drink it at all times of the day and in vast quantities, always over-sweetened and often without even a drop of milk.

Fangs laid a piece of bread in the ashes by his fire and after waiting for it to toast itself he munched it hungrily with a piece of cold bacon. With a dirt-caked hand he scratched thoughtfully at his cheek, which was covered by four or five days' growth of black stubble.

"Did you git a paper last night, brother?" he shouted across to me, in an effort to make himself heard above the singing of his small daughter.

"No—did you?"

"Nah! Wuz too fly fer 'em. My Sonner wuz led down in the *poove* wi' *his* pony an' he on'y got out jest in time."

After a while, when Fangs and the other men had handed cups of tea up into their wagons for the women and the younger children, these too began emerging—to begin their task of frying something for their family's breakfast; for although the men always light the fire and make the tea it is usual for the women actually to cook the breakfast whenever they are able. Gradually the aroma of frying bacon and potatoes and of various other mixtures wafted its way to us from the line of fires stretching up the lane. We made some more toast, having already eaten two fried bantam's eggs each, and I made some more tea which we slowly sipped.

The others quickly ate their meals—travelling people learn to eat fast—and, wiping their plates clean with bread or rags, replaced them in their food-baskets. We then all gathered in a group near Samson's van to confer on the best place for us to go next. In this discussion I was condemned to silence because I had little or no knowledge either of the country or of the stopping-places in the area.

"I reckons we'd be best off up agin the fuzzy-brake," a man known as Snaky stated.

"That ain't no good, mush. You wouldn't git five minutes there afore the *gavvers'd* come an' shift you," Fangs sneered.

"Wot about the Sawmill Lane, then?" suggested Liberty. "I've bid there a week meself 'fore now."

"Yeah, that ain't a bad ole place," Young Bob agreed.

"You'll be summonsed there fer sure," a woman called Freedom said pessimistically.

"They policemans won't be back. Let's bide here, you won't find no better place fer the *grais*, that's certain," Little Caroline stoutly declared, her wizened face tight with annoyance.

"I'm a-goin' to *Dinilo's* Corner—is any o' you comin'?" Samson declared.

"Wot! *Dinilo's* Corner? Why that's fenced-in, man! Bin fenced-in these last six months," announced Snaky, whose knowledge of the country was generally assumed to be fairly good.

"That ain't fenced-in," Samson persisted, unconvinced.

"I tells you 'tis fenced-in!" Snaky hotly rejoined. "Why me Uncle Joe an' me cousin Billeen tole me that on'y a month ago when I seed 'em at Reading 'bloc'—an' they sez they couldn't draw-in there."

"I tell you where we can go—an' we kin bide there till we'm grey-headed!" exclaimed Fangs dramatically. "That's Martin Marsh!"

"Martin Marsh?" repeated two women and a man in one awestruck breath.

After some more heated argument and consultation,

and for want of a better suggestion, all decided to follow this course. Suddenly, however, it was realised that, owing to the amount of rain that had fallen the previous week, the Marsh would be under water.

"... foxin' wagons'd sink down to their axles an' we'd never git out," moaned Caroline, her thin face more drawn-in than ever.

"Then let's have a day or two agin' 'Vizes Trees," suggested Samson, still somewhat aggrieved that his earlier suggestion had been rejected.

Finally, no definite flaw being found in this suggestion, it was agreed upon by all, except Caroline who was opposed to our moving at all. ' 'Vizes Trees,' I gathered, was some five or six miles away in the Devizes direction, and was an old right-of-way lane running off a main road. It did not sound very encouraging.

Gradually, the women and children, having combed soapy water through their hair—each member of the family using the same comb in the increasingly brackish water—began to busy themselves haphazardly and un-methodically with the preparations for our departure. The women would have gone out 'calling' had it not been Good Friday.

Some of the smaller children began to cry, as they so often do just prior to a move, and their mothers cried out: "Stop that cryin' my baby—we've got to go away now. We'm goin' away. . . ."

The older children, however, were excited at the prospect of moving—some even going so far as to help their elders to bundle together cooking utensils, baskets, rags, old prams, buckets, canvas sheets, piles of rags, odd harness, old boots, scrap-iron and all the other hundreds of bits and pieces which are part of our life, piling them on to the spare trolleys and carts. The bantams had to be caught, the harness had to be sorted out, the dogs tied on behind the wagons or on the trolleys, the plug-chains wound up, and the horses harnessed. As nobody is allotted any specific tasks, a move for our people generally takes far longer than it might for a more organised and efficient society. However, it is the raggle-taggle quality of muddle and noise and dirt and disorder which is the fascination—both for us and for outsiders also. The world-drive for efficiency, higher standards of living, mechanisation, and living 'by numbers' has happily passed us by.

Everything was eventually ready for the move. The horses were all harnessed and hitched-in to the various wagons and carts and trolleys, and the children were all stowed away inside the wagons or on the footboards. Some of the adults walked, a few pushed old prams loaded with baskets or rags, others rode, the men leading the horses. Samson's van was first in the line, his leadership being acknowledged; then came his little pony and governess cart, driven by his eldest daughter, Lavinia, followed by Snaky's open lot and trolley, followed in turn by a long procession made up of the rest of us—with Beshlie's and my wagon, as the last-comers, bringing up the rear.

The pony pulling Young Siddy's tiny open lot suddenly reared up, but Siddy clung to the bit and beat the pony vigorously about the face with a thick holly stick, kicking it in the stomach for good measure until, eyes rolling, it quietened down.

"I don't like a lazy pony!" he laughed, displaying black

teeth and pretending not to be upset by his pony's show of bad behaviour. Privately, of course, we realised that he was furious—for news of a wild wagon-horse travels swiftly amongst our people, and is greatly detrimental to the horse's value.

Samson's great skylight van moved steadily forwards, the grey cob, tall and thickset, easing it gently off the verge on to the road with practised experience. And slowly we all followed, rumbling and bumping in pursuit, the length of our procession stretching over a hundred yards. We shouted to one another, our voices feeble above the noise of the hooves and wheels. Two of the girls were singing—each a different song; others were whistling, high-pitched and tunelessly. Sonner, driving a quick black pony in a small trolley laden high with sacks of rags, was singing at the top of his voice, in imitation of cinema heroes, a ballad which expressed his hopes we should soon reach ". . . cow country, where no Injuns there will be. . . ." Thus we wound onwards into, as far as I was concerned, unknown country. Round a bend and up a hill, then down—applying our brake full on, whilst others had to let down their 'drug shoes.' Then we could see the foremost wagons ahead of us, round another bend, ascending to the crest of another hill, winding upwards still in our view. And we trailed on behind, a few feet from Old Hannah's wagon, which was being driven by her crippled son, Smiler. Up the hill, down another, over a crossroads, and still onwards: we had covered, in my estimation, about three miles when suddenly great consternation broke out towards the head of the line and there were roars and shouts of "Stop! Stop!"

"O *dordi!* O the baby's killed! . . . The wagon's over"

. . . and various other highly alarming exclamations reached us. I jumped quickly down from the wagon and joined the others who were hurrying forwards to investigate the cause of the outcries, and was just in time to see a shabby, yellow-painted wheel roll slowly and ponderously across the grass verge, finally toppling heavily over into the ditch where it vanished from sight. It was sharply pursued by the distraught figure of Nelson, cap awry and coat flying. He too disappeared into the ditch but reappeared a few seconds later dragging the heavy wheel after him. It had, I saw, detached itself from his wagon whilst we were actually travelling along. It was a rear wheel and the wagon leant drunkenly at a tilt.

"O my poor dead mother! O my blessed Jesus!" shouted little Caroline, jumping up and down with agitation, wrath and shame. "O me poor wagon—'tis all to pieces! O 'tis all broke up! O my dead father, I wishes I'd never gone wi' that man! Wots ever that wheel a-comed off fer?"

"Sammy! Siddy! Walty! Snaky!" shouted Nelson in his low gruff voice. "Will you push the wagon up straight agin so as I can put the wheel back on to him? He ain't broke up—'tis on'y the pin wots a-comed out of him. Look! Ain't that right?"

The others gathered round, offering suggestions and rolling cigarettes. After much talk they eventually heaved the wagon upright so that the wheel could be slipped back on to the axle and a nail attached in place of the missing pin. After a short search we discovered the oil-cap in the grass and screwed it back on.

"Never knew sich a thing to happen in all me life," muttered Nelson, jerking viciously at the horse's head, which was lowered as he cropped the roadside grass.

"You bin a-makin' that ole wagon shake too much at night, that's wot loosed they wheels!" grinned Snaky from under his moustache.

"Wot?" exclaimed little Caroline, her pointed face still working with wrath that such a thing should have happened to her wagon in front of the others. "That man's half a *dinilo*! He ain't a-broke the banns wi' me fer these last six months—an' he won't fer six months, my brother, that's fer sure!"

We all laughed and laughed, until Caroline, spitting brown saliva vehemently on the road, climbed back cursing into the wagon, pulling the torn front curtain across after her.

Rejoining our own wagons and horses, we started off again on the final lap of our journey. On the by-roads we had travelled we had not encountered much traffic of any kind. As we neared our destination, however, it was necessary to follow a stretch of the main Bath road; and along this busy highway traffic roared. Coaches, lorries, family-eights and sports cars sped past, our long line of slowly moving wagons throwing them into some confusion. We passed through a hamlet, edged our way down another steep hill—those without brakes again having to lock their rear wheels in their 'drug shoes'—and then we reached our goal: a rough lane, stretching off at right angles from the road. It lasted for about fifty yards before fading out into a tiny footpath which ended in a black swampy wood. The lane was muddy and pitted with deep ruts and holes; large stones and broken bricks were scattered, half-embedded in the mud. The foremost wagons lurched, unmindful of the ruts, into the lane, swaying and shaking alarmingly. Samson's tall heavy skylight van looked especially precarious as, top heavy, it swung wildly from side to side. Samson, however, completely disregarded its rocking and continued up the track. The smaller, lighter, open lots did not fare so badly, their lack of weight allowing them to jolt and bounce without suffering harm to anything save perhaps their wheels.

"I wouldn't take my lot up there," shouted Fangs, disturbed at the surface, for his was a large top-heavy open lot. "It'll beat the wagons all to pieces!"

We were inclined to agree with him; and so we remained opposite each other on either side of the lane's entrance, whilst the others pulled-in a little further up it.

By the time we had unharnessed the horses and tethered them in the lane and along the side of the main road it was past midday. Most of the men decided to drive down to a public-house, about three miles away. They knew that the landlord would serve them. None of the public-houses in the villages close at hand would have travelling-people on the premises.

To a Romani, when entering a public-house, there is always the likelihood that he will suffer the indignity of being refused service with a curt, "No gypsies served here!" or a brusque, "No, sorry—not here." The refusal follows the same pattern, whatever its phrasing, and amounts to the same thing: racial discrimination plus a dash of snobbery. Many years ago the English public-house was a place which I greatly liked, and many hours have I spent in them. Nowadays, having only too often suffered refusal of service both when in the company of other travelling-people and also when alone, I hesitate to approach these delicately run hostels—feeling almost a criminal in my attempt to patronise them.

Possibly the peak in discrimination and snobbery has been reached at R—— in Hampshire, where *none* of the inns will serve Romanies—whether living in wagons or in houses. On one occasion, when stopping just outside the town on our way back from the Hampshire hop-fields with some other travellers, we were visited by a very well-to-do Romani and his wife and son, who drove over in their glittering new lorry to see us. It was suggested that we should venture out on a mild celebration. Thereupon six of us—five men and one old lady—clambered on to the lorry and drove into R——. Alas, we were sadly mistaken in hoping that our money would be received as readily as that of the *gaujes*. Nine public-houses refused us service—without so much as a moment's hesitation. No customers in any of those full houses came forward to suggest that we had a right to be served. I found it a very depressing experience. One landlord, a very embittered and uninteresting-looking man, when I requested a reason for his refusal to accept our orders, savagely hissed, "You know your creed, don't you? Go on—get out!" All his customers—puffy-faced and shorn-headed men, tubby dull-faced women—seemed to approve of his action, or at best remained noncommittal.

But on this occasion the public-house was known to be hospitable, so a boy re-harnessed Samson's little odd-coloured pony and hitched her into the tub-cart, and the five men crowded themselves into it, scarcely having room to sit down. Samson drove, whirring the whip lash round by the little pony's flank and striking it once or twice, and they swept forward and sped out on to the main road at a fine pace, the clickety-clacking of the pony's tiny hooves soon becoming lost in the perpetual humming of the Easter traffic.

Sonner, Jobi (Samson's eldest son) and I then decided to go together to fetch some water; and we slouched off up the main road, carrying two buckets apiece, swung up over our shoulders by their handles so that their mouths lay flat against our backs. On reaching the top of the hill which we had come down with the wagons we went into the first cottage and knocked loudly on the back door. It was opened by an ancient crone whose face bore no trace of intelligence or character in its broad flat contours, only age. She recoiled slightly on seeing us, standing ragged and dirty on her doorstep, and her mean little eyes peered at us through cheap round spectacles.

"Wadja want?" she demanded.

"Can-we-have-a-drop-o'-water-please-lady?" Jobi asked in a well-tongued traveller's phrase.

"Water? No, you can't. Go away out of here quick, before I set the dog on you!" And so saying she quickly slammed the door.

"God's cuss that ole mother's tit!" spat Sonner, his eyes hard and flat-looking. "Come on!"

We tried the next house with no better luck. We tried at the public-house—the landlord of which said that the water had been cut off, which was a statement we had cause to doubt. Another man, watering his garden, refused us curtly.

Wishing them all ill-luck and cursing them soundly, Sonner and I decided to walk to the next village, which he said was about a mile away. Little Jobi said that he was too tired and that he was going back to the camp. Sonner knew a short cut, he said, so we set off. I could not dispute its distance-saving qualities, but its disadvantages were many, for it entailed climbing through impenetrable thorn hedges, leaping down vertical banks, and climbing innumerable barbed-wire fences. We passed several cattle troughs in various fields, but these, after a brief testing in the palm of his hand by Sonner, were deemed impure. He spat vigorously on each occasion after his trial of their contents.

At last we reached the hamlet, appropriately called Water End, and there better luck befell us, for the occupants of the first house at which we called allowed us to fill our buckets from a garden tap.

"Thank-you-sir. Got-any-ole-car-batteries-or-ole-rags-lyin'-about-please-sir?" enquired the resourceful Sonner, all in one breath.

The householder, however, was unable to oblige in that respect.

On the homeward journey I dissuaded Sonner from following his hazardous long short-cut route in favour of a more level course along the road; the full buckets could never have survived the precarious ascents and descents of the other way.

By the time we returned to the encampment we found that nearly two hours had gone by and that the men were due back from their drinking bout.

Beshlie's and my catering had proved inadequate for the day and our meal was a dull one. However, we munched hungrily at all our larder could provide, namely bread, butter, and cold fried bacon, with an enjoyment fostered by genuine hunger.

We were in the middle of this feast when the sound of the pony's trotting hooves warned us that the men were returning from their celebrations. The little tub-cart swung sharply into the lane, bouncing in and out of the ruts, and halted abruptly by our fire, spilling its human contents untidily out. They had, of course, followed the normal Romani's principle. On finding a public-house which *would* serve them, they had remained there until closing time, drinking enormous amounts of beer by the pint and spending liberally. Not for them the 'half of bitter' and 'Good evening,' but heavy drinking in the best tradition. This occasion had obviously been no exception to the rule. Liberty and Fangs swayed shakily round us, before dropping to the ground beside our fire, while Samson, Snaky, Young Eli and Siddy walked primly across the main road and relieved themselves against the opposite hedgerow. A haze of beer-tainted tobacco smoke enveloped us, and snatches of disjointed, maudlin conversation ensued, and it was not until the furious calling of the women told them that their food was ready that they moved. Then, watery-eyed and shivering, they swayed and tottered towards their respective families, who received them with singularly few signs of love and affection.

We were still munching stolidly at our bacon and bread when Sonner called suddenly across to us in an undertone:

"*Muskeros*—in a control car."

And as he spoke a long, dark green police patrol car slid smoothly to a standstill at the lane entrance, and its two occupants got out and walked over to us. They stood for an instant gazing sternly at the row of wagons and trolleys and at the horses tethered in the lane and by the roadside.

One constable carried a large report sheet, on which he carefully wrote all our names and ages. Having completed that formality, they drove off. Their report of our presence there was, of course, relayed by radio to the local county constabulary, and if any of the names on the list tallied with those of travelling-people who had not answered summonses there would assuredly be a further visit from the control 'car'. A certain amount of confusion was caused during the name-and-age taking when two of the men inadvertently gave the same name! This, however, they quickly explained away by stating that they were cousins.

Not an hour had passed, however, when exactly the same procedure was repeated by a second patrol car, which in turn departed.

We were all somewhat disturbed at the amount of interest being shown in us and the older people thought these visits meant disaster.

"I reckons they'm out to git we fer something," remarked Old Hannah ominously, adding: " 'Twas in this country me dear man wuz *took* jest fer havin' the *yog* agin the roadside. They gie him three months—'cos he hit the *gavmush* when he kicked the fire over us."

As the day wore on we sat in groups by our fires, some making pegs, others—like myself—making hazel baskets.

These hazel baskets are of the simplest construction. They consist merely of hazel-wood sticks, about half an inch or more in diameter, which are cut into lengths of from ten or twelve inches—depending how large one wishes the finished object to be. Starting from the base a

square is made, and from then onwards two or three
further layers are built up as it were at right-angles to one
another, each square becoming larger as the basket is
built upwards. The sticks are tacked together with three-
quarter inch nails and a hoop of hazel is added at the end
to form a decorative handle. The baskets are then filled
with moss and primroses—or artificial flowers if wild
ones are out of season. They are really rather ugly little
things, but seem to find a fairly ready market amongst
house-dwellers who hang them up. I have sold many for
three and four shillings apiece, which is clear profit as
almost any hedgerow or copse will yield sufficient hazel
'withies' to make several dozen of these baskets. Beshlie
and I have, however, found that the making of tiny
model gardens and other rather precious little objects,
made from natural materials, generally proves to be more
profitable. It is surprising what can be achieved with
some moss, a few flowers, some twigs and a log of silver
birchwood!

While we worked, many of our neighbours merely sat
or lay, talking and sleeping, beside the smoking *yogs*.
Snaky's son Freddie played his portable radio whilst his
girl Celia lay near him on the ground. She was 'going
with' Freddie and they were much wrapt up in each other.
Later perhaps, if they did not tire of one another, they
would have their own wagon and pony, which their
respective parents would provide if they approved the
match. Thus, with but little celebration when they actually
moved into their wagon, they would slip easily and
naturally into the pattern of the traveller's life. Although
this would still be known as a 'broomstick marriage'—
with no official *gaujo* marriage taking place—there would

be none of the ritualistic traditional festivities which once marked most Romani marriages.

The radio played loud and clear. It was a new model, which had cost Freddie eighteen guineas, and it was kept constantly tuned to stations which were playing only music. Actually, most travellers prefer a gramophone, because it is more readily controllable than a wireless. Old Hannah informed me that she had possessed a radio but had sold it in disgust.

". . . Waren't never hardly no music playing," she had said. "Why, 't were allus a-wastin' its time a-talkin'!"

"All the way from China!" shouted Freddie suddenly, chancing upon some folk-music from West Africa.

"Wots ever that boy a-playin' on that gramyphone?" inquired Hannah, half-hearing. "Sounds like they'm foxin' Germans a-singin'!"

"Where's Germans? Wot Germans?" ejaculated Nelson, starting up in alarm from his fire where he had been dozing in its heat.

Two world wars have been sufficient to instil into all travellers a wholehearted fear and dislike of all things German—a nation which they still regard as the epitome of all evil. To call a traveller 'a German' is viewed as being a supreme insult.

"Wot Germans?" scoffed little Caroline. "Why, man, you'm half outa yer mind. You wuz led there sleepin'. Wots you talking about Germans fer?"

"Me Aunt Hannah there wuz sayin' she seed some Germans a . . .," began Nelson earnestly.

"God's cuss that man!" spat Caroline disgustedly. "Look wot you'va brought me to." She cast her eyes over her wagon and round about her, looking on her two small daughters—black-haired and wild-looking—with evident distaste. "On me dead mother's grave I wishes I'd never set me eyes on yer!"

"O *dordi!* They two's a–cussin' each other agin," shouted Snaky with delight, for all travellers like to witness a family row or disturbance.

Little Caroline eyed Snaky with distaste, her black eyes gleaming with malice.

"Listen to that man," she said to Nelson. "Why I wouldn't travel wi' him agin. Never no more. An' let the God A'mighty hisself come down outa the sky an strike me dead iffen that ain't the truth!"

Soon it was too dark for any further work, so we made ourselves more tea and I toasted two or three thick slices of bread.

After we had eaten, Beshlie and I walked down to Samson's van in order to try to do a deal over some old coins and silver brooches which they had.

"Come up into the wagon an' I'll show 'em to you," said Samson when we arrived. So we climbed up the steps into his tall van. It was dimly lit by two candles, guttering naked on the edge of the built-in chest of drawers. The younger children were asleep on the floor beneath their parents' crossways bed at the rear end of the van; for Samson, although only twenty-six years old, already had four children. His wife appeared black as a negro in the poor light. It was a pleasant wagon inside, with traditional layout and a considerable amount of shining brasswork, especially round the fireplace. Mary-Anne was proud of her home and kept it neater and cleaner than any of the other travellers there; and it lacked the strong sickly-sweet odour which is characteristic of

65

many Romani vans, being made up, I suppose, of the combined scents of tobacco, wood-smoke, old clothes, and unwashed bodies. I myself am unable to detect it; but friends whose lives rarely cross the paths of Romanies have frequently remarked on it.

"Well, what have you got? Would you sell that silver *foni*?" I asked Samson, pointing to a broad snake ring on his finger.

"I wouldn't part from that, brother, not fer all the money in the world. 'Twas gid to me by me poor dear mother jest afore she died; an' I couldn't part from it, could I?"

I agreed with him, and inquired again what they *had* got to sell.

"We ain't a-got much—we'm too poor," grinned Mary-Anne.

"Too poor? O *dordi!* I'll bet you've got more pound notes than I've got hairs on me head!" I laughed.

"Where's they 'spade-guineas' to?" Samson asked his wife.

"They'm here," answered Mary-Anne, taking out two George III golden guineas from a tiny box behind the chimney.

Samson took them from her and laid them in the palm of his hand in the candlelight in order that we might survey their full glory.

"A man offered me eight pun fer they t'other day," he remarked casually.

Mary-Anne then produced a rather fine old silver brooch and a pair of ear-rings made from pierced silver three-penny pieces—which are held in high esteem by travelling-people.

At this point one of our large dogs loosed himself from his chain under our wagon and leapt savagely amongst several of the small cross-bred terriers of the encampment. I had hastily to jump out of the van and dive headlong amongst the writhing, yelping, growling mass of curs to disentangle one from his jaws—and then disengage two terriers whose teeth were embedded in *his* leg.

"Beat they dogs off! Beat 'em off!" shouted several women.

I re-tied Naylor under the wagon, and was about to return to Samson's van when Fangs appeared beside me, silent and dark, his hat brim obscuring his eyes.

"I ain't a-*poovin'* me horses tonight, mush, is you?" he whispered, for the others had already turned most of their ponies out into the adjoining fields.

"I reckons they *gavs*'ll be back," he continued. "Let's *chur* a cake of hay—I knows where there's a good rick."

Having had no cause to view the inhabitants of this particular neighbourhood with anything but antagonism, I readily agreed.

"Down here," said Fangs, and he led the way along the main road for a few yards. We ducked down under some low barbed-wire fencing and made our way across two fields. We reached the rick, which was already partly used. The bales were scattered untidily about on one side of it, so I knew that one would not be missed.

Fangs cut the binding string of a bale, lifted half of it, and handed it across to me; then he put the other half under his arm. A small glimmering light suddenly appeared in the middle of the next field and we darted back against the rick. However, the wavering light gradually disappeared away to our right. Apparently it had been a farm-worker taking a short cut over the fields. We breathed more easily and moved swiftly back, waiting until no car headlamps were approaching before making our brief journey down the main highway.

When we reached the camp I put the half-bale down by our mare's head and she greedily started munching. She was partly hidden behind a bush so that I knew it was unlikely that the evidence would be discovered. I hoped that Fangs would not be careless in the matter of disposing of any hay that *his* horses might leave scattered about the lane.

"Them bastards wouldn't *gie* it to you, and they wouldn't *sell* it to you—so wot can you do but *chur* it?" Fangs asked logically.

When I did eventually return to Samson's van to see how matters were progressing I discovered that the deal had been concluded—although I gathered that it had been rather a severe test on both sides.

However, Beshlie had waged a fairly satisfactory war and had obtained both the gold coins and also the silver brooch, in exchange for which she had *chopped* a small amount of tawdry modern jewellery of the fairground-prize type. But Mary-Anne seemed quite happy about the deal. Samson, however, was a little disappointed that his sales talk and 'flyness' had not brought him a better bargain.

"Cah! I reckons you'm the masterest 'oman wot ever I dealed wi'!" he said, in a somewhat awed tone.

Having concluded the deal, and having talked for some time of our mutual journeyings and experiences, we bid them good night and returned to our own wagon. The lines of fires were dimmer now, the embers glowing in the darkness.

3

The following morning dawned with the promise of another fine day, and I repeated my previous achievement of being first afoot. This time, however, I realised that no one had slipped from their beds before daybreak to fetch the horses from the *poove*, and, at seven o'clock, they were clearly visible dotted about in the field. Realising that this would lead to trouble if it was not attended to at once, I hastened along the line of wagons shouting the names of the men whose horses were in the *poove*. But by the time any one of them had summoned up the energy to come out all but young Siddy's pony had vanished.

"Cah! The buggers have *lelled* 'em!" exclaimed Samson disgustedly.

"That's the fust time as ever I've a-bid up in the bed wi'-out wakin' up to git the *grais* out the *poove*," Liberty moaned sadly.

"Well, we'll jest have to git 'em—how much do you think he'll make we pay?" said Snaky, blowing through his moustache, his cap and neckerchief askew.

"I'll bet we has to gie half a *bar* apiece," Liberty rejoined pessimistically.

Liberty, Samson and Snaky shouted to young Siddy who, having emerged creased and rumpled from his old bender-tent, which consisted of an old carpet thrown over some hazel-rods, was advised to catch his pony without more ado. Then they stumped mournfully over the fields in the direction of the farm, gradually disappearing, mat and smoke-dulled in the morning light.

I returned to our wagon and lit the fire; and while the

kettle was boiling I investigated the ground where our mare was tethered to find out how much evidence of the hay was left. Luckily she had eaten all but a few wisps, and so had Fangs's horses.

After nearly half an hour the other men returned, leading their horses. They were deeply mortified, for the farmer had insisted upon the payment of a pound apiece for the horses which he had caught in his field and had threatened the men with violence if he found the horses there again. He had also telephoned the police for good measure. This combination of events made it seem unlikely that we should be allowed to prolong our stay in the lane even for the rest of that day. I expressed these views to the others—who received them with the utmost scorn.

"Wot? Move we today?" Samson exclaimed. "I ain't a-movin' out o' this lane today—not fer all the policemen in the world, I ain't!"

This announcement was unanimously approved.

Some little time later, after the women had gone out 'calling' and I was sitting by the fireside on an upturned bucket, smoking and talking to Fangs, a small shooting-brake suddenly drove at speed into the lane, pulling up abruptly beside us. I knew at once that it was the farmer whose land bordered the lane. He climbed out of the car, a tall, fair, pugnacious man wearing a cap.

"You've had your horses in my fields once too often," he said, his face tight with wrath. "I told them this morning, when they came for the horses, that if they weren't gone from here by nine o'clock I should fetch the police and get you all summonsed. And it's half-past nine now—so that's what I'm going to do!"

"Hold hard!" replied Fangs calmly, his face assuming a

somewhat hurt expression. "You'm a-talkin' to the wrong men, farmer. Do you know where *my* horses was last night?"

"I know all right—in my field!" snapped the farmer.

"An' that's where you'm wrong, farmer. My horses waren't in yer fields—nor his waren't neither, that's so true as I'm here! Now, do you know where they wuz?"

"Well, where were they?" inquired the farmer suspiciously.

"I'll tell you where they wuz, farmer," Fangs answered complacently. "They wuz tied up in this lane—God strike me an' all me children dead iffen that ain't the truth. Now you speak to the right ones, farmer, not to we!"

This happened, of course, to be quite true; and whether the righteousness of true innocence had impressed itself in Fangs's oily tones I do not know, but the irate farmer climbed back into his car without another word and drove past us up the lane to the rest of the men, who were huddled in a group round another smouldering fire, gambling on the turn of a card.

As the car approached, some of them rose to their feet, standing dark and suspicious beside the wagons. We could not catch all that was being said, but the farmer was gesticulating, and some of the men were cursing. Finally, with a shouted threat, the farmer, disregarding the ruts, drove rapidly back up the lane to the road—a barrage of stones and sticks descending on his car's roof, aimed by the men and boys—whose rage had finally got the better of them.

"God's cuss that bloody foxin' bastard — the mother's . . . !" Snaky shouted, his lined face black and hard like a rodent's.

71

" 'Twas lucky we didn't kill the bastard!" Samson muttered. "Cah! Iffen the 'omans had bin here they'd a-kilt 'im fer sure."

Four or five of the smaller boys suddenly appeared in our midst, carrying a cardboard box full of day-old chicks which they had brought to the fire for our inspection. The incident of the farmer was quickly forgotten in this new excitement, for all Romanies are fascinated by young birds or animals.

"Look wot we've a-got!" shouted Samson's son Amos, his tiny dirt-streaked face beaming and his black eyes shining through his long dark hair which hung rough and uncombed about his face.

"Where d'you git they little *kanis*, boy?" Samson demanded suspiciously.

"Did you *chur* 'em?" Snaky asked with interest.

"No, the man gid 'em to us," answered his son Jonah, turning his wizened young-old face upon us.

"Wot man?" asked Samson.

"The farmer gid 'em to us," said Jonah, looking to the others for confirmation.

"Yeah, the man gid 'em to us," said Liberty's child, Benny.

"Wot man gid you they birds?" Samson persisted.

"The man up in the farm—on the cross," replied Amos informatively.

"Yeah, they wuz feedin' 'em to the pigs, so the man gid us these—'least we had to gie 'im a shillin' fer 'em," said a tiny girl with huge eyes and braided hair, clad in a man's tattered jacket that reached to her ankles.

"Wuz the man feedin' 'em to the pigs alive?" Liberty asked with curiosity.

"Some wuz 'live an' others wuz bein' drownded in a sack in the rain-water tub," Jonah replied.

"Cah!" murmured Liberty.

"They'm all cock-birds, ain't 'em, boy?" asked Samson.

"Yeah, most on 'em. They come straight outa the inky-bator—an' then he wuz giein' they to the pigs," repeated Jonah.

"Let 'em out," Samson commanded.

Amos obligingly tipped all the tiny yellow chicks out on to the ground by the fire. There were about fifteen of them, and, righting themselves, they cheeped and ran feebly in all directions. Three ran into the fire. One was burnt to death, its feathers sending out a ghastly smell. The other two escaped the fire's jaws and thus, by experiencing its fierce touch, became proof against its grasp. A little girl cried at the burning of the chick; but her father hastily comforted her by letting her fondle one of the others. Within about ten minutes, strangely enough, the rest of the chicks began to realise that the warmth of the fire was pleasant and they huddled together a foot or so away from its edge, only occasionally forgetting themselves and dashing suicidally into its heat, turning back, cheeping with fear and pain, at the last moment. In this rough-and-tumble life, amidst violence and hazards of every description, providing a tiny bird or animal survives its first day it will probably live to an old age: only the hardy survive.

Beshlie has a special love of birds and we are never without a variety of them. Among the aviary-bred wild species we have a bullfinch, a greenfinch, a goldfinch and also two crested border canaries. The wagon often resounds and echoes to various bird-songs, which are frequently audible even when we are travelling along the roads. In one especially large skylight wagon which we owned we had a number of small foreign hardbills—Zebras, Cut-throats, Nuns, Waxbills and Strawberry finches. One pair of Zebra finches actually went so far as to nest in a tiny wicker basket provided for them, rearing four young, in spite of the fact that we were travelling almost every day during their incubation. We have had two small experiences with cage-birds which are unusual enough, perhaps, to deserve mention. One winter evening, a tiny Strawberry finch escaped from its cage, flying out of the wagon into darkness. Horror-struck by this tragedy, Beshlie snatched up a candle-lantern and hurried out over the snow-covered ground round the wagon, calling to the little bird and holding up its cage in the light of the flickering candle. After a few minutes of what seemed to me to be the most futile calling, a tiny form fluttered to the ground by her foot and, stooping down, Beshlie was able to pick up the cold little finch and replace it in the cage.

On another occasion, some two years later, in the heat of a midsummer's day, the door of one of our canaries' cages became unfastened and its occupant flew out past us as we were eating our lunch by the fire. That, we were convinced, was definitely the last of the canary. The little yellow object, gleaming in the sun, flew away and round the field in which we were stopping, eventually disappearing from view. We resigned ourselves mournfully to its loss. But within ten minutes it was back and had landed on the wagon roof, chirping in a rather alarmed manner. Beshlie immediately called to it, using the call that she used when feeding it; and swiftly yet smoothly she swung its cage from the hook in the wagon's porch, moving it up gently on to the wagon roof a yard or so from the bird. Chirruping happily, the little bird, after a few suspicious hops, entered the open cage door and was soon on the topmost perch, singing with his usual vigour. This astonishing happening was repeated on two other occasions.

Not that I would suggest for a moment that any bird or animal should be kept caged unless it has been hatched or born to such a life and has known no other!

Another time I persuaded a keeper to give me four tiny magpie fledglings that he had removed from their nest to destroy. Beshlie devoted much attention to these tiny naked creatures and her perseverance was rewarded by the fact that all four survived and thrived—their diet consisting of soaked bread, tinned dog meat and, later, insects and carrion of all kinds. Eventually we presented them, in pairs, to an aviary enthusiast and to a naturalist. Their artificial upbringing had rendered them entirely unfit for the battle of survival if they had been released in their natural surroundings.

At the same time as we had the magpies we also acquired a tiny rook fledgling. This bird, whom we named Amos, proved to be far more intelligent and interesting as a pet than the magpies, and from his earliest days evinced marked signs of individuality and character that firmly endeared him to us. After we had given the magpies away we were able to devote more attention to Amos. He was always allowed complete freedom during the day— except when we were actually moving—and was shut up only at night, in a large wicker cage which he soon came to recognise as his home. He became very friendly with

75

all the other animals, and he especially liked a white cat that we had with us then. He did, however, have an extreme dislike of tractors and should one pass near our wagon he would invariably hide himself away until it had become inaudible. Amos was particularly fond of our greyhound bitch, on whose back he would perch and sit preening himself at every opportunity. Unlike most tamed members of the crow family he would evince not the slightest interest in any of his wild brethren whenever they flew, cawing, over the wagon. At the age of nine months he began to talk and also to give absolutely perfect imitations of the barking of the small dogs, the mewing of the cat and the clucking of the bantams. His vocabulary was neither particularly large nor especially original, as it had never been our aim or intention to teach him to talk —so all his words and phrases and other noises were simply those which he had picked up himself of his own accord. We grew very attached to Amos and were con- stantly astounded by his curious ways and tricks—includ- ing one which I have never before or since encountered in a tamed bird, that of shamming death by lying on his side, remaining immune to proddings or comments. When he first performed this trick we were convinced that he *was* dead and were deeply grieved. Another of his favourite habits was to insert his beak into the spout of the teapot and sit in front of it flapping and fluttering his wings as though it were a parent bird ready to feed him! In the end, however, when he was nearly two years old, we found ourselves moving in country where everyone's hand seemed to be turned against the rooks and crows, large shoots being regularly organised. And so, rather than keep Amos caged or see him fall a victim to the ever-ready aim of some 'sportsman', we decided to present him to a lady in Berkshire who had always expressed an affection for him. With a surprising sense of regret—for we are rarely sentimental about parting with animals or birds—I despatched him, complete with wicker cage, to the lady's address in a quiet village where we knew that he would be able to wander about with far greater scope for exploration than we had been able to give him in our own unsettled existence. All our animals and birds have to pin-point the wagon itself as their home, for if they chance to wander away any distance from it they inevitably become lost.

From time to time we have also had a number of temporary bird visitors staying with us in the wagon, including a heron with a gangrenous leg, another rook, an injured carrion crow and a tawny owl—all of whom we later released when they had recovered sufficiently; and numerous smaller birds with varying injuries which we doctored whenever possible, releasing them when cured or killing them if they were too badly damaged.

An experiment which proved most interesting was when we allowed one of our bantams to sit on a clutch of six pheasant's eggs. All hatched successfully and we even kept one of the cockbirds as a pet for some time. None of the other five shy chicks ever really became tame at all, but the one which we kept back did. He would feed from our hands, allow himself to be picked up, and would come and bask in the heat of the fire beside us. Alas, his life was short. He was lost as the result of being mauled by a stranger's dog when he had wandered too far from the safety of our wagon. Both his legs were shattered before

I could rescue him, and it was the kindest thing to put him out of his misery—which I did.

4

We sat or lay round Samson's fire, talking and smoking, watching the chicks. Old Hannah, who had not bothered to go out 'calling', moved slowly across from her wagon, leaning heavily on her stick. A brightly patterned silk scarf was pulled, as usual, low over her forehead. Two large tins were suspended, one each side of her, by a rope round her neck. In these tins, under her coat, she was reputed to carry large sums of money.

No matter how great or small her fortune might actually be, there could be no doubt that her social conscience was highly developed, for unlike most travellers of over seventy, she drew no non-contributory old-age pension.

"I leaves it fer they as needs it," she remarked graciously.

"I seen dear ole Jabez the other day—he wuz axin' fer you. I tole him you wuz ready to go wi' him!" laughed Sonner, mocking her.

"You foxin' black-headed bastard!" Old Hannah boomed quaveringly. "Iffen you gits too close agin me, young man, I'll lay me stick agin yer y'ears!"

"O you wicked ole 'oman—you're wusser'n ole Biddy Skeen!" shouted Noah, amidst loud laughter from the rest of us.

" 'Tis hard fer you to git about wi' all that *vongar* in they tins—can I borree twenty pun, please?" Snaky asked, with a mock-serious face.

"Iffen you gits too close agin me, young man, I'll lay me stick agin yer y'ears!"

An outburst of cursing answered this sally, to the immense enjoyment of everyone.

"Gie me some baccy, Eli," Old Hannah commanded, and the tin was obediently passed to her. She extracted a little and placed it in the bowl of her short-stemmed clay pipe and, lighting it with a burning twig from the fire, puffed happily, and then placed a fragment of red-hot wood on top of the tobacco, which, she stoutly declared, much improved the flavour.

A muddy, chipped, aluminium teapot was lying in the ashes by the fire, and the children were handing it from one to another, each taking a swig from the spout, swallowing its cold contents with evident enjoyment.

"Put that pot down, gal," Liberty told one of his young daughters, but without enough force to make her feel it worthwhile to obey.

"Look at that brazen child," he murmured resignedly.

Time had passed quickly and soon the first of the two traps with three of the women in it returned. They had sold their wares quite quickly, and now in place of the flowers and pegs in their baskets there was food in abundance for their families. Large white loaves, lumps of bacon, tea and sugar, tins of milk, candles, and potatoes —these formed the main bulk of their purchases. The children ran out to meet them, crying out for the sweets and chocolates which they knew would have been brought back for them—and sure enough, within a few moments, their mouths were full of all manner of cheap, sugary sweets, chocolate mice, marshmallows and dolly-mixture! The men did not move—but shouted for the boys to unharness the pony and tether it to graze. A few minutes later the second trap returned and the scene was repeated.

The families then separated and moved back to their own fires to cook the main meal of the day—the time of which frequently varies from two o'clock until five o'clock, depending upon how soon the women return. On a Saturday, however, the women can often sell out and be back home at the encampment soon after noon. Sundays and Mondays are the only two days on which the women never go 'calling.'

We had scarcely finished our meal when the half-expected police car arrived; this time containing a sergeant and a driver. The sergeant glanced at us and strode past us to the further end of the lane where the vans were huddled closest. His was a quietly-spoken manner, official but reasonably polite. He was just explaining that he had received a complaint about our presence there and must, therefore, insist upon our moving there and then when a screech of brakes on the main road attracted our attention and one of the boys ran up, shouting that there had been an accident. The sergeant hurriedly ceased his interrogations and, accompanied by his driver, hastened towards the scene of the accident, a hundred and fifty yards or so along the main road.

After vigorously cross-questioning the little boy, we gathered that a boy had been knocked off his bicycle by a passing car. Our informant, who had hastily withdrawn from the scene lest he should be called as a witness, did not know if he had been hurt.

Great excitement broke out. The men set off in a group to see the gory mess at close quarters, while the women and children surged to the lane entrance and stood in a ragged motley array, gazing down the main road at the little knot of people which had gathered around the motor-car that had done the damage.

"Wuz he kilt?" young Siddy's wife asked curiously.

"I 'spects he wuz," said Polly.

"That dee-little child wuz kilt—stone dead he wuz," announced little Caroline dramatically, romancing wildly, and adding further credence to her statement by continuing, "O *dordi!* An' him a dear little child of only four years old. Why he've a-got a brother an' a sister too; an' his poor mother's too bad wi' the shock to come down the road to see him—jest a-led there kilt, wi' his dee-little guts an' blood all out on the road by him!"

"Kilt? O my blessed Jesus ain't that terrible," breathed Rosie.

The group by the car began to disperse, and a tractor-driver, who had been working nearby and had stopped as a witness, drove along the main road towards us. This was an opportunity for Caroline and so, followed by a horde of other women and children, she marched out and held up the driver, a young man in his early twenties, demanding an instant description of the unfortunate child's death-throes.

I remained by our fire and watched. After a minute or two the tractor continued on its way and the women and children, obviously disgruntled, returned slowly to the lane.

"Was the boy killed?" I asked.

"Kilt?" repeated little Caroline indignantly. "Wot, man? Kilt? Why, he weren't no more'n knocked offen his *treader*. An' now he've rid off home on it!"

The excitement and drama had gone. Romance and sentiment were shattered. Everybody felt slightly cheated.

When the sergeant returned to his task of hastening our departure the previous stubbornness soon resolved itself into movement, as I had predicted it would have to; and our group split up. Most of the other wagons were still not ready to go, but we left with Fangs and Old Hannah, and started for "a lovely place—up agin the sawmill, in a nice ole green lane." Our only cause for optimism came from the fact that it sounded somewhat pleasanter than the destination of the others—ominously named 'Fever-hospital Lane.'

The *'atchin' tan* "up agin the sawmill" proved, however, to be quite unendurable to both Beshlie and myself. It was overlooked, overcrowded, and noisy in the extreme, with the screaming of electric saws going on all day. We stayed there two days—amazingly without any interruption from the police—and then decided to leave the others and to make another circle before the Fair.

None of the others was anxious to move, so we pulled-out alone, after brief farewells. We had decided to head in the Chippenham direction, where I knew of a static Romani who wanted us to paint his showman's wagon. If the weather held good there might just be time enough to complete it before the Fair—and thus furnish ourselves with a reasonable amount of spending or dealing money.

So it was that we reached the outskirts of Chippenham and pulled in on the old Romani's ground—amidst a mass of old lorries and buses, all bought-in for scrap. It was curious to see our tiny wagon hedged in by these dead, inactive monsters.

The old man showed us his ornate wagon in which he lived with his ancient crone-like wife, and we discussed terms. Eventually we fixed upon a price which was agreeable to both sides—I having taken the precaution to ask more than three times what we were prepared to accept! And we agreed to start work next morning. It promised to be a good Devizes Fair for us that spring.

'Vizes Fair

1

THERE were eleven wagons on the marsh, counting our own, and about twelve others in the nearby lanes of the country surrounding Devizes, for it was the day before the Spring Fair. Some thirty horses were tethered or roamed loose about the marsh and on the green of the nearby hamlet. The majority were flashy odd-coloureds, which are so much favoured by travelling-people, who always like a showy animal, although, of course, the old and oft-repeated remark "a good horse ain't never a bad colour" is an eternal truism. Nevertheless many a wild and ill-natured animal has had ten or twenty pounds added to its price because of its colour.

We had arrived that morning, in company with old Sylvester and Tea-Annie and their younger son and his wife. We had met them on the road near Chippenham just after we had finished painting the showman's van—the word having been passed to us that they were stopping there; and we had joined up with them on the journey to Devizes.

The spring and autumn fairs at Devizes are an old-established institution, and once hundreds of horses would change hands amongst our people at them. Nowadays, alas, the number of horses at the fairs has diminished beyond belief, and now they are really only an excuse for a gathering—and for hard drinking. The once-enchanting fun-fair, with its steam organs, rococo round-abouts and swings, and coconut-shies and spinners is now a gigantic dieselled and electrified monster of garish sideshows and slick roundabouts, drowned in the blare of loudspeaker-conveyed American records and the chugging heartbeats of the great looming power-plant lorries. Nevertheless, in the two public-houses in which the travelling-people gather, the riotous atmosphere of bygone fairs survives. And there are always the old to talk to.

Sam and Jobi pulled-in later that day, their dull un-painted little open lots drawn by dejected ponies, their harness mended with string and wire. Jobi stopped with us, whilst Sam joined his brothers Orphie and Albert further across the marsh.

Beshlie and the other women were all out hawking and shopping: even Sam and Jobi had brought their wagons and children on alone. Hard is the lot of the Romani woman, for it is she who keeps the family in 'bread and meat' throughout most of the year except for short periods when the entire family is engaged in some form of casual piece-work farm employment, or, of course, for a short time after she has had a child. And as the family increases in size so the woman's earnings must increase accordingly—more articles have to be made to hawk, and more clothing has to be *monged*. Most of the women—and certainly all those who live in the tradi-tional manner—go out each morning with their full baskets of wares (either flowers or pegs) and with only a few coppers in their pockets. The need for them to dis-pose of their goods, in order that the family may eat that day, spurs them on to greater pains in persuading the often unwilling householders to make a purchase.

At about four o'clock in the afternoon a trolley, drawn by a quick grey pony with a shaggy coat, returned with seven of the women aboard—their baskets filled with food. The children and the dogs rushed out to greet them, the children's hands outstretched for their sweets. By five o'clock all the women were back, and still another wagon had arrived—belonging to 'Hard-times Bob,' the elder of old Sylvester's sons.

Sylvester and Tea-Annie were sharing one large *yog* with their younger son Vesta and his wife and three children, whilst their daughter Tranet and her husband, Indian-Bob, had their own fire next to ours. Old Sylvester and Tea-Annie were both over seventy-five years old and had travelled the roads of Devon, Somerset and Wiltshire all their lives. Tea-Annie was withered and leathery like an ancient monkey, her sparse white hair scraped back flat from her forehead; but Sylvester was light-skinned, wisps of fine grey hair protruding from beneath his hat and falling about his cadaverous and rather aristocratic face. Out of this environment and in different clothes he might have been taken for an elderly retired cleric or scholar. But *in* this environment he was a pure Dickensian character, bent-backed and bow-legged, wearing two ragged well-cut jackets, a red silk neckerchief and stove-pipe corduroy trousers of the old-fashioned Romani man's favourite style. All Romani men are dandies—though the uninitiated might never guess it!

The actual blood relationship between Sylvester and Tea-Annie was close—Tea-Annie being his aunt! I have often wondered if this may have accounted for two of their married offspring being childless—a rare event amongst travelling-people, to whom birth-control is unknown and who frequently measure a man by the size of his family.

I have also noticed that quite often when a 'deep' Romani marries a complete *gaujo* or *gauji*, as the case may be, there is often no issue from their marriage—or at most only *one* child; whereas brothers and sisters on each side who have married into their own races frequently have very *large* families. I have seen so many instances of these happenings that it would appear to be more than mere coincidence.

One of Vesta's children came over to our fire whilst we were having our meal, but was hastily called back.

"Come outa the man's face when he'm eatin' his vittles!" Vesta's wife, Lily, shouted angrily.

It is regarded as ill-mannered by travellers for anyone to sit at another's fire when they are eating, except by strong invitation. Such an example of intuitive good manners by such a much-maligned race could well be followed by some of the less polite *gaujes* when they pass along the roads staring inquisitively at ourselves and our wagons whilst we are sitting eating or cooking our food. To pass between a seated person and the fire is also regarded as being highly impolite.

When we had all finished our meal we went over and sat on the ground by Sylvester's and Tea-Annie's fire to discuss how we should get to Devizes the next day, a distance of some five miles. It was at length decided that we should all go in together on Jobi's trolley, pulled by Vesta's black horse. We ourselves had, at that moment, no extra vehicle with us.

That being decided, old Sylvester's mind began

to turn to half-forgotten fairs of years long gone by.

". . . ar, I used to be a terrible one fer drinkin'," he murmured. "Many's the times as I can mind a-waitin' fer she (pointing at Tea-Annie) to finish callin' in a road, an' then I'd take all the money she'd jest a-got from the houses, an' goo into a public an' spend every penny o' it till I wuz filled up wi' the beer into me. Then one day, when I wuz in a public down agin Frome, I had some poisin in me *livena!* I just wuz a-drinkin' from me pint pot when all on a sudden I gits a terrible pain in me guts —like a knife it were—an' I falls down on the floor." Old Sylvester paused for a moment to let the full impact of his story be absorbed before continuing. "I knowed I'd bin a-poisoned! So I crawls outa the house into the yard where I wuz sickified till I wuz near *mullo*. When the doctor comes he sez that I wuz took bad through a-drinkin' ole beer wot had bin about in they ole lead pipes fer too long, an' that's wot had poisoned me. An' I sez: 'Doctor,' I sez, 'I knows I bin a-poisoned—but 'tweren't by no ole pipes but 'twas by one o' me own delations wot thought I'd done his gal wrong.' An' from that day to this I ain't a-never touched a drop o' beer—ain't that right?"

He looked to his family for confirmation. All nodded seriously in agreement with his oft-repeated story, all that is with the exception of Tea-Annie who continued smoking her pipe imperviously.

During old Sylvester's story-telling a tiny cross-bred whippet puppy had been annoying him by sitting in front of his feet by the fire, and in spite of its having been kicked away half a dozen times or more it insisted, with the obstinacy of extreme youth, on returning to that one particular position. Much enraged by such open disregard for his wishes, old Sylvester grasped the offending puppy in both hands, struggled laboriously to his feet and hobbled over towards a deep ditch some dozen yards behind our wagons. When he had almost reached the ditch he hurled the puppy bodily towards its edge. The puppy bounced once on the barbed-wire fence and disappeared from view, to land, screaming and yelping with pain and fright, in the muddy water of the ditch—where it remained howling and splashing for five minutes or so until it gradually realised that none but its own efforts would bring salvation. Eventually it managed to struggle up the bank to safety, sodden, waterlogged and miserable. Once up, it ran to an old bitch, whose puppies had just been sold, but she snarled and drove it off as it vainly endeavoured to seek shelter under her still-enlarged teats. Nobody save myself had appeared to take any further interest in the puppy from the time it left old Sylvester's hands and dived into the ditch.

"He'll larn," remarked Tranet casually, as a wiser and more wary puppy lay watchfully by her feet. Rough treatment, and the need for scavenging, usually combine to encourage an early maturity in dogs. Of course, since the disappearance of rabbits, dogs are not highly valued, and few travellers would care to pay more than five shillings for one! As is the case with many primitive peoples, the thing that has cost its owner but little is rarely valued for itself. In fairness, I would add that dogs are rarely subjected to any *sustained* chastisement for misdeeds—it is all over very quickly. Even as regards their values there are exceptions. For instance, I myself once began to bid for a dog at half a crown—and rose in stages to three pounds! Yet still its owner would not sell, because the dog belonged to his youngest daughter, aged three, and she did not wish to part from it. The baby often owns the most valuable possession of the family—and rarely wants to part from it!

At the time of writing I see (by taking a careful count) that we have six dogs in all—four small and two large. We have Mossy, the tiny Griffon, who stands only eight and a half inches at shoulder, and his son—this last being the product of a union between Mossy and a tiny Toy Manchester terrier bitch which we kept for some time, only parting from her because of her inability, caused by her very fine coat, to stand the winters in a wagon with any degree of comfort. The son, named Zabett, has proved to be a freakish little creature, even smaller than his father, but a quick and fearless little guard—quick and sure as a weasel. Being born to the life of wagons, Zabett thoroughly enjoys our travelling, leaping with excitement whenever the horses are harnessed-up. We have recently become the owners of a pair of cream, ruby-eyed Chihuahua puppies. As yet, however, these two have not had time fully to accustom themselves to the life and have not developed any marked signs of individuality. The two wagon dogs, a greyhound and a labrador cross Alsatian, are both fairly large, and they appear enormous beside the 'tinies.' Both are excellent watchdogs, refusing to allow any strangers to approach the wagon unless reassured by Beshlie or myself that all is well. We have owned several pure-bred Alsatians in the past, but of them all only one ever proved himself to be either really sensible, free from neurotic tendencies and fully adaptable. Great Danes have always been our favourite. Those noble dogs

have a nature all of their own and almost invariably—
when acquired as puppies—develop in just the way that
their owners desire. Unfortunately the cost of feeding
such immense creatures is almost prohibitive, which is
why we had to sell Naylor. As in other spheres of
life people may dream of being able permanently to
afford a car, so it is our ambition to be able to afford a
Great Dane—and any other livestock we feel inclined to
keep! The linear beauty of greyhounds has always
fascinated us and we invariably own one or two of those
sagacious beasts. I remember one patch-faced white one
whom we called Mumblers owing to his habit of baring
all his teeth when pleased. We also had a rather character-
ful orange brindle dog which came from other travellers,
named, with marked unoriginality, Brin. We also had
an ex-track dog which proved to be rather useless; and a
white show dog who was little better; and another fine-
looking tall dark brindle dog called Chaser who unfortunately developed an incurable mange. Two or three
years ago I bought a Scottish deerhound—hoping that
its combination of the lines of a greyhound plus a tough
weather-resisting coat would fit it admirably to our form
of existence. But our one experiment with that breed
proved so disastrous—the puppy being highly-strung to
an unbearable degree—that we abandoned any further
thought of the breed.

Vesta's wife, Lily, had their year-old baby son at her
breast.

"Do he bite?" inquired Tranet thoughtfully.

"Yes, he do," smiled Lily, gazing fondly at the dark-
faced infant.

"Why don't you put him down an' let un crawl about a bit, gal?" old Tea-Annie asked, looking with some scorn at her daughter-in-law and adding: " 'Twill help make him hard."

The mother placed the baby down on the muddy ground; whereupon he began to cry loudly, so he was whisked back to his place without more ado.

"Why's he got them snaps in his y'ears?" whispered one of Vesta's pretty children, eyeing my ear-rings with some wonder.

"Don't be brazen, gal," snapped her mother.

"He wears they fer the sight o' his *yoks*," informed her grandmother. "They'm good fer the eyes. Why, iffen I gid up a-wearin' these wot I've a-got in *me* y'ears I'd be so blind I couldn't tell silver from gold, nor a half-sovereign note from a green pound 'un."

"O my granny, can I have me y'ears done now . . . ?" began the little girl, her large eyes round with wonder.

"Goo an' hide yer face, gal—you'm too brazen," snapped old Tea-Annie in reply.

Tea-Annie's ears were pendulous and torn and jagged, like so many of the older women's, from the times when 'bad-minded 'omans' had torn her rings through her lobes during fights. Her own ear-rings were solid gold hoops, much larger than mine. I offered to 'have a *chop*' with her but she was not at all enthusiastic at this proposal.

"Wot?" she exclaimed. "*Chop* these away? I wouldn't part from they, no not fer all the money in the world, my brother. Why they wuz gid to me by me poor dear oldest daughter wot's bin dead an' buried these last twenty-two years, an' they 'longed to me dear mother afore that. So I couldn't part from 'em, could I?"

I tactfully agreed that she could not, and the talk turned to other matters, drifting on until the daylight had completely faded. Old Sylvester placed a bit of sacking on the ground by the fire and lay down on it, curled up on his side like an aged sheepdog, his head resting on an upturned bucket.

Tranet and Indian-Bob left to go to bed.

"I'm a-gwin t'have a dee-little baby daughter afor this year's out," grinned Tranet, as they climbed into their little open lot.

"Wot? Why he ain't man enough to make you one!" old Tea-Annie insensitively announced, amidst laughter from the rest and gazing contemptuously upon the unfortunate Indian.

The Indian looked somewhat hurt and they disappeared from view.

"I reckons that man's three parts *dinilo*," muttered Tea-Annie, laughing gutturally to herself.

"Here, old man!" she suddenly shouted, kicking the sleeping Sylvester sharply in the stomach. "Git up into the *verdo* an' take a bit o' fire up fer the stove."

The ancient man obediently levered himself into a sitting position and, filling a cracked enamel bowl with red-hot embers from the fire, crawled unsteadily up into their wagon.

With a muttered "good night" to Vesta and Lily I also withdrew for the night and to the strains of a gramophone from the other wagons across the marsh I fell asleep.

2

The day of 'Vizes Fair dawned bright. A slight pall of mist still hung over the marsh when I awoke, and the sky was pink and glowing. The horses were hungrily cropping the dew-covered grass, their 'plug chains' rattling as they moved, and our mare greeted me as I jumped down from the wagon. I unchained the dogs, and set off to fetch some wood from a nearby copse. The owner of the copse, which was the only source of wood in the neighbourhood, was very hostile to our people, and the night before our arrival there had been a violent quarrel between some of the owner's farm-workers and our men which had culminated in the arrival of the police to restore order. However, as there was no other supply of wood, we had no alternative but to continue our trespassing no matter how great the opposition. Sam and Orphie had their fires already alight when I passed their wagons, though their women and children had not risen, and they were toasting pieces of bread.

"Mawnun'," observed Sam. "Is you goin' arter a bit o' wood?"

I assented.

"You wants to mind how you goes, then," warned Sam. "They guards that *kosh* like it wuz made o' golt— an' the place is 'live wi' *veshengros*."

Thus forewarned I climbed the barbed-wire fence surrounding the copse and moved quietly and furtively into the wood. There was abundant dead wood lying everywhere and I had soon gathered a large amount, which I packed together and secured in a tight bundle with a piece of rope which I had taken with me for that purpose. Suddenly the hackles rose along the greyhound's back and I caught sight of a man's figure moving stealthily in my direction. The man was about a hundred yards away through the trees. I hissed at the dogs and ordered them to return to the wagons, and they slunk quietly away ahead of me. I did not want either of them to be shot. I picked up the wood and, swinging it on to my back, hurried as quickly as I could towards the fence which marked the boundary between the copse and the common land of the marsh. I could hear the twigs snapping behind me as the keeper began rapidly to overtake me. However, with an extra spurt, I made the fence, hurled the bundle over, and swung after it as rapidly as I was able. The man, red-faced and heavy, crashed through some bushes a yard or two behind me, a double-barrelled shotgun under his arm.

"What the hell do you mean by coming in here?" he shouted, his breath coming in gulps. "Haven't I told you buggers to keep out—we don't want you in here, nor anywhere round these parts neither!"

"Good morning," I said politely.

"The next time any of you comes in here I'll see he gets something to remember me by!"

He patted his gun with a pudgy white hand.

"I've just been picking up dead wood," I remarked.

"I knows all about your sort of people," he continued ominously. "Next time I catches any of you in here there's goin' to be *real* trouble. You people ought to be banned from the roads. You leaves dirt and mess about wherever. . . ."

"It's been a great pleasure to meet you," I murmured sarcastically, "and I trust that your devotion to duty brings you great rewards."

Without listening to his reply, I shouldered the wood and set off back across the marsh track.

"Wuz you *lelled*, mush?" Sam inquired as I neared his wagon.

95

"Said he's going to shoot the next one he catches in there," I answered briefly.

" 'Tain't no good fer him to talk like that—'cos we shall still goo in there fer *kosh* jest the same," commented Sam philosophically, creasing his wizened brown face against the smoke from his fire and spitting ruminantly over his shoulder.

By the time I had reached our wagon all the men were up and the blue smoke was curling upwards from the fires beside the wagons. Perhaps, in that quiet age-old scene, its pattern unchanging through the generations, the onlooker might have caught the true glint of romanticism which lies inescapably beneath the dirt, the noise and often the squalor of the rough patchwork that is our people's life: a life of uncertainty, humiliation, movement and chance—a life of no privacy, no property to call one's own—save perhaps an often-rough little wagon and a pony. It is a life in which permanence plays but little part, since landowner or policeman is liable to move one at almost any hour of the day or night. Even 'calling' is a chancy business, in which one is quite liable to have dogs set on one, have doors slammed in one's face, or suffer innumerable other insults and humiliations—often, ironically, from people who, fifty years ago, would probably have suffered the same treatment at the hands of the upper middle-classes. It is a sad thought, which sometimes springs to one's mind, that perhaps, after all, man's pleas for equality are false and that snobbery and discrimination are natural instincts born of situation.

I have even, on two occasions, encountered blacksmiths who refused to shoe my horses on the grounds that they were not willing to assist "you road people." One might speculate with some awe on the inevitable results of a garage-proprietor refusing to sell petrol to a 'working man'!

Some farmers—rapidly decreasing in number—will employ our people for occasional casual piece-work such as hoeing, potato-lifting or other lowly tasks, but the majority regard travelling-people as their natural enemy. The average 'working man' does not view us too kindly —envying, perhaps, our people's apparent escape from his own fixed pattern of toil. The now nebulous 'middle-classes,' however, tend to regard us either with distant interest and condescension, perhaps giving us their cast-off clothing; or, much more rarely (and these are a good find for us!) as some kind of ethereal creatures unworried by mundane things, existing on a diet of berries, nuts and milk; practising strange esoteric rites and engaging in our own deep folk-culture! Such people are, of course, pleasant enough to meet, but unfortunately they are not always in a position to assist us materially themselves— though they may often have friends or relatives who can. On one occasion a would-be romantic of this genus did present me with five shillings as a token of his admiration and esteem for 'gypsies,' expressing at the same time a strong wish that his wife would join him in a whole-hearted emulation of our way of life! I hastily tried to dissuade him from such a rash step, which must inevitably have led him to disillusionment in one heavy jolt.

As there was little likelihood of our returning from the Fair before the late afternoon we all ate a substantial break-fast of fried bacon and eggs, with a few potatoes and onions thrown in for good measure. We had all got up that morning in our motley—ragged, mat, everyday clothes; but after breakfasting almost everyone changed, either fully or partially, into 'Fair-day' clothing. The children's hands and faces were washed more carefully than usual, and much of the soapy, dirty water was combed through their hair, which was slicked back close to their skulls. When this was completed the women followed the same procedure, tying their braids with ribbons of bright colours. Old Tea-Annie rubbed nearly half a cake of damp greenish soap into her sparse hair and combed it flat and greasy over her head, finally covering it with a very old-fashioned travellers'-style purple silk handkerchief with a pattern of white diamonds and squares. She was wearing her best brown button-boots, and a vivid shocking-pink 'pinna' over several brightly-coloured dresses. A huge silver brooch was at her throat, and numerous large silver and gold rings adorned her brown old hands. She sat on an upturned bucket helping Lily to dress the little girls, who were attired for the occasion in some beautifully worked, lacy, frilled, clean and new-looking Victorian children's dresses which had been given to Lily by the occupants of a large house at which she had called.

The men were shaving in turn from an old condensed-milk tin, each using the same razor and brush and scraping hard at the accumulation of stubble which adorned the cheeks of most of them, old Sylvester being an exception. He had performed the operation only two days previously and saw no point in repeating it so soon.

A slight misunderstanding had arisen between Tranet and the Indian which resulted in both deciding not to go to the Fair at all. However, nobody else seemed to be greatly distressed by their decision.

"They'm full of fadiments!" observed Tea-Annie very scornfully, adding, "They've a-nested theirselves wi' the *beng* I reckons."

In time, everyone was ready. The women and children were finely arrayed in a medley of vivid colours, in clothes of contrasting fabrics and clashing designs all happily placed one against the other in merry abandon. All this combined to produce the silhouette which belongs, inevitably and unavoidably, to the Romani.

Most of the older men were dressed in the 'rough' manner of Romani men. All wore hats or caps and brightly-coloured silk neckerchiefs knotted round their necks. The younger men were mostly clad in second-hand 'drape' suits, or in tailor-made modern versions of the old-fashioned 'dealer's suits'—wide-shouldered coats in striped worsted, and many-pocketed; the trousers wide with pleated seams down each leg. On their heads, worn far back, crouched snap-brim hats of the kind associated with cinema gangsters of the 'twenties. Some wore American ties, others knotted scarves. (Many a big-town 'wide boy,' scrap or 'general' dealer, thus attired, is of Romani blood—though he would probably be the last to admit it to anyone outside his kin.)

At that moment Orphie and his wife Freedom drove up, their leggy bay pony drawing them in a tall-wheeled, old-fashioned shooting-brake with long graceful independent shafts, each fixed to the dainty, carved-out lock. These fine, graceful, delicate vehicles, beautifully sprung and designed for any kind of country, are hard to find today. Most of those which fall into travellers' hands meet a sad end when used for scrap-iron collecting or similar heavy work, since their springs, so fine and pliable, crumble under such rough usage. But Orphie's brake was still in remarkably good condition. He and Freedom sat on the front seat, whilst their five younger children were on the floor behind them. They stopped beside our wagons to have a few minutes conversation until we were ready to join them on the journey. Orphie was clad in a very loud, ill-fitting plaid suit in which yellow predominated, a red *diklo*, a green hat and very large muddy boots laced with string. His gorgeous apparel was the subject of some comment.

"*Dordi!*" exclaimed Jobi. "Here comes a dear ole Romani-*rai!*"

"Will you *chop* that suit o' clothes, Orphie?" inquired young Vesta, offering his own faded blue jacket and torn corduroy trousers in exchange.

"He puts me in mind of a dee-little cock *kani*," grinned old Tea-Annie from her seat by the fire.

Orphie became a little embarrassed by these remarks and swivelled his thin cigarette along his lips from one side to the other before announcing, in an enthusiastic attempt to gain face, "I'm in the mood fer a deal today! I reckons I'll *chop* me horse an' wagon away at 'Vizes Fair today. An' mebbe git meself a *kushti* new *juvel* as well!" he added, winking vigorously in all directions.

As he was talking a flat trolley, drawn by a little bay pony, came speeding up from the lower end of the marsh. On it Sam and his family were precariously perched. One of his young cousins and a striking, dark girl with whom he was 'going' were also clinging aboard the little trolley. These two were staying with Sam during the Fair time.

"*Kushti dik*-ing *rackli*, ain't she?" commented Jobi,

"Dordi!" exclaimed Jobi. "Here comes a dear ole Romani-*rai!*"

staring admiringly at the dark girl, who smiled but turned her eyes away and said nothing.

Tea-Annie and old Sylvester decided to ride in to the Fair with Sam and his family despite the crowded state of the little trolley. Sam's wife, lean and jet-haired, over-bright eyes set deep under her brows, was a little put out of countenance when she suddenly recollected that she had forgotten her 'mumblers.' However, she was dissuaded from returning for them, and when Sylvester and Tea-Annie had clambered on to the trolley, the two parties set off with much shouting and occasional bursts of singing.

Young Vesta, the last to reach the milk-tin, was still shaving. This he did rapidly and erratically, cutting himself several times and leaving long sideburns lower than the lobes of his ears. Slicking his fair hair down with a comb dipped into the brackish bristle-filled remains of the soapy water in the milk-tin, he pulled on his old cap, far back over one ear so that its peak stood up vertically. Jobi had harnessed up the black horse and Vesta ran and fetched a clean new canvas sheet which he laid carefully over the bed of the trolley to protect our Fair-day clothes from harm. Young Vesta, it being his horse, took the driving seat and Jobi and I sat on either side of him while his wife and three children, Beshlie, and two other women sat behind.

"We'll soon kitch they up wots gone on," pronounced young Vesta, who was a cruel and reckless driver. It was a point of honour with him that his horse should arrive first at the Fair, no matter how great the others' start might be.

A long ash bough in his hand, Vesta gave the black

horse a switch and it leapt forward. It was a tall, leggy
animal, hard-mouthed and unresponsive after years of
rough handling. Yet even so it hardly deserved the treatment meted out to it on that hazardous five-mile journey.
We soon swung and jolted over the rough marsh track
and out on to the road, the horse's hooves clattering and
echoing on the metal surface. The other two parties were
long out of sight. Young Vesta jerked and tugged the
reins alternately every few seconds and we dashed onwards. When we reached the first village we came upon
some other travelling-people waiting at a bus stop. Young
Vesta pulled the horse so sharply to a halt that it went back
on its haunches, and invited the waiting party to ride with
us, which offer they readily accepted. It was Walty and
his wife, five more children, and two or three unattached
girls—their faces inexpertly rouged and powdered, which
made them look like tiny brittle harlots. There were now
over twenty people aboard the trolley. It was a tight
squeeze, with Walty joining us on the footboard. We
started off again along a stretch of straight road with a
series of bends and hills ahead. Young Vesta thwacked
the ash pole across each of the horse's flanks in quick
succession and we flashed onwards at full gallop to the
consternation of a few of the women behind.

On the first bend we caught a glimpse of the two other
carts and their passengers on the crest of a short hill about
three-quarters of a mile ahead. Our own road began to
climb and we rattled along, young Vesta allowing no
slackening of pace; and then the road fell away in a long
steady downward slope. Walty turned the brake wheel
until the traces remained taut and the horse, having no
weight to hold back, continued at a fast trot down the

hill, snorting half in fear and half in annoyance at the rashness of the driver in forcing such a suicidal pace on the slippery, glassy surface. Nevertheless, we reached the bottom without mishap, and then began a stiff climb. The horse began to lather and steam as young Vesta, with many a vicious 'stripe' from the pole and a hack from the reins, callously endeavoured to keep it trotting *up* the gradient. Nobody dismounted from the trolley: and all praised the horse's stamina. Eventually the crest was reached, the brakes were reapplied and we sped down-hill once again, through a small village with the cottage doors open for the inhabitants to watch 'the gypsies' speeding past. We clattered round a corner and there saw the vehicles of Sam and Orphie only a matter of a hundred yards or so ahead of us. Applying the ash stick in heartless cracking blows, young Vesta urged the horse forwards, cursing to himself, his small yellow face set hard, his tiny eyes half-closed. Another uphill pull confronted us and most of Sam's and Orphie's passengers dismounted to lighten their ponies' loads, being more thoughtful for their horses than Vesta, who would not allow any of *us* to do so. We passed the others with cries of derision and mockery and soon we left them far behind and out of sight. But as we rounded another bend a mile or so farther on disaster nearly struck us. A steam-roller was moving ponderously back and forth on some road workings a little distance ahead of us. I sensed that the horse would not like this strange monster and warned young Vesta.

"Wot?" he ejaculated in scorn. "Why, this horse'll pass anything on the road, mush—an' I'm the man as knows."

My doubts were soon justified as we neared the roller —the driver of which had neither the sense nor the courtesy to remain still until we had passed. The black horse veered sharply away from the oncoming roller, and the trolley's wheels mounted the kerb with a mighty jolt, almost driving the trolley's side against the walls of the village cottages which were set on the roadside. Suddenly the horse shied up, rearing on to its hind legs and snorting and panting. Some of the women gasped, and one shouted that her baby was dead. Young Vesta, however, was not deterred by this, and seizing the thinner end of the ash pole, he administered harsh resounding blows against the horse's flanks, back, and hocks with all his force—standing up on the trolley's footboard to gain greater play. A few moments of hazard, with the horse wavering between fear of the monster and pain of its beating, and then its mind was made up. With a leap and a rush it broke into full bolting gallop, sending us careering forwards past the steam-roller, through the village and far along the road at a harrowing rate, the roadmen pausing in their work to gape aghast and horrified as we flashed past. Vesta was much annoyed at his horse's show of bad behaviour and nerves and he kept up the pace for half a mile or more, letting the horse have his head. Then he pulled the horse back into a fast trot, continuing to beat him with the pole until, enraged and puzzled, the distraught and exhausted animal began 'hopping'—jumping with all four legs held stiff in the manner of an unbroken horse attempting to unseat his rider—until shouts and stick drove him on again. But our journey was almost over, and in a few minutes we arrived at the fairground—sweat pouring off the horse and leaving a trail like a leaking barrel on the road behind us.

3

We drew up on the green beside the fun-fair, where a large number of other travelling-people had already congregated. Several horse-drawn vehicles of different kinds were parked against the far side of the green. Some of the horses were tethered to the railings, others were still harnessed in their carts, while still others had been left loose to wander about and crop the short grass of the green before returning home that night. One small bay pony had been left fully harnessed except for its headstall and was grazing while still drawing a small tub-cart about behind it.

We dismounted from the trolley and walked over to the far side of the green where the groups of travellers were gathered, seated in small rings as though around imaginary fires, chattering and laughing and exchanging gossip and family news. No one is as interested in the Romani and his relatives as he is himself. The student's enthusiasm and scientific dissection may hold him in good stead when studying the race as a whole—but his interest, if not his knowledge, is always exceeded by the Romani himself, whose natural egocentricity and preoccupation with himself and his own kind is never lacking.

Indeed, at any Romani gathering it is always to matters of the race and purely family talk that conversation turns —never to the affairs of the outside world in any form at all.

As large numbers of travellers, both of the static hut- or house-dwelling kind (who still, of course, call themselves 'travellers' as it is a recognised race name) and of the wandering wagon-dwelling sort gather at Devizes

Fair, a strict vigil is kept by the police throughout the day and evening. They patrol in pairs, sometimes with a dog, their eyes for ever on our people on their day of enjoyment. The police are also on the lookout for travellers who have not answered summonses and also for those to whom to *issue* them. Pouncing on the merrymakers in the public-house has always seemed to me to be a rather third-rate trick to play.

A young constable, leading a rather undersized collie-like Alsatian dog and obviously unfamiliar with travellers, was passing near to our group as we were seated on the green talking. Old Miella Skeen, with whom I was in conversation, saw the dog and, noting its size, addressed the young constable in her best *monging* tones:

"Would you gie me that puppy, policeman? I wants one fer me little granchile wot's bin bad wi' the branichals an' the yaller gandice. . . . Would you gie me that puppy, please, policeman? *Gie* me that puppy, please. . . ."

Her voice trailed off as the constable, his face paling slightly at this affront to his dignity, led his dejected cur quickly away without a word.

And the talk flowed on about me, quick, jabbering, almost unintelligible to an outsider.

"Where's you '*atched* to now?"

"Up agin the milk factory. . . ."

"Bob's bin bad, so' my Britty, an' my Lias an' my Violet. . . ."

". . . an' the policeman come to us, brother, an' he sez iffen we ain't a-gone be the middle o' the day. . . ."

"Wot? Dead? O my mother! I never heered, so help me God I never heered. . . ."

"He wuz led down agin the *yog* an' we thought he

wuz just a–sleepin', then me granny wot's got the rheumatickses bad. . . ."

". . . he'd bring we a paper—an' one fer everyone on
us wot owned a *grai* in that lane that. . . ."

"Wot's bin the matter wi' 'em, gal?"

"Dead an' buried! O *dordi,* an' we never heered one
word, an' that's so true as I'm yere. . . ."

". . . don't be brazen I sez. . . ."

". . . make me a *chavi!* Pass me the baccy. . . ."

"That's the most God's-cussed place wot ever I've
a-bid into. . . ."

". . . an' may the blessed God hisself come down outa
the sky this minute and strike me an' all me children dead
iffen that ain't the truth wot I'm a-tellin' of you now. . . ."

"An' I'm the man as'll gie it yer as soon as look at yer!"

". . . come to we last Sunday an' axes to buy the
grey mare wot we bought offen me dear Uncle Jobi. . . ."

"Fifty-five pun he offers me for that mare. . . ."

"Better'n I have bin, thank you. . . ."

". . . up agin the ole *kenner* wi' me Auntie Mary-
Jaynette. . . ."

"Mawnun', lady—could you spare me sixpence fer the
baby, lady? It'd be sure to bring you luck. . . ."

"Goooooooaaaaaan! Fox yer mother! You never gid
no more'n fifty pun for un. . . ."

". . . best wagon in this country, brother. If you can
find me a better'n I'll *gie* you that wagon fer nuthin'!"

"She've jest had another—baby gal 'tis. . . ."

"Omy Annie! Wot? I've a got fifteen now. . . ."

"Rosie—she wots got Speary, don't you know. . . ."

"Tilly lost her's. . . . No, I means the one wot's got
German, don't you know, Lias's brother. . . ."

". . . we can bide there till we'm grey-headed. . . ."

And the sun grew hotter and the fairground music increased in volume. More and more travellers arrived, some in lorries, some in traps or on trolleys, others in motor-vans, all easily distinguishable no matter what their transport and no matter, as happened in some cases, how good their attempt at *gaujo* disguise. It is very disheartening to see how many travelling-people—particularly when no longer travelling the roads—prefer to try to pass themselves off as *gaujes* rather than face the snubs and indignities that almost inevitably befall the Romani who, by way of his dress or bearing, openly asserts his race.

There began a steady drift towards each of the two public-houses which consented to serve our sort of people. One, very small and gloomy, and set in a back street, was mostly frequented by the horse-and-wagon travellers; the other, being slightly superior in situation, tended to draw the more well-to-do dealers and ex-wagon people, showmen and even a few *gaujes*.

I naturally preferred the first—'The Greyhound'—and we soon made our way in that direction. Although only noon, the place was full to over-capacity: both rooms, the courtyard and all the passages were seething with travellers. There were 'deep' Romanies, *diddikais* like myself; men, women, and lots of children. So far as I could judge, except behind the bars, there was not a single *gaujo* present. Within five minutes I had bought Jobi and Vesta a drink apiece, and had had my own cup refilled by another traveller—a tall man wearing a black hat with a hole in it. Brown, creased faces and glittering dark eyes were everywhere in the haze of tobacco smoke.

"Take them children out!" shouted the landlady in a high-pitched voice, noticing four or five tiny children crawling about amongst the men's legs, as well as a baby being fed by its mother from a beer bottle with a teat affixed to it!

As the time passed and the amount of beer consumed increased, so the whole tempo quickened. The older people sat round the walls conversing happily of the joys of long-past fairs, while the younger men and women filled the floor-space. Rough sentences became caught and entwined in the spirals of smoke drifting ceilingwards from countless cheap cigarettes and clay pipes, and fragments of a mouth-organ's melody reached us from the other room. The ripening atmosphere drove Beshlie and many of the other women out into the courtyard or on to the pavement outside the house itself, where they sat down unselfconsciously in groups to continue their conversations. To the men, however, the scene spelled enchantment. For the moment their personal troubles were forgotten in a celebration of Hogarthian robustness.

I moved temporarily out into the passage to have a drink with old Leander, who had been beckoning me fetchingly from the door. She was seventy-eight years old, yet her eyes were bright and undimmed in her brown wrinkled face and her ungreyed hair fell in ringlets about her face. Large silver rings hung from her ears, and she was smoking a snapped-off clay pipe.

"Most of these wot's yere today's me delations," she remarked thoughtfully, after we had been talking for some little time, "but I doesn't speak to many on 'em, 'cos you cain't put no pendation in 'em—an' they ain't wuth that!" And she spat vehemently on to the floor at her feet, grinding the nicotine-stained saliva into the boards with her toe and grinning at me.

After two or three glasses of black beer with her—all of which she insisted on buying *me*—and indulging in a few bed-jokes which culminated in our promising to spend the night in each other's company—to the vast enjoyment and amusement of some other people who had been listening—I withdrew to the rear parlour where I found old Sylvester and a mass of the older Romanies listening to various singers demonstrating their prowess.

Contrary to the chorus songs of the *gaujes'* public-house celebrations, our people always sing alone and in turn— being listened to politely by all present until their song has ended, in spite of the fact that very often almost every-one present knows their song by heart. There were only two definitely *gaujo* songs that I heard—one, a modern sentimental ballad concerning a paper doll, which was offered by a young man in an American hat and a gaberdine drape suit; the other a magnificent if somewhat obscure lyrical melody which I had some difficulty in following. Its singer was a vast middle-aged man, only his eyes suggesting his Romani ancestry, flabby and paunchy, with cap over one ear and a cigarette end behind the other; and his delivery was operatic and filled with extravagant gestures and dramatic pauses. Indeed, in the song's extremes of sentimentality the singer was reduced almost to tears. It was a surprising work and appeared to be dedicated to the praise of Christmas-trees! It was so well done that it brought thunderous applause from the audience—for who loves sentiment more than the Romanies?

Unfortunately, at this point I became involved in a

rather energetic argument concerning horses, and so was unable to listen very attentively to the several men and women whose songs followed 'The Christmas Tree.' This grieved me as one woman, especially, had seemed to be performing a really fine old Romani ballad, her voice, harsh, long-drawn and melancholy, filling the whole room with sadness. I recognised the tune as one which my grandmother used to hum, but the words, long forgotten, were new to me.

A minor disturbance broke out when a young traveller of slick appearance endeavoured to plant a kiss on the forehead of a young girl seated with her mother by the wall. The girl's mother, however, who possessed the fascinating name of Cinderella Bull, strongly disapproved and brought an empty beer bottle sharply down on the back of the youth's head and floored him. He lay cursing roundly and vowing that he was fatally injured. Fortunately further trouble was prevented by the people near him, all of whom declared him thoroughly 'brazen.'

Meanwhile the singer continued, quite unabashed by the disturbance. She ended her song almost in a trance, and fell back into her chair. Her place was immediately taken by a young man of ragged appearance, with black hair and yellow *diklo*. His song was, alas, sung in a disappointingly nervous manner, his mother frequently backing him up and prodding him sharply when he lagged. His further performance was completely shattered by the sight of two constables entering the room and shouting 'Time!' in unison. For a few seconds there was complete uproar, until it was definitely established beyond any doubt that it really *was* 'time.' That no 'extra time' had been applied for by the landlady came as a great shock to us all, for it had been generally assumed and accepted that service would continue until four o'clock. Peace and goodwill was further strained by the fact that several more constables had come in and had begun searching among us for travelling-people who should have had summonses served upon them, but who had, so far, been untraceable.

"Wot! Black Horse Green?" I heard Samson ejaculating in wrathful indignation. "Where's that to, policeman? I've a-never bin to that place in all me life—an' that's so true as I'm yere, policeman."

"Name and age. . . ." The constable's voice droned on, moving among us and edging us gently but firmly towards the doors.

In a few more minutes I found myself outside and amidst a swarming mass of swaying, unsteady travellers. A few were singing, others step-dancing. A fight broke out between two dealer-type travellers, but it was immediately quelled by three constables who converged speedily on the revellers. Devizes Fair has been the scene of much violence on the part of travelling-people in days gone by, and it has long been thought advisable by the local authorities to place a strong police control upon our section of it.

I found Beshlie with the others, and slowly, in a wave of ragged smoke-dulled colour, we all drifted back to the green beside the fun-fair and the small auction-ring for horses. Most of our people in nearly every fair conduct the greater part of their dealings outside the actual auction, and on this occasion several travellers had already started dealing before we reached the green. A young Romani was running a large grey cob up and down one of the

113

8

green's smooth asphalt paths, followed closely by a small middle-aged traveller, armed with a thick cudgel with which he was unceasingly beating the unfortunate animal. Despite the small man's zeal, however, no one bid for the cob, which was withdrawn after a short time, with much cursing. The instant the cob was out of the running a short crippled traveller, spectacularly clad in a bowler hat and neckerchief and round-collared 'dealer's suit', came forward. He was Smiler Joe Scamp and he had a complete turnout for sale, comprising a large odd-coloured cob and harness, and a good flat trolley with yellow wheels. In an effort to impress possible buyers he and Black Orphie took it in turns to drive at breakneck speed up and down the narrow path—speeding far up the path and then wheeling round and tearing down towards us. The watchers who crowded on to the path as the turnout galloped away leapt aside on its return in the nick of time to avoid being knocked aside by the galloping cob. Walking, trotting, galloping—then backing, stopping, starting, stopping: and all accompanied by a constant flow of loud sales-talk by Orphie or Smiler.

". . . an' tell you what, mister," shouted Smiler, limping round in circles and addressing us all, "you can put that cob in a wagon wi' all the wheels locked—an' I'll bet any man here fifty pun as that cob'd pull it! An' he'd goo on fer twenty mile or more! An' if there's a man yere today who's man enough to have a deal then I'm the man as'll gie you a *good* hoss, wuth the money!"

The spectators nodded. The cob raced back towards us again. We leapt back. Black Orphie suddenly and forcefully drew the horse back to a halt and, tossing the reins down on to its back, jumped off the trolley.

"Cah! Wi'out tellin' a word of a lie that's the best hoss as ever I druv!" he announced with conviction.

Up jumped Smiler, shook the reins, emitted a harsh shout, and away they went, turning round a hundred yards away and speeding back straight at us—only pulling up sharp at the last moment with the horse's dilated nostrils within inches of us. Several men spat nonchalantly.

"Now is there anyone here who'll make me a reasonable bid fer the turnout?" inquired Smiler, his little black eyes darting over our group.

"I'll gie you forty pun fer the lot," remarked a small hunch-backed Romani casually. Ragged ill-fitting clothing hung about his malformed body and run-down unpolished shoes were on his feet. The uninitiated would have judged that he did not possess forty *pence*.

"Wot? My bloody Gawd!" exclaimed Smiler and Orphie simultaneously. "My dead mother! Why I'd git more'n that fer the *grai* alone, jest fer death!"

"Goooooaaaaan! I'll gie you forty-two pun fer the lot—an' that's me last word!" the hunch-backed man, Mushy, shouted doggedly.

"I tell you wot I'll do," replied Smiler ingratiatingly. "I'll take sixty pun fer the turnout!"

A tall dark man, part-Romani, with one leg and a crutch and wearing an American hat and well-tailored suit, shouted:

"I'll gie you forty-five pun, Smiler."

"That ain't no bid! Ain't no one got any money yere today?"

"Ar, I've got the money all right—an' I'm aimin' to keep it too!" replied the large man nastily.

Smiler made a derogatory comment regarding the other's conception, which evoked such a flow of oaths and curses that a rather colourless *gaujo* and his wife, who had stopped for a moment to watch the dealings, hastened away, paling slightly.

Smiler soon decided that there was no sale to be had in that quarter and returned to his former tactics with renewed vigour and fervour, his moods oscillating between contemptuous scorn at his prospective buyers' timidity in not availing themselves of his fine offer and fury at their stupidity. But when neither brought forth a bid in excess of the one already offered he turned to wheedling and pleading with them, eventually announcing that he had no further intention of selling to them at all as, in his opinion, they obviously had not sufficient money to pay his price. But all these tricks and insults failed to raise the price above forty-eight pounds, which was bid by Nelson Black; and eventually, after further argument, their palms met with a crack and the deal was sealed. Nelson called to his wife and she produced a thick wad of notes from her bosom and the requisite sum was counted out. It is an old custom for the women to look after all the money—especially at fairs, where it is quite possible that the men may become roaring drunk and lose it all!

During this major deal Sam had '*chopped* away' his tall bay pony—a four-year-old—for a black one, which was obviously older and appeared to be less sound. This, combined with the fact that he had to give a pound to *chop*, led other bystanders and myself to conclude that he had had the worst of that deal. Even his wife, carrying their money, seemed loath to give him the note to clinch the deal. However, Sam was stubborn, and in spite of whispered advice from several of his older 'delations' he insisted on having the deal settled. In the lives of Romanies

there are few secrets! And in the harsh and selfish struggle
for survival there is but little genuine love lost between
the families: resentment and back-biting go hand in hand.
Feuds and fierce family ties are strong. The path of love is
thorny among the travellers, although children are plentiful, and happiness has to be snatched from the uncertainty
that is our life.

"O can we stop by the road tonight, policeman,
    Jest fer the night, please, dear sir. . . ."

The gramophone crooners from the Fair's loudspeakers
poured around us still. More horses were being run up
and down, and more gesticulating deals were in progress.

Then young Vesta came up to Beshlie and me and asked
if we were ready to return to the encampment as his
father and mother had seen enough of the Fair. So with
some regret to be leaving the others who were staying on we
climbed aboard the trolley which young Vesta had ready.

Old Sylvester and Tea-Annie sat with us going home.

An olive-skinned Romani man, in early middle-age,
remarked to old Tea-Annie: "Shall I come back 'long
wi' you—an' p'rhaps I kin make you a *chavi* tonight!"

Old Tea-Annie's lined brown face broke into a
thousand wrinkles as her little old face creased into a
monkey-smile of appreciation of this suggestion.

"Goooooaaaaaan!" she laughed with mock severity.
"You go on wi' yer own *juvel*!"

And with much laughter and shouting we drove off.
Several Romani women who had been waving us farewell suddenly raised their skirts above their knees and
shook an upraised leg apiece at our departing trolley—
surely to the astonishment of various non-travellers who
happened to witness it!

4

The homeward journey was slightly easier for the horse, there being only ten persons on the trolley, counting young Vesta's children. But we kept up much the same pace as in the morning and even had the ill-luck to meet the same steam-roller—and with much the same effect as before!

It was nearly five o'clock when we finally drove across the marsh to the wagons. Old Tea-Annie's wagon was gleaming yellow in the evening sun, the dogs raced out barking, and those tied under the wagons bayed furiously and tugged at their chains in excitement. Tranet and Indian-Bob both stood up by their fire to watch our approach, their faces inscrutable. We were the first back, and by invitation we joined the others at the Indian's fire; and we hung our kettle in its flames in order to have a speedy cup of tea, for our throats were parched from the dusty roads and the smoke-laden atmosphere of the public-house.

After we had all eaten some 'bread and meat' and had drunk considerable amounts of '*meskie* we sat and talked of the Fair and of the people who were there.

Old Tea-Annie lit her pipe.

"I'd sooner go wi'out me *moro* an' *mass* than wi'out me ole *swigler*," she muttered, puffing stolidly.

As it happened we possessed at that time a very big hoop-handled stew-pot which was far too large for us; so when I noticed a little half-gallon sized pot lying near the fire I suggested that Tea-Annie should give me a pound note to *chop*.

Viewing this suggestion with great scorn, old Tea-

Annie nevertheless asked to be allowed to inspect our pot. I fetched it from where it was hanging under our wagon, and gave it to her to look at. Inspecting its unchipped and moderately clean interior she put it down with mock disgust.

"He'm all a-cracked inside. He ain't no good, brother. Still, iffen you gies me fifteen shillin' to *chop* you kin have my little un there wot's so good as new."

We haggled and squabbled for an hour or so, after which time old Tea-Annie had agreed to give *me* five shillings to *chop*!

" 'Tis me snail pot, don't you know—an' I ain't really particular about partin' from un," she remarked, her eyes squinting at me from behind a pall of smoke from her pipe.

Some of the southern travelling-people still collect and eat snails, stewing them for several hours and then draining off the liquid. Although I have often eaten hedgehogs, badgers and many different kinds of birds, I have never eaten snails.

"Look, my pretty old 'oman," I tried. "I tell you what I'll do. Now—because I like your face, and because I know you'd help me—I'll take ten shillings to *chop*. Quick! Give me the ten shillings. . . ."

"Go and hide yer face, man! I ain't a-gwin to gie no more'n five shillin' to *chop*—an' that's me last word!"

Our haggling continued. Then old Tea-Annie, with feigned wrath, spat out: "I'll gie you seven shillin's and sixpence to *chop*!"

My hand met hers in a clap, palm to palm, and the deal was done—or so I thought.

Then, in a last effort to get the better of me, she said:

"But I ain't a-got no money at this moment—so will you let me gie it you the next time I sees you? I shall sure to see you again."

"What?" I ejaculated, much outraged at such an old trick. "Do you think I'm a *dinilo*?"

"Well I ain't a-got no money an' so help me God iffen that ain't the truth. 'Tis so true as I'm yere, so I'll gie it you next time I sees you—else'n we cain't have no deal. You trustys me, doesn't you?"

However, to Tea-Annie's mortification, old Sylvester, who had been sleeping beside the fire, suddenly awoke and, gathering that I was owed seven and sixpence, placed his hand in his pocket and without more ado gave me three half-crowns!

Old Tea-Annie was amazed, and regarded him with astonished horror.

I was unable to restrain my laughter and the others, quick to appreciate a joke against their mother, joined in loudly.

Poor old Sylvester, still only half awake, gazed feebly around him trying to discover what was amiss.

The situation, from his point of view, was somewhat relieved by the return of Sam and his family driving their new horse. Sam's wife Britannia was a niece of Sylvester's, and she had been to the mental hospital to see her eldest son who had been confined there following 'a funny 'tack' in which he had injured another Romani boy rather badly with a kettle-crane.

Britannia joined us at the fire whilst Sam and the children drove on over the marsh to their wagon.

"Did you go down the 'sylum, gal?" asked old Tea-Annie.

"Yeah, I went in there an' . . ." began Britannia.

"Cah! Did you go in there by yerself?" interrupted young Vesta's wife, her eyes wide with awe.

"Yeah, I jest walked straight inside the . . ." began Britannia again.

"You has to be careful o' they people wot's shet in they places," advised old Sylvester sagely. "Why iffen one on 'em wuz to bite you then you'd go outa yer mind so bad as they—an no doctors couldn't do nuthin' fer yer!"

This statement produced a fearful and awestruck silence. I had a mental picture of poor Britannia being gnawed hungrily by numbers of the institution's inmates.

"There weren't no *nusses*—they wuz all *doctors*," continued Britannia, her rather beautiful dark features creased at the memory. "An' I wuz a-walkin' through one o' they rooms when a mush jumps up on to his bed—balls-nekkid he wuz—an' starts a-hollerin' an' dancin'. *Dordi!* I wuz so *trashed* I nearly felled down. Then three o' they doctors kitched hold on 'im an' pushed un down in the bed. One o' they told me as he'd bin a-havin' they fits every hour fer the last six months—an' his wife had revorced un! Then they takes me through some more big rooms till we gits the garden—an' there wuz my Awkie a-workin' there. They've gid him work to do now, see, 'cos he'm so much better. So now he'm doin' a bit o' gardenin' an' hoein' an' that. . . ."

"Wuz he bad?" interrupted young Vesta.

"Nah! He wuz better!" exclaimed Britannia. "Why he wuz full o' sensible talk—jest like we is yere—an' he axed about every one o' yous. The doctors tole me as they may let un out on license by the fall o' the year."

Britannia pondered over this for a moment or two, then added a little pathetically: "Cah! I should like to have my Awkie back a-travellin' wi' us agin."

A variety of other questions followed this account, especially concerning other travelling-people—of whom there appeared to be a considerable number—who were resident in the mental institution.

Then, as the daylight was fading, the last trolley returned, its passengers singing and laughing.

"Ar, they've a-got the beer into 'em all right," observed Tea-Annie, adding maliciously: "They sez that's a 'bouncer' wot Orphie's a-drivin' now."

"He'm 'nappy' iffen he ain't a 'bouncer' anyways," remarked Sylvester.

Some time later in the evening most of the men went out to the nearest public-house whose landlord would serve them. And while the women remained by their fires or in their wagons, old Sylvester, the Indian and I stayed by our fire and talked of horses, dogs, stopping-places, wagons, other travelling-people and the like until the time had passed and most of the men returned.

They all came back together, on a lorry driven by a part-Romani from Gloucester, some too drunk to stand, most exceedingly merry or morose. Wisdom and another man had come back with the others to see Orphie's wagon, which he was considering selling, and while they were there Sam insisted on demonstrating the prowess of his new horse and, despite the fact that it was nearly eleven o'clock, promptly harnessed it up and hitched it into the wagon-shafts. Unfortunately Sam, who was partially drunk, had omitted to inform his wife and children of his plans or intentions. Thus, the instant the horse moved the little open lot forwards, Sam's wife and children leapt from their beds screaming with fear at the unexpected movement.

"O my blessed Jesus!" screamed Sam's wife. "We'm all kilt! O my Jesus! The baby's dead. . . ."

This, combined with the darkness, was too much for the new horse, which had probably never pulled a wagon before. It promptly reared up, Sam lost his hold, and before anyone could grab its head, it had dashed sharply round with the wagon on a hard lock, turning itself and the complete wagon over.

Screams and shouts broke out. Three men rushed to the horse, pulled it to its feet, and began beating it about the head and back. The man who had come with Wisdom was quick enough to unhitch the traces and the horse was loosed. The others, with much heaving, spitting and cursing, eventually managed to hoist the little wagon upright again. It was found that, by some strange piece of luck, none of the wheels was damaged and that, apart from a lot of mud on its side, the wagon was unharmed.

The screams and shouts had awakened all those who had been asleep, and dozens of women and children crowded round in excitement. A rather sheepish Sam was endeavouring to placate his wife, who vowed that she would leave him in the morning. After a time all was quiet again and I withdrew to bed, leaving a few of the men still trying to have a deal at the far end of the marsh.

We were all up early the next morning and hastened to make ready to be off before the 'control' cars began their rounds of our people's stopping-places to start us moving again.

We agreed to accompany old Tea-Annie and Sylvester and their sons and daughters as far as the Dorset borders, where our ways would part.

Despite the fact that we were all abroad at sunup, it was nearly half-past nine before we were ready to move. Old Sylvester had hitched-in his large odd-coloured mare and had taken the wagon out over the marsh and on to the road where he left the turnout and returned to us to help the rest of the family prepare for departure. The canary-coloured wagon, long and squat, and the thick mare, were a pleasing sight in the morning sunlight; and two lurcher dogs were tied to the rear of the wagon, where they stood restively and anxious to be off.

Gradually the horses were harnessed and put in the shafts, the bantams caught and the kettle-cranes, pots, food-hampers and plug-chains all stowed away on the wagon-racks or trolleys. Then, when the children were safely up in the wagons, we started off over the marsh, our wagon first, then Jobi's, then a trolley, followed by the Indian's and Vesta's, a pony and trap driven by a young boy and two more carts. The embers from the fires were still smouldering as we left, pulling-out on to the road in a line behind old Sylvester's patiently waiting horse and van.

And so we were off once more, on our respective circles, some short enough to embrace the Devizes Autumn Fair, others so long that it would be hard to make the next Spring Fair in time. However, even if we did not encounter the others again for a year, we could remain reasonably confident that their lives would remain unchanged. The lack of fundamental change is one of the few comforts of our lives when all around us the pattern of existence is ever changing and ever re-forming.

PART TWO

"Sorta Diserable"

PART TWO

"Sorta Diserable"

EVEN though it was mid-June a strong wind was blowing, bringing with it a saturating drizzle. Having spent the previous night on a verge beside the road, within sight and sound of a vast new council house estate on the outskirts of the gloomily named town of Basingstoke in Hampshire, Beshlie and I were anxious to *jal* on as soon as possible. There was no food left, so we breakfasted on two cups of tea each, and sat for a while absorbing the warmth from the fire—our wet clothes steaming in its heat. A few early morning workmen passed by on their bicycles, grey in silhouette against the rain. One shouted: "Good mornin'." The others glanced at us curiously and said nothing.

By half-past seven I had untethered the mare and had harnessed her up. Beshlie replaced the cups in the basket on the rack of the wagon, and placed the plug-chain in its canvas bag, hanging it up under the wagon. Then she called to the bantams, who had been let out when I came down and, as they were all hand-tame, picked them up one by one and placed them in their respective houses—also made of basket-work for lightness—under the wagon. When this was done it only remained to make fast the bullfinch's and canary's cages, which hung each side of the wagon door suspended from the roof. Naylor jumped

127

up on to the footboard, sitting in his accustomed travelling position, one eye on the road ahead. I had sold the greyhound so that we had only Naylor and our toy dogs—which travelled inside the wagon. Beshlie also climbed into the wagon and sat just inside the door and I sat beside Naylor on the footboard and we moved forwards once again. Even to the meanest traveller there is a certain thrill and a feeling of elation at the moment when the wagon lurches forward, the horse sometimes quick and anxious through cold or lack of work, at other times slow and unwilling through tiredness or regret at leaving a particularly pleasant piece of grazing. To move behind a horse which is drawing one's only home and all one's worldly possessions is oh so different from the careless abandon of a pony and trap.

The journeying in that part of Hampshire is not, in my opinion, very agreeable. For one thing there is the carelessness of motorists to contend with. They have a habit of veering swiftly round the wagon from the rear, cutting sharply in again, and almost slicing off the horse's head. Now and again motorists, apparently unable to appreciate the slow pace of our progress, have rammed us from behind—fortunately causing more damage to the fluted fronts of their cars than to our wagon. But it is very disquieting to hear a car hurtling towards the rear of your equipage and being forced to wait, helplessly, for the crash!

On the morning of which I am writing, as we neared Odiham, the perpetual screaming and roaring of the jet aircraft from the local aerodrome was an added plague. On the edge of the town I noticed two youths, aged about twenty and of rough appearance, 'tatting'—that is, collecting old clothes and rags from door to door in sacks. When the sacks were filled they emptied their contents into the back of a battered, hand-painted motor-van. Their interest in us was marked, for they were, of course, sedentary travellers. However, as we discovered after a few minutes' conversation with them, their world and ours had not a great deal in common, and sensing their slight uneasiness at being seen in conversation with us humbler travellers, our talk was of a somewhat short duration. Their link (for despite their differing appearance they were brothers) with actual wagon-dwelling travellers had been broken by their grandparents, and it seemed unlikely that it would be reforged by their generation.

It was necessary for us to halt in the town in order to collect some provisions. Having completed my scant purchasings and having stored them away at the back of the wagon, I went to the mare's head and was about to lead her out into the stream of traffic passing through the town when I became aware of the presence of an expensively-dressed middle-aged woman, with blonde hair in tight curls, standing almost directly in front of me. Before I had quite realised what was happening a red-nailed hand had swept downwards to my own and deposited sixpence in it with an expansive gesture. The lady then stepped back one pace, and focused an immaculate camera upon me. Luckily, however, my reactions had speeded-up by then and I managed to make it clear that this woman was not going to buy the right to take my photograph for sixpence.

"Hm!" she sniffed with annoyance. "You look as though you *need* sixpence!"

And so saying she stalked off on clickety heels in a

9

state of high indignation and ill-temper—which was scarcely lessened by my remarking that it was unlikely that anyone would wish to photograph *her!*

Taking the Guildford road, we soon left the town and came upon wide green verges, tree-lined and pleasant, where we began to look out for a suitable *'atchin' tan*. A police patrol-car glided softly past us in the opposite direction, and its two occupants' white faces swung in our direction, grim pale masks under their incongruous taxi-driver's caps. I feel that all police cars should be equipped with specially built-in turrets to accommodate the fine tall headgear which is the symbol of dignity and trustworthiness synonymous with the British constable.

We continued along at a steady unhurried pace, then suddenly, through the trees on our right, my glance fell on a large skylight van. It was pulled-in as far from the roadside as possible against a hedgerow.

"There's travellers through the trees," I said to Beshlie, who was seated inside the wagon, and drew her attention to the van. "I'll go across and see who it is."

I crossed the road, noticing as I got nearer that there seemed to be only the van and one large roan horse. There were no trolleys or traps of any description—which is very unusual, for few Romanies move about with less than two horses and a trolley as well as a living-wagon, an exception being the 'mumpers'—who quite often have no horse at all, and merely push their belongings about on old perambulators or carts.

Three small girls were playing with a broken bicycle beside the van, and a woman with dark complexion and braided black hair was sitting smoking a thin cigarette on the footboard of the tall van. The man—dull and mat as an old railway engine—stood nearby, watching me approach, his face impassive and pale.

"'Mornin'," I said tonelessly. These were strangers to me and we were mutually suspicious.

"'Mawnun'," replied the man, running his cigarette rapidly along his lips from one corner of his mouth to the other.

He was quite young, not more than thirty I judged, and his face, round and rather chinless with a flabby roll of fat just beginning to appear at his throat, was white and unshaven. His old grey hat was several sizes too large, its weight pressing downwards on his ears and bending them over like those of a terrier. Long strands of mouse-coloured hair protruded from the back and front of this hat and a dull neckerchief of indeterminate colour was loosely knotted at his throat. His *monged* suit, once proudly bearing the label of some glorious ready-to-wear tailoring emporium, was now frayed, torn and shapeless—with even its stripes worn off! He possessed a singularly mournful, down-trodden, listless air.

"'As you come a long ways, brother?" asked the woman. And the children stopped playing and silently watched.

"We were over agin Basingstoke last night," I replied.

"Agin Basingstoke?" repeated the woman characteristically. "Did you see any travellers over that way?"

"No, we didn't see anyone at all. Is there anybody stopping in that country just now?"

"That ole Lush is that way somewheres," she said, eyeing me hard. I knew that she was testing me to see if I knew whom she meant.

"You mean that old Lush King—what's got dear old Mary Janette Jess?"

My reply was correct, and our suspicions lessened.

"His boy wuz yere two daays ago," remarked the man, in a curious drawling accent, rather Australian, which marked him as a Kent traveller.

"Which boy wuz here?" I asked.

"The one wot they calls German," continued the man. "Him wot's got the cross-eyed 'oman. He bid yere fer near on three weeks afore anyone come to 'im."

By 'anyone' the man had meant the police.

"What are they like round here now?" I inquired, for we had not travelled that area for a considerable time.

"They ain't too bad, brother, if you keeps yerself up together an' don't make too much mess."

His eye roved complacently and unseeingly over the immediate area of his own van which was strewn with old tins, paper, rags, broken dolls, bits of harness, bread-crusts, old meat and flies.

"Why don't you pull-in along o' we fer a daay or two? We'd like yer comp'ny," suggested the woman.

"Yes, we'll pull-in with you," I assured her.

We drew into the trees about twenty yards from their van, our own little wagon quite dwarfed by the height and size of the enormous skylight van.

Over the years, we had ourselves owned and sold or 'chopped away' or exchanged a large number of wagons from the meanest canvas-topped open lot, through a series of different types of wagons to the huge ornate Reading wagons.

In the latter class a large Chertsey Showman's wagon which we acquired some years ago deserves special mention. This magnificent van was built at the turn of the century by men who in their hearts still envied the Victorians their passion for rococo decoration. Some of this decoration may have been in bad taste, but as applied to wagons it produced magnificent results, and these huge glittering vehicles were largely responsible for the creation of the romantic myth which has clung to the Romanies ever since. Our Chertsey wagon was over a ton in weight even when empty. The underworks were decorated with intricately carved floral motifs, and the wheels possessed fine brass bell-shaped hubs that glittered and shone. The body of the van was made of 'penny-farthing' wood, an old-fashioned size which is the width of a penny and a farthing laid edge to edge. The ribs were also liberally scalloped, and these we picked out to great effect in vividly contrasting colours. All over the wagon's sides, front and rear, was a veritable riot of carving, mostly of grapes and vines; and little gargoyles were fastened at each corner of the roof on the guttering, the water pouring through their open mouths in rainy weather. During very wet spells we were able to collect sufficient supplies in that way to last us for several days. But such a wagon was not practicable on the smooth contemporary road surfaces owing to its vast weight and the consequent size of the horse required to pull it. Nowadays, such big wagons as are left are mostly kept by fairly short-distance travelling-people in the flatter parts of the country.

It was nearly midday and we both became aware of sharp hunger pains, so, having tethered the mare nearby, I hastily collected some wood from the trees and hedge, and soon had the *yog* blazing under the kettle—for which we had luckily brought some water with us.

133

The rain had almost stopped and the other family sat dejectedly by their van, having had their lunch.

I fried some meat and bread and two of our bantams' eggs and then placed a tin of beans in the ashes to heat. This repast would probably prove sufficient for the rest of the day.

After we had eaten our meal we walked over to the large van. The children had resumed their endless bicycle game, and the man and woman were half-lying, one on each side of their fire. They did not alter their positions as we approached, but invited us to sit down, which we did. The man was of a Romani family which had originally travelled exclusively in South Wales, and the woman was a Newman—a family which had become fairly inter-mingled with the *gaujes*. Wisdom, for that was the man's name, was one of the most lachrymose travellers I have ever met; and Annie, the woman, was little better. Their mournfulness was not of the kind affected by most travellers—who find that an outward show of ill-luck is often profitable. They were infected with a deep sorrow-ful sadness which seemed to enshroud them. Their con-versation bore out this impression.

"Bad ole weather—fer the like o' we, ain't it?" re-marked Annie.

I agreed that it was bad.

Wisdom, I gathered, had been given a piece-work job by the nearest farmer to cut back an almost impenetrable tangled hawthorn and bramble hedge which was about fifteen feet in height and thickness. He was just about half-way through the task; but that day the weather, combined with his natural inclinations, had persuaded him that it was not a day for work.

"I worked on it all daay yisterdaay . . . an' I didn't sorta feel like a-doin' no more todaay," he explained, adding, " 'Tis all accordin' to how the fit takes me."

"Sunday's a long-seemin' ole daay, ain't it, brother?" said Annie unexpectedly, for that day was a Thursday.

"Yes, but it's a good day for a deal, and it's a restful day, isn't it?" I answered helpfully.

"I reckons 'tis a long ole daay," rejoined Annie, unconvinced and obviously no sabbatarian. "Sometimes we jest lays up into the bed all mawnun'—specially iffen the weather's bad. Wotsever the use in a-comin' down outa the van fer? You gits sorta *diserable* jest a-sittin' about doin' nothin', don't you?"

"Sometimes," began Wisdom philosophically, squinting through the smoke, "I jist gits up on to an ole *treader* and jist rides about. . . . Why, one Sunday I rid the *treader* forty mile there an' back to see some o' me delations wot wuz stoppin' agin the New Forest. 'Tis better'n jist a-layin' about a-doin' nothin', ain't it?"

"Do you ever make the hazel baskets, or wooden flowers or paper flowers?" I asked, in an effort to break new ground.

"Not much now, brother," replied Annie pessimistically. "Don't seem to be many as wants any no more round yere."

Their horse was tethered by a long chain which was mended here and there with wire and string. Suddenly he galloped sharply along the chain's length, starting from the pin, and snapped it smartly in two. He galloped off and disappeared through the trees.

"He'm a sorta playful horse, that," remarked Wisdom,

chuckling approvingly and rolling himself another cigarette.

"Does he often break off?" I inquired with some alarm, for we had previously lost a pony through its being kicked badly by a horse belonging to another traveller.

"Ain't no chain as'd hold him," added Wisdom, smiling broadly.

"Does he kick?" I asked.

"He don't never kick," Wisdom reassured me, adding as an afterthought, " 'Less'n he gits in a funny temper, o' course. Iffen he gits funny tempered then he'll kick any horse wots about."

This news was hardly comforting, for our own mare was also apt to be unfriendly with strange horses, and the likelihood of one or both of the horses being maimed because of the inability of Wisdom to tether his on a reasonably strong chain was somewhat annoying.

"Well, one of them will have to go in the *poove* tonight, that's sure," I said firmly.

"Iffen the old mush kitches 'im you'll have to pay two *bars* to git him back in the mawnun'," Annie muttered.

"My bloody God!" I exclaimed. "Then you'd better *poove* yours!"

It was eventually agreed that their horse should go in the farmer's field that night and we would tether ours by the roadside.

On close inspection, we were sad to discover that Wisdom's van, which from a distance had looked so grand, proved—like so many of these ancient vehicles— to be riddled with worm and dry-rot. New panels of wood had been clumsily let-in or nailed-on about the underworks, the lock was mended with chain and wire and the shafts were rotted away at the ends almost to the 'stops.' With the abandon of some travellers Wisdom, with only about half a pint of paint, had happily set about painting one side of the van blue. Thus the blue gradually merged into an earlier-applied green; the back was red, and the other side greyish.

"When I gits the time I'm a-goin' to paint that old *verdo* up, an' then p'rhaps I'll sell him to someone," Wisdom observed on seeing me looking at the van.

"There goes the ole five o'clock busty," said Annie suddenly, as a double-decker bus filled with homeward-bound workers roared past. "We ain't a-got no clock so we has to tell the time by them ole bustys. We *did* have a clock an' he wuz good till one o' the *chavies* washed him in some soap an' water. Never did seem to keep the time after that, though. I 'spects the water rusted in them ole works."

"Better go an' git a drop o' water now," said Wisdom, adding for my benefit: "We has to git it at five o'clock in the afternoon, 'cos that's the only time the ole *rackli*'ll gie us any."

I picked up our carrier and walked with him for the half-mile or so to the nearest house, where a sour-faced, short-haired, breeches-clad woman answered the back door.

"Hm! More of you, are there?" she commented rudely upon seeing me as well. "Well, I have to *pay* for the water, you know. I can only let you have a little—and only come at five o'clock!"

With that she withdrew and we filled our containers at the hosepipe tap just outside the back door.

"Thank you very much, lady," called Wisdom

ingratiatingly as we left. Adding to me in an undertone: "That's a poxy ole bitch, you know. Why, the other day me young cousin rid over to see us, and he walked over wi' me to git a drop o' water, sorta jist fer the company, an' she wouldn't let him inside the gate. Told him to git on, she did. An' he weren't a-doin' no harm—jest havin' a talk, he wuz."

Thus simmering over the injustices of humanity we trudged back to the vans to have some more tea.

Our *yogs* were fairly close to one another and we were able to conduct a sporadic conversation during our tea-drinking. The three small girls, Rosie, Lily and Amie, came over to sit with us.

"Come outa that man's face, you brazen gals!" shouted Annie as the children crouched beside our fire.

"That's all right—let them bide," I called to her.

"They'm the unbelievingest children in the world," complained Annie resignedly. She continued: "Some-times I could jest git hold on 'em an' gie 'em a good ole stripin' wi' a stick. Still, it don't do no good to hit 'em, do it? I likes 'em to have their own way an' jest do wot they wants—cos I reckons it makes 'em happier like that."

I was once again reminded of the fact that all travellers' offspring live in a veritable children's paradise. There is little washing—except perhaps the hands and face once a day; they are allowed to play all day, unhampered by discipline or inhibitions for they are never hit—only *threatened*; they are scarcely ever sent to school; and their linguistic mode of expression is delightfully unrepressed. It has often amused me to hear minute children of both sexes express their feelings in phrases at which a grown man, in other spheres of life, would blench, and which would reduce most mothers to near-unconsciousness! There are probably few healthier or happier children in any other branch of society.

"Have you got a photy-taker?" Annie asked after a while.

I admitted we had a very old cheap box-camera which I had managed to *mong* from a house-dweller.

"Does he take a good photy?" she persisted.

"Best in the world," I assured her.

"Would you take one o' me little gals up on the horse, an' send 'em to the post office fer us to git?"

"Certainly I will," I agreed.

Travelling-people love to have their photographs taken when they know that they will actually receive the photographs. Many of the older people have charming collections dating back over nearly a century.

So, in the summer evening light, I took three shots of three tiny girls astride the tall roan horse, and one of Wisdom and Annie beside their van.

"Pay him fer 'em now, Wisdom," insisted Annie.

I accepted the sum offered to cover the charge of the developing and printing.

"If you sends we the negatees we can have some took off to gie to me delations, ain't that right, mush?" said Wisdom.

"That's right," I confirmed. "And can we have one too?"

"Sure you can, mush. Why, you can have so many as you wants."

"Be careful with the negatives," I warned. "Don't touch them with your fingers too much."

"I knows about that, mush," Wisdom reassured me. Informing Annie he went on: "Don't you touch they negatees when we gits 'em—'cos they'm like a butterfly's wing, an' the pitcher gits kinda wore off."

I have, over the years, taken many hundreds of snap-shots of travelling-people of many families. I do not show them outside the race for they were taken for private enjoyment and for the people concerned.

Gradually, as the evening wore on and we talked, slowly and waveringly, I realised more and more that these were Romanies whose percentage of *gaujes'* blood had certainly not proved advantageous to them. They possessed the slowness of speech and mind characteristic of the true peasant, and little of quick alertness which is so much a part of the dealings, and hagglings, of the purer Romani.

However, our evening did not pass without one deal. Noticing my black corduroy trousers, made for me in the old-fashioned travellers' style, Annie remarked:

"I 'spects you got they trousers made in Ockford, ain't that right?"

I agreed that such was the case.

"Me dead father used to allus git his made fer him there. Is they lined right through?"

"Yes, sure they are," I admitted.

"Well, my Wisdom's got a pair jest like they; only he don't like 'em, sez they'm too heavy. They'm up in the wagon—fetch 'em down, Rosie—an' they'm jest like new. Why, they've still a-got the price ticket a-sewed on to 'em. We gie two pun ten shillins fer 'em down in the hop-country last year. Would you like to buy 'em, brother?"

"I might do," I replied cautiously, "if they're cheap enough—to a poor man."

Rosie soon reappeared with the trousers. They were, to my surprise, of very high quality corduroy and, apart from being too wide for my taste, were otherwise quite reasonable.

"How much are you going to ask me fer 'em?" I inquired.

Wisdom sat still, rolling another of his innumerable thin cigarettes, a near-idiot smile overspreading his round countenance.

The dark eyes of Annie narrowed.

"I'll take two pun fer 'em," she tried.

"I'll gie you ten shillings fer 'em," I replied quickly.

"Wot?" cried Annie in feigned indignation. "Why, me dear Uncle Nashun bid me thirty-five shillings fer 'em on'y last Sunday."

"Ah, that was a good bid—you should have sold 'em," I answered sadly. "I'll give you twelve shillings for 'em— and that's all the money I've got."

"Huh! You've a-got more pound notes than there's flowers in the garden!" announced Annie somewhat surprisingly.

"I'll take thirty-five shillings from you for 'em," she snapped.

"You've had that bid once—or perhaps you didn't like to take the man's money?"

"Wot? Why, them trousers is like new. They ain't a-bin worn—my mother, he ain'ta never worn 'em no more'n once. I'll take thirty-seven shillin's and a six-pence fer 'em—an' not a penny less."

"My dear woman, I couldn't give you any more than twelve shillings for 'em at the most. Why, I've got to get them altered, and even then they won't fit," I rejoined with as much spirit as I could muster.

Wisdom still puffed contentedly at his cigarette. The children sat quite still. I hung the trousers on a briar bush. We all gazed at them appreciatively.

"You'm too hard to deal wi'," said Annie after a minute or so. "I keeps on tryin' to have a deal, but you jest won't make me a sensible bid. Gie me thirty shillin's an' that's me last word!"

"They'm lovely old trousers, good quality and old-fashioned," I agreed with mock sorrow. "But the truth is you're speaking to a poor man—one that hasn't got as many pound notes as he has fingers on his one hand! Still I'd like to have a deal with you and I'm in a generous way of mind so I tell you what I'll do. You give me that old pair of trousers that don't fit me, and I'll give you fifteen shillings and a banty chick for'em—and that's the best I can do."

So saying, I affected to walk off in disgust.

The woman weakened slightly.

"Gie me twenty-five shillin's an' the bird an' you kin have they trousers . . ." she began.

"My bloody God, no!" I interjected swiftly. "I'll give you what I've just said—and that's a good deal for you. Nobody else in this country would want to wear those poor old-fashioned trousers today. You have a deal—take my money now . . . here it is . . . and you shall have the dee-little bird for the children. Quick! Quick now! Take the money quick. . . ."

"Go on then!" said Annie suddenly—and our palms met in the smart clap to clinch the deal.

I had never before, or since, had to have a deal with a woman in the presence of her man. It was a curious experience. However, once the deal was concluded, we were all the best of friends again although each affected to feel hard done by.

The humidity of the atmosphere had increased during the evening, and soon after Wisdom had *pooved* his *grai* and we had all gone to bed a fierce thunderstorm broke over our neighbourhood. Sheet lightning flashed through the trees above our vans and a torrential downpour of rain descended on us, beating like a drum on the thin roof of our little wagon and making sleep impossible. The storm lasted until the early hours of the morning and we lay sleepless and somewhat alarmed by its intensity. In the quiet of the early morning, however, just before daybreak, I glanced out at the other van, dimly visible through the trees, and saw that its light was still burning as it had done all through the night. Alas, on top of all his other troubles Wisdom, it would seem, had become possessed of a van plagued by 'London Bugs.' Those vicious little creatures, who will nip so readily and so painfully, are only kept at bay during the night by means of the light, which must be kept burning. It is a wretched, disheartening, and thoroughly uncomfortable experience to have the misfortune to acquire a 'buggy' wagon.

I woke again at half-past six, put on my boots, for I had slept otherwise fully clothed, and climbed down into the slippery mud where the previous night's *yog* had been. I scratched some fairly dryish wood from the hedgerow, and with the aid of an inch or so of candle—half of it lit and the remaining half allowed to melt downwards from above—I lit the morning's fire, filled the kettle, and hung it on the 'crane.' Searching in the food-basket I found a piece of bread, toasted it, and ate it with a slice of cold bacon. I then prepared the same meal for Beshlie

143

and handed it up into the wagon for her. Soon the kettle
boiled and the water gushed puffingly out of the spout,
sending up clouds of steam from the fire. I swung the
'crane' to one side and filled up our old enamel teapot—
which had belonged to three different families of
travelling-people before it reached us by way of a
chop.

There was no sign of life from the other van, and I
guessed that they would not be afoot much before nine
o'clock as the night had been so bad. Travelling-people,
unlike the 'working man,' have no particular need to
arise at an early hour in the morning and—unless 'the fit
takes them'—frequently do not bother to emerge from
their wagons before eight or nine in the mornings.
Romantics who think of these 'children of nature' as
getting up with the light and going to bed with the dark
are, alas, misled.

We were anxious to be off early so as to avoid the
turmoil of holiday motor-traffic which swarms along the
roads of southern England during the summer months.
I had heard of a farmer who might possibly allow us to
camp on his land for two or three days, and we hoped
this would give us enough time to produce some hazel-
wood baskets, or perhaps make some baskets from
'bennets' or engage in some other pursuit to produce
enough saleable objects to provide sufficient money for
our immediate needs. We were not, however, entirely
without funds as we were still living on ten pounds which
I had made, as clear profit, by selling a governess cart to a
lady for ten guineas. I had bought it only a few days
previously from another traveller for ten shillings! In the
field of buying and selling horses and vehicles I must

admit to having experienced a considerable amount of good luck during the past few years.

Although Beshlie always buys materials with which to make up her own clothes, I buy myself no other garments except trousers, which I like to have made for me. The rest of my clothes I beg, as do the majority of Romanies.

An old and experienced traveller once observed to me: "Iffen yer goes out, my son, to beg yerself a suit o' clothes, mind you goes to some big house or mansion of a *bori rai* or the likes, then, my son, you'm sure—iffen you *pukkers* the tell right—to git the best sorta coats an' the like. Iffen you doesn't git the best then you'd jest so well pick up wot you wants offen the ole rag-trolley after you've bin out *a-tattin'*."

I rapidly finished the tea. There was no water left, so it would have been impossible for me to have washed, even if I had wished to do so. Anyway I *had* washed a day or two previously, so it didn't really matter.

I harnessed up the mare, who was cold from the night's rain. Beshlie was soon down and we went through our ritual of departing preparations. Just as we were ready to move off, the unhatted, tousled head of Wisdom appeared at the upper half of his van door.

"You goin'?" he inquired rather unnecessarily.

"Just off," I replied.

We exchanged hasty farewells, and with mutual wishes for good luck we jolted through the trees and out on to the hard black road, and headed for Surrey.

PART THREE

"'Ware of the Varmints"

PART THREE

"'Ware of the Varmints"

1

THE afternoon sun beat hard down on us, its heat being greater than that of the fire. We lay on the ground, the dogs panted beneath the wagons, and the horses stamped and pushed themselves far backwards into the rough moorland thickets of the common in an effort to dislodge the flies that constantly pestered them.

"Shall we go and have a drink at that *livnoker* down the road?" I suggested to Righteous.

"He won't serve you there, brother," Righteous replied, pushing his black hat far back on his head and revealing a full head of tight curls. "Why, I went down there yesterday afore you come yere. 'A pint o' brown, please, sir,' I sez. 'Sorry,' he sez, 'I don't serve none o' your sorta people yere.' 'Then can I have a packet o' fag-papers, sir?' I sez. An' he sells me them all right."

"I wouldn't have bought anything from the man," I exclaimed angrily.

"Ar, 'tis some as makes it bad fer the others," commented Righteous philosophically. "Trouble wi' so many travellers," he continued, "is that they gits into a public an' there they bids till closing-time—a-drinkin', a-cussin', and a-fightin' and a-spittin' all over the place, an' it sorta h'upsets the *gaujes*—them not bein' used to them ways.

But it makes you feel bad at times when they won't even gie you one drink, an' jest bids there lookin' despiciously at yer."

"Well he served *me* last night," announced Nelson, one of Righteous's sons. He was a round-faced, happy-looking youth of about nineteen. His hair was slicked down with water, flat to his head, ending suddenly in one long straight scissored line at his collar.

"He axed me where I wuz from," he continued, grinning. "So I sez 140 Green Street, Bristol, and he sez: 'So long as you ain't from they caravans on the common I don't mind where you'm from.' So I bid there all the evening. But it ain't much of a place, an' its bittery-tastin' ole beer wot he sells—bin layin' about in they barrels fer too long, I reckons."

"Well, he wouldn't serve me, an' that's so true as I'm yere," said Righteous, as though he had been disbelieved. "Fax the matter is I weren't perticular to have a drink at all, but I thought it on'y right to buy one seein' as how I wuz wantin' some fag-papers an' baccy—an' then he wouldn't serve me! I can mind times when that's happened an' travellers have knocked the place about a bit; else'n they've a-bid outside an' beat-up the ole man's pub-sign and knocked him offen the hooks. Don't do to make too much trouble round these parts, though, 'cos they've got a big *gavmush's* training college up agin they trees—an' they'm about yere in droves 'most every day an' night a-studyin' out fer murders an' the like."

Righteous dropped his voice a little and became somewhat awestruck as he recalled rumours of various happenings at night along the main road across the common.

"I wouldn't walk along that road at night—no not fer a hundred pun," he breathed. "There's people wi' knives gits about 'long there at night times." As though this statement were not terrifying enough he added for even greater effect: "The police sergeant wot come to us the other day told me as there's two an' three murders 'long that ole road every year!"

We all lay in silence after this alarming account, absorbing its implications.

Noah, another son, was the first to speak again:

"I seen a funny-lookin' little black 'oman 'long that road this mornin' . . ." he began, his eyes sliding closer together in the effort at self-expression.

"Go an' hide yer face, boy!" interrupted his father sharply. "Wotsever the matter wi' you? You didn't see no little black 'oman 'long there today."

"God strike me dead, my father, I seen a funny-lookin' little black 'oman I tells you. She wuz out a-callin' wi' some flowers an'. . . ."

"Goooooooooaaaaaaaaannnnnnhhhh!" shouted the others in a chorus of derision.

"My dead mother!" exclaimed Nelson. "Why, the *dinilo* means as he seed her wot's 'long wi' White Boy!"

"Which White Boy?" I asked, unintentionally confusing the issue, for I was acquainted with two travellers bearing that improbable name.

"Which White Boy?" repeated Nelson, appearing dazed at the complexity of the question.

"He means the one as had Milletty Loveridge's gal— she wot dropped down dead in the street one day when she wuz out callin'. Then he had this one wot comes from somewheres down the country—more in your country, brother—an' I reckons she'm one o' the Pinfolds' or the Eweses',," his father explained with conviction.

"No, he can't mean that one," I insisted, "because he's down country *now*. He's pulled-in for the summer, hoeing a hundred acres on a big farm."

"Whichever one do he mean then?" murmured Righteous, temporarily beaten.

"I knows which un he means . . ." began Noah, but his asserted knowledge was drowned in explosive laughter and mockery.

"O *dordi! Dordi!*" laughed Nelson. "Was there ever sich a *dinilo?*"

At last, however, we managed to sort out just which White Boy it was whose wife Noah believed he had seen—and, having dove-tailed relationships together, we were all much relieved.

It was a pleasant common on which we were stopping, and one could be reasonably sure of at least four or five days there before anyone would complain to the police of our presence. Once a complaint *was* made, however, the police would, of necessity, have to seek us out and in all probability move us on.

Personally I have the greatest contempt for those farmers, landowners, or mere busybodies who, at the first sight of a horse-drawn van drawn on to a roadside verge or common, will immediately telephone the police. Such furtive behaviour is, to my mind, not above the level of writing anonymous letters—yet it is only too often practised by the most respectable and complacent people, many of whom in all probability sit in church on Sunday and listen unconscience-stricken to sermons on the brotherhood of man. Yet these same people frequently view the travellers almost as though they are some strange scourge or disease—something to be rapidly removed from their sight and sound at the earliest possible moment.

Righteous was wearing a wide silver ring, with an ornate design engraved upon it, on one of his fingers. It was a ring which only a traveller could wear, and I liked it. And so, after a prolonged contest of haggling and bargaining, we managed to have a deal whereby I gave Righteous one of our Old English game bantam hens and one young mongrel 'tom bird,' and he agreed to give me half-a-crown and the ring as a *chop*. That, considering that the wily Righteous had asked ten shillings *and* the two bantams from me at the start, was a fairly successful deal. (I will never forget witnessing a traveller sell an old skylight van to a *gaujo* as an "an-tick, sir," for eighty pounds when, from another traveller, he would not have expected to receive more than ten or fifteen pounds. Of its kind, that deal was a gem.)

That evening two young *gaujo* men came over to see two flat trolleys which belonged to Righteous. At first I had thought that they were interested in buying one to convert into a farm-trailer; however, I soon discovered that I was wrong in that respect. Trolleys, providing that they are light, are always highly valued by travelling-people who use them for rag-collecting and 'iron-carting,' and very often they put tilts on to them and make them up themselves into rough open lots to live in.

It appeared that the younger man had been taken by the latter idea himself, and expressed his intention of travelling the country and engaging in temporary casual farm work

153

on his travels. A brief conversation with him, however, convinced me that he had not the right temperament and outlook to take such an irrevocable step. I asked whether he knew many travellers personally. He replied innocently that he did not actually *know* many, but that he had "seen a lot about."

"Well, sir," Righteous began, assuming great humility. "Now I suppose you'm after a good, sound trolley, sir?"

The young men agreed that such was their quest.

"Then you've a-comed to the right man," announced Righteous with enthusiasm. "Why, sir, I owns *six* good trolleys an' all on 'em is fer trade—'ceptin' one, an' that 'longed to me poor dead wife. An' I wouldn't sell that un—no not fer all the money in the world! 'Twouldn't be right now, sir, would it?"

The sentimentality of this last observation obviously struck the young men as right and proper, and they nodded in approval.

"Fax the matter is," continued Righteous amiably, "I've a-got these two trolleys yere, both on which I might sell; an' me others is led in some sheds on a piece o' ground wot 'longs to me father, down the country agin Bristol. But I'll sell you either o' these trolleys wot you sees yere—an' I'll sell 'em to yer wuth the money!"

The two carts in question differed very greatly in condition. The smaller of the two was a genuine traveller's trolley, with carved-out underworks, dainty lock, and bell-shaped brass wheel hubs. It had been a delightful little vehicle. Now, alas, it was very poor; its bed was very thin and the boards were rotted and old, the underworks were also rot-filled and had been clumsily joined in several places, while several of the 'villies' on three of the four wheels were cracked and loose and the iron bonds were worn thin. The once-gay yellow paintwork was flaking and dry, falling off to reveal its previous colour of blue. The other trolley, however, was in far better condition, with four good 'bowlers,' and the whole devoid of rot. It was, though, an unromantic plain, unadorned, purely utilitarian trolley. But there was no doubt that it would stand up to a great deal of ill-usage without coming to harm, and it did not appear to be more than three or four years old. A professional's hand had been responsible for its gloomy colouring of dark green, 'lined out' very skilfully with yellow.

It was obvious that Righteous had vague hopes of being able to palm off the fast-collapsing one first.

"Now, sir, if you wants a *good* sound little trolley fer a pony to pull then this un's the trolley fer you yere. Why, I've a-got a titty little pony, on'y twelve hands high, wot'll pull that trolley *anywheres*—ain't that right, boy?" And he looked to Nelson for confirmation.

"Certainly it is," agreed Nelson quickly, adding: "That's the lightest trolley wot ever I've a-drove, sir. Why, you could take un up over any hill in this country, sir, wi' a little pony, sir, an' you'd be sure to git over wi'out no trouble, sir."

The young men, who had been prodding at it in a professional manner with a pen-knife and scanning the tell-tale underworks with serious faces, rather mournfully complained of the rot in the wood and expressed doubt as to the length of time that the trolley would remain intact.

"Wot?" exploded Righteous indignantly. "Fallin' to pieces? My dear young men, that trolley'll hold together fer ten years an' more yet. Now is you men enough to gie me a reasonable bid for un?"

"Go on, make the man a bid, sir!" prompted Nelson.

"A lovely little trolley. There aren't many about like that today," I added helpfully.

"I'd tek eight pun offen you, sir—seein' as you'm in need o' one an' I'd like to help you," said Righteous, eyeing them closely.

"No, I'm sorry, it's too far gone for us," answered the elder of the two young men, pushing his small-check cap back slightly and scraping with a large hand at the back of his bristly neck.

"Well, sir, then you jest have alook at this un yere," persuaded Righteous, and was about to move across to the other one when the dogs suddenly began furiously barking.

"*Gavmush*," called Noah briefly from beside the fire.

"Excuse me, young men, but the policeman's jest a-come to have a word wi' me," remarked Righteous casually; and the two young men stepped aside, faintly embarrassed, as the constable approached. He was apparently from a patrol car. He wore a peaked cap, and was smoking a pipe. He produced his notebook.

" 'Evenin', policeman," observed Righteous, leaning nonchalantly against the trolley.

The policeman wandered round the wagons and trolleys glancing over them with assumed casualness. He looked at me with some astonishment.

"Who are you?" he asked, curtly.

"A poor *diddikai*, constable," I replied.

"Um," he said in a somewhat sinister tone, stiffening and puffing harder at his pipe. "What is your name and age, please?"

I gave him those details, as we all have to, to so many constables, on so many occasions and in so many places.

He moved among us, ignoring the two young *gaujo* men, asking the same questions and writing down the answers.

". . . from Hereford—where the white-faced uns comes from," grinned Righteous in connection with his place of origin.

"We'm all right yere, ain't we, policeman?" inquired Nelson.

"Um, I should think you'll be able to stay here a night —that is if I don't get any complaints. Make sure you're gone in the morning. And make sure all the horses are tied up all night."

He was about to depart when Righteous reported the loss of his youngest son, Lukey, who had disappeared some time before.

"He wuz yere, see, policeman—ain't that right, Noah? Up till dinner-time. Then we seed un walkin' off over the ole common—an' next thing we knowed is he'd gone! Gits funny 'tacks, he does, an' jest goos off wi'out a word; done it afore, he have. I 'spect he'm off to find some o' his delations. But it ain't right fer a boy o' his age to be gittin' about on his own like that an' a-worryin' us all grey-headed, is it, policeman?"

The constable puffed thoughtfully and with some dignity at his pipe and considered the question ponderously for a few moments.

"What's the name of the boy?" he inquired at length, pencil poised.

"Luke, policeman, Luke Black—teks his mother's name he do."

"How old is he?"

"Why, he'm on'y 'bout twelve years old, policeman, 'tain't right. . . ."

"How tall is he?" interrupted the policeman.

"We ain't never measured un," replied Righteous, taken aback. "But I should judge 'im to be not far off my son Noah in height."

"Is he fat or thin?"

"Well, policeman, he'm sorta thick-set, as you might say," muttered Righteous unsurely.

"What colour hair has he got?" pursued the policeman, obviously one for detail.

"Wot colour hair have he got?" repeated Righteous, slightly stunned. "Why 'tis a kinda brownish-grey—lightish—why, I should say meself he'm wot they calls blondy-eaded," concluded Righteous in a sudden gush of inspiration.

"I'll report the matter," said the constable, putting away his book and pencil.

"Iffen you sees him, policeman, will you please tell him we shall be a-stoppin' in Scrags Lane—an' he'll know where we'm to."

The constable departed, and a minute or two later we heard the smooth purr of a motor as his car drove away.

Righteous, unperturbed, immediately resumed his business as though nothing had interrupted it. "Now, sir, you jest come over an' look at this other trolley—why, he'm on'y a twelve-month old, made in Gloucester he wuz. I bought un new offen the man wot made un. Now ain't that a good trolley, young men?"

"A very good trolley," agreed the young men.

"Ain't that jest wot you'm a-lookin' fer?" pressed Righteous.

"Yes—if you're not asking too much for it," the younger man said cautiously.

"I'm a man," began Righteous, pushing his hat back and assuming a complacent expression, "who likes to do anyone a good turn—like you do yerselves, I 'spect—an' I ain't a man as'll ask a big price fer a thing wot ain't no good. Wot I believes in doin' is axin' a fair price fer a *good* thing; an' when I sez me price then that's it! I ain't like some—an' if anyone's got the money they'll be sure to buy wot I'm a-sellin' 'cos they knows it's wuth the money." He paused for a moment, rolled another cigarette between black fingers and scanned his listeners keenly. "Now this is how it is, young men. I gie thirty pun fer that trolley—an' so help me God iffen that ain't the truth! But I'll sell un to you fer thirty-two pun jests to make a quick profit. My dear ole father, wots dead an' buried, used to allus say: 'Take a small quick profit rather'n hang about a-waiting fer a big un.' Now, young men, no messin' me about—do you want to make me a bid fer un? Or ain't you got the money?"

The young men paled and flushed respectively at this last intended insult, which was intended to act as a bait to their pride. They walked slowly round the vehicle, muttering to one another, whilst we all sat or stood, smoking and watching them in silence, hoping to embarrass them into a quick decision. Now and then someone would make a casual comment regarding the fine qualities of the trolley.

"To tell you the truth I ain't perticular 'bout sellin' that trolley," mused Righteous, "but seein' as you *wants* a good trolley I'd help you out by lettin' you have this un cheap."

The check-capped one lit a cigarette from a packet, puffed at it with some emotion and remarked:

"We'll give you fifteen pounds for it."

"Fifteen pun! O my poor dead mother! O *dordi!* Do you think I could afford to *lose* on it?" exclaimed Righteous in horror. "My dear man, I'd a-sooner see it rot where it lies than I would part from un fer fifteen pun—fifteen pun!"

And he ejected a stream of nicotine-stained saliva in a jet from the corner of his mouth.

"How much did I gie fer that trolley, Nelson?" he demanded of his son.

"You gie thirty pun fer it—an' may God strike me dead iffen that ain't the truth," corroborated Nelson dutifully.

Righteous sprang to his feet and paced up and down, his cigarette whirring from one side of his mouth to the other, so great was his emotion.

"Why, young men, you can git fifty buckets o' water an' pour 'em into the bed o' that trolley—an' if one drop goes through they boards then you can *have* that trolley fer nothin'! Why you can go all over the country—an' I've a-bin to every place 'ceptin' London—an' you'll never find a sounder trolley 'an that one there—not fer the money I'm axin' you. But I'm the man to have a deal wi', an' I'm allus fair so this is wot I'll do: I likes yer faces, see, so iffen you likes to gie me thirty pun, an' half a quid on top fer luck, you can take him on now, an' you can be sure you've a-got one o' the best trolleys in this country. Now, is you men enough to have a deal wi' me or not?"

"A *good* trolley, that is," murmured Noah, almost to

himself, rolling a cigarette of black tobacco from a piece of newspaper which he used in place of a cigarette-paper. Large cheap silver rings glittered on his brown, dirt- and smoke-stained hands. One of the dogs—a small 'whippy'—slunk close to the fire and Noah picked up a thick piece of wood lying by the fire and cracked it cruelly across the dog's back. It uttered a sharp yelp of surprise and pain and dived back under the wagon. The two young men looked in its direction. Nobody else glanced up. Noah smiled, displaying stumps of black, decayed teeth.

The young men looked a little worried and stood without speaking.

"We couldn't do it," one of them said eventually. "We wouldn't give you any more than twenty pounds for it, at the most."

"Is that yer last word? 'Cos if it is then it don't seem like you an' me's goin' to have a deal," said Righteous in mock disgust, pretending to walk away. Then wheeling suddenly round, he came back and snapped: "Gie me twenty-five pun—an' we'll have a deal!"

"Go on now, sir," urged Nelson enthusiastically. "Be a man, sir, an' gie him twenty-five pun fer it. 'Tis wuth every penny o' that—an' he'm losin' money on the deal jest to help you out."

"Quick! Quick!" shouted Righteous. "Quick, young men! Gie me the money now while I'm a-minded to have a deal, case I changes me mind, an' the trolley's yourn."

But the young men were not so easy as we had thought they would be. After a further muttered consultation the elder one announced with spirit:

161

II

"We'll give you twenty-two pounds for it—and that's all."

"Make it twenty-three pun an' we'll have a deal," rejoined Righteous, his face set hard.

"We couldn't do it," said the young men.

"Goo on! Don't let a green pound note part you!" advised Nelson, his face earnest as the climax of the deal neared.

"Twenty-two pun ten—an' I'll gie you back fiver shillin's fer luck," spat Righteous, his face working, eyes like glass, and his black hat pulled down over them and almost obscuring their intensity. In a deal even the lowliest *diddikai* comes into his own, the cunning, quickness and Eastern quality of the Romani triumphing over the phlegmatic peasant-slowness which has gradually been acquired in most other aspects of his life and conversation.

Then suddenly it was over—the young men accepting this final offer, on condition that the trolley would be delivered at their farm that evening, a distance of only two miles.

So Nelson's little odd-coloured pony was hastily untethered, harnessed up and hitched-in. The two young men sat at the back on the 'bed' of the trolley, swinging their legs down over the side and Nelson, catching up a long hazel switch from near his wagon, jumped up on to the driver's seat, brought the switch down sharply on the pony's flank, and off they went at a fine pace.

"Ain't that a pony fer speed, brother?" laughed Righteous to me as we listened to its fast-tropping hooves gradually growing fainter over the common-road.

"Times is hard when I have to let a good trolley like

that go on fer on'y twenty-two pun or thereabouts," he remarked, a pretended sobriety thinly veiling his elation. For I knew—and he was aware of it—that he had bought the trolley a week or two previously from another traveller for only eight pounds. Times were hard indeed.

"Reckons it'll be dark afore Nelson gits back—I'm *jallin'* on to *voodrus,*" said Noah, yawning.

"Where's you sleepin' boy—in the 'bender' or up into the wagon?" Righteous demanded.

" 'Tis hot tonight. I'm goin' to bide out in the 'bender'," Noah replied.

A small low igloo-shaped 'bender' tent had been erected from hazel-rods covered with a piece of stained canvas and part of an old carpet. Straw and rags lay on the ground inside to form its floor and the bed. An old white greyhound bitch lay inside. She had belonged to Noah's dead mother, and she was the only dog which received any consideration. Noah removed his boots, flung himself down on the rags, and in a few moments was sound asleep, his stubble-covered face pressed into the straw, his never-bright eyes tightly closed. His simplicity of life was matched in many ways by his mind; yet few could make pegs faster, or fashion such finely-shaved chrysanthemums from elder wood as Noah. He was good-natured and generous to those whom he liked; but if goaded or crossed his uncontrollable temper would assert itself and he would fling himself on his tormentor with thoughtless fury. On one occasion in a drunken brawl at a shack-settlement of ex-roaming travellers, it had taken five of us to drag him from the inert body of another Romani whom he was cudgelling violently with an iron kettle-crane.

"Father wouldn't let me have a *yauker*," he said to me one morning. " 'Cos he knows I wouldn't be safe wi' it. Why, I'd so like as not jest put a shot into the fust person wot made me nerves bad, an' kill him dead."

His eyes glinted as he said this, and he glanced furtively round. Noah, like a great many other travellers of his mentality, was a product of a family *very* closely in-bred; and although I have no knowledge of genetics I have often pondered on the standards and outlook of all too many of those closely in-bred Romanies with whom I have had immediate personal contact. Their likenesses are very marked.

He was known to be 'many-minded,' that is to say inconsistent, vain and cruel. To us, however, he was always helpful and kind; on many occasions he would fetch our water, sometimes several times a day, from sources often more than half a mile distant, and perform many other little personal services.

Our *yog* was still burning and the kettle was boiling on the crane so I made a last drink of tea, pouring one out for Righteous also. And we sat in silence for some time, listening to the flying insects and the settling birds, and all the time keeping our ears tuned for the sound of the returning pony.

"Cah! Look at they batty-mices!" Righteous exclaimed, as two horseshoe bats swooped down just above the wagon tops, flitting silently away into the gloom.

"Where's you goin' from yere, brother?" he inquired. He was himself staying on as one of the wheels of his wagon was undergoing repair at a wheelwright's shop a few miles away. One of the chief reasons for concern

over damage to a wagon is the difficulty of securing the
services of anyone willing or able to undertake the work
of repair—particularly if the damage is to the wheels.
Wheelwrights capable of repairing or rebuilding old-
fashioned wooden wheels with iron-bonds are very
scarce, and even when sought out are often either senile
or truculent. Each year wheels become harder to replace.
To complicate matters further, each set of wheels has to
have its own individual cap-spanner without which the
wheel cannot be removed for repair, the spanners being
quite unlike any other tools in use today. A hammer and
chisel *can*, of course, be used, but such a method damages
and disfigures both cap and nuts. The wheels must be
kept covered up with damp cloths in the summer,
lest they contract and the bonds become loose, and
should be turned fairly frequently, especially if the
wagon is standing on soft ground, for they will sink readily
into the damp earth and the damp-affected 'villies' will
rot. Although a few travellers nowadays have their
wagons on inflated motor-car wheels such a step is, in
my opinion, decadent and out of key with the life. Such
moves could only lead to spring mattresses, end-kitchens,
and similar follies!

"I'm going Oxford way," I replied, for I hoped that I
would be able to find a little fruit-picking or hoeing
work in that county or on its borders. Anyway I knew
the roads and the *'atchin'tans* quite well there, which
always makes life for our people infinitely easier. There
is nothing more arduous or nerve-straining than travelling blind into 'strange country.' It entails all the hazards
of pioneering; and necessitates constant inquiries as to the
hills one is likely to encounter round every corner.

Often, of course, such inquiries meet with thoroughly unintelligent answers. On two occasions I have been airily directed up hills with a one in six gradient with a confident: "Oh, nothing much of a hill: you'll get up it *easily*." The mental parallel which some people appear to draw between the capabilities of a heavy horse-drawn van and a 'family-eight' car is truly astonishing, and is a somewhat depressing reflection of our times. It is depressing, too, that in spite of two world wars for Democracy any wayfarers other than those with car and egg-shaped trailer van or lop-handled bicycle and knapsack are viewed with the gravest suspicion and mistrust, often with open hostility. There are exceptions, of course, particularly among old people, whose bent and frail figures may often be seen moving to their garden gates to watch us pass.

"Ockford way?" Righteous repeated. "That's where you gits them old-fashioned trousers made, ain't it?"

"Not *these*. But I *have* had them made there," I replied.

We talked a little of Oxford and Oxford Fair—which still has a little of its bygone splendour left. I often go to the Fair, but I used to visit it mainly for the pleasure of meeting an elderly friend whom I knew I would find there. This excellent old man was one of the few non-Romanies who, until the outbreak of the second World War, had consistently travelled Britain's roads with horse-drawn wagons. A scholar, he was one of the most thorough men I have ever met, and his knowledge of almost every by-road fit for wagons in southern England and Wales was truly phenomenal. Clad always in fine-quality tailor-made clothes—yoke-backed jackets, pleated trousers, a spotted handkerchief at his throat and a black

soft felt hat upon his head—he looked in every way a
Romani-*rai* of the old school; and he had had the varied
experiences which many lacked. He had always remained
self-employed, and he now owned a large house, several
lorries and a car. Yet he was gentleman enough not to be
ashamed to come and sit by our roadside fire on many
occasions in Oxford and Gloucestershire.

It was almost dark and Nelson had still not returned, so
Righteous decided to go to bed himself. Beshlie and I sat
on by the glowing embers of the fire for a little longer.
Finding a little tobacco left in my pocket, I rolled myself
a last cigarette, lighting it from a smouldering piece of
wood from the fire and inhaling the acrid smoke. Naylor
lay near the fire, savouring its last warmth, half-asleep
yet constantly alert and ready to fade away from the
fire and into the shadows should any strange noise or
scent arouse his suspicions. We had just bought another
greyhound bitch—a lemon and white one, and, as she
was very large for a greyhound, we had hopes that,
later, the result of a cross between her and Naylor might
prove to be useful dogs. She was quite unused to the
travelling life, so I chained her under the wagon to help
her realise that that (during the summer, anyhow) was
to be her home. She whined, in the high-pitched way
that greyhounds have if all is not entirely to their liking,
so I opened my ex-laundry food-hamper and took out a
piece of bacon and threw it to her. Naylor, being quick
to anticipate my action, swiftly lurched over towards her,
but I saw his move and recalled him at once before he
could steal her food. I spoke encouragingly to the bitch
and she eyed me with less suspicion. In a day or two, I
thought, she could be safely left unchained.

Though not lately, I have seen travellers' dogs encouraged to fight for the amusement of their owners and often to the accompaniment of spirited betting. The victor would be much acclaimed and the unhappy loser left to crawl away, sometimes partially maimed, to lick its wounds as best it could.

On one occasion, in Devonshire, I was stopping with some travellers when two of the younger men 'poleaxed' a greyhound to death as it was badly infected with mange.

". . . I wouldn't keep a dog like that," one of them had said indignantly. "Why, iffen the 'Umane Man (R.S.P.C.A. Inspector) had seen 'im he'd a-gid me six months fer sure."

I did not have the heart to tell him what would have happened to him if the official had been a witness of such amateurish—though admittedly effective—slaughter.

I also recollect on another occasion being only just in time to prevent a traveller from worming his dog with some not too finely powdered glass!

Nevertheless, in many respects, the dogs belonging to travellers do have a very natural and enjoyable life. They can generally find companions amongst the dogs of other travellers, and are able to scavenge to their heart's content.

Still pondering on dogs in general, I lifted the food-basket back on to the wagon rack, chained Naylor under a bush near to the fire, and clambered up into the wagon to bed.

2

I woke early the next morning and was up by half-past five. There seemed to be the promise of yet another hot day. I loosed Naylor and quelled his exuberance with a stern word; then I unchained the greyhound, rechaining her again after a few minutes. It was pleasant to see the horses dotted about the common, the flashy odd-coloureds showing up so strongly, while our black mare and Righteous's chestnut were scarcely visible on the heath. Nelson's little pony, its fur still caked with patches of congealed sweat from the previous evening's trolley journey, had wound itself up so intricately in the plug-chain that it could hardly stand, so I hastily untied the chain and tied the pony by its rough rope halter to a gorse bush whilst I disentangled the chain from around its legs. Luckily no injury had been done, and I replaced the chain on the halter. Snorting loudly, the pony moved off within the circle of its restricted grazing patch.

It is astonishing how some horses will entangle themselves quite hopelessly in their tethering chains or ropes, whilst others will untangle themselves most expertly. An uncle of mine once had a small pony which, tethered by the neck, choked itself to death in a night of storm in its efforts to get free. Fortunately such major disasters are rare.

There were five horses grazing over the heath, and the rest appeared to be quite happy. I moved our mare to a fresh patch, hammered in the iron pin and left her. She was a pure-bred Welsh cob of the old sort, and her beauty of stance and line never failed to excite my admiration. We had had many bids for her, but she was not 'for trade.' It is usually only 'spares' or 'rubbish' that are. A good, quiet, honest wagon-pulling cob is hard to acquire today. The ideal 'vanner,' which may vary in size according to the type and weight of the wagon it is required to pull, *must* be dead-quiet in traffic, free from any vice, must allow itself to be tethered by a 'plug-chain,' and should preferably be a good doer on poor feed—few travellers give their horses any hay or corn or anything else apart from grazing, but with constant change of feeding grounds they rarely need it. A wagon horse must also learn to draw a heavy van out of a 'stiff pull' over muddy or soft ground, and must pull slowly and gently and steadily so as to avoid turning the wagon over as it lurches into ruts and dips. It must also be willing to do a lot of backing in order to get the wagon into narrow tree-grown places where it would be impossible to turn round to come out when leaving.

We *usually*, though by no means always, have a pony and trap besides the wagon and cob. The former is often 'for trade,' but the latter never—unless faulty! In the past I have sometimes had as many as five or six cobs in a year before finding a really good vanner. Few Romanies will '*chop* away' or sell their wagon horse if it is devoid of vice or fault. Many are the cobs and ponies who refuse to pass such horrors as road-drills, steam-rollers, mechanical hedge-cutters, red flags, milk churns, etc. Very few operators of hedge-cutters or drills or similar implements have the courtesy to stop working when horses are passing.

I walked over to a clump of fire-blackened furze-stumps and began pulling out large sticks, my hands and clothes rapidly blackening with charcoal as the pile grew in size. I packed them together and, tying them into a bundle with an old piece of rope which I had taken with me, swung them over my shoulder, called Naylor, and walked slowly back to the wagons.

It was strange, I reflected as I neared the encampment, how *full* and permanent everything seemed, and how *much* of everything there seemed to be. A casual observer might have marvelled that everything could possibly be packed up on to the trolleys and into the wagons when the time came to move. Of course, the paths of muddy trodden ground round the standing-place of each wagon would be left, and so would the black and white scars of the fires and the inevitable empty tins, the few remnants of coloured rags and probably a few wood shavings from the *koshtis* of the pegs. A Romani *'atchin' tan* always leaves its own evidence and is quite unmistakable. The beauty of an encampment lies, I think, in the unconscious muddle of objects, the haphazard placing of wagons and trolleys and harness, and the crude but glowing colours. Ugliness only predominates when the traveller becomes afraid of colour and unaware of crudeness and ill-arrangement. Too often he strives after a neatness which he will never achieve in an effort to emulate the colourless uniformity of the house-dwellers.

I have only been made fully *aware* of dirt or squalor when I have been among travellers who try to ape the more unintelligent type of working man in clothes, speech and way of life. Then pride of race fails, colour and vigour fade, and everything but the restlessness vanishes. But this is quite rare.

Of course, vast quantities of travelling-people today are unquestionably *diddikais* or part-Romanies, but they *are* almost without exception *part*-Romani—in spite of the fact that the police and other authorities, quite without knowledge of their pedigrees and without any real evidence, deny it. They deny it in order to strengthen their case that they are not, after all, persecuting "real gypsies—but only riff-raff, you know." Their theory is, of course, somewhat strengthened and helped by the fact that nearly all travelling-people will hotly deny that they are 'gypsies,' a term they regard as being highly derogatory. "We ain't gypsies—gypsies is furrin! We'm English, like yerself. We'm Romanies—roamers—travelling peoples sir."

Such a statement is often repeated in court, to police, or to *gaujes* generally. In actual fact, almost all the contemporary wagon-dwellers *are* more than half-Romani, and many are pure-blooded. It is ironical that the police and others will happily persecute and often unjustly ill-treat the *diddikais*—that is to say someone who is partly of their own blood—while affecting—at any rate in their absence—to idolise and sentimentalise the memory of the ethereal '*real* gypsies!'

Noah's old white greyhound bitch emerged from the 'bender' as I passed and sniffed lethargically at the morning air.

I threw the bundle of black wood down beside the remnants of the previous night's fire and, after placing a little dry straw and some twigs in the ash, I lit it. In a few seconds and after a little blowing, the fire was alight. This lighting of a fire is a monotonous ritual, but not without significance. "If the fire won't burn in the morning then it won't all the day"—and once achieved it is a satisfying action.

There was just enough water left to make some tea when the kettle had boiled; and I left it to brew while I toasted a piece of bread on a stick by the fire. I spread some butter on it and breakfasted thoughtfully, pouring myself some tea into one of our cups which was decorated with what Righteous described as a "Weepin' Willies patten," and handing another up into the wagon for Beshlie.

Our finances were in a rather poor state, as we had only three pounds left. Earlier, we were rather apt to 'lie on' our money until it was all spent before seeking any more. But advancing years and experience had taught us the inadvisability of such a course. Anyway, when one is down to one's last few coppers—as I had often been in past years—and when one is living a life divorced from the national forms of assistance, the bleakness of extreme poverty tends to cloud one's judgment, and thus opportunities are often lost. Successful deals are more often those which do not *have* to take place because of necessity.

We decided to remain a few more days on the common before moving. It was not really the right season for wooden flowers or hazel-basket making—and I did not feel like going out rag-collecting. 'Tatting' is a gloomy task. We toyed with the idea of fashioning some baskets from the grass known as 'bennets.' These are woven on the principle of the old-fashioned 'bee-skeps' and usually sell quite well. But we decided against it when we saw the quality of the 'bennets' which the common could provide. Some travellers make the same kind of baskets from coarse straw, but the effect is never so pleasant.

Eventually we decided that Beshlie should do a few very small and very 'commercial' flower-pieces and landscapes. When executed with the correct degree of 'pretty-prettyness' and placed in a simple painted frame, these masterpieces would usually find a fairly ready sale among the ladies of the council house estates—ladies of unvaryingly bad taste, who always knew exactly what they liked and liked nothing else. This decision having been arrived at, I hastened to erect a 'studio' from a canvas sheet pulled round some bushes to form a shield—for Beshlie did not like to be watched at work as it tended to distract her.

By the time these preparations were completed the others had crawled from their respective wagons and 'benders' and were sitting, tousle-headed, round their *yog* frying themselves some breakfast while Noah toasted slices of bread, putting each completed piece in the ashes by the fireside.

"O *dordi!*" Righteous exclaimed, seeing Beshlie with the box of paints. "Is you goin' to oil-paint we? You shoulda told us—we'd a-had a wash fer you!" He laughed loudly at his joke.

"A man come to us once, brother," he continued. "Up the country—a *bori rai*, he wuz—an' he oil-painted me poor dead wife an' me dear ole father as well. Marked 'em out lovely he did. Gie every one on us the right feature, he did. Then he gie me father half a *bar*, got in his moty-car an' druv off—an' we never seed un no more. That wuz a good painter, mind. Why, I 'spects he made hisself hundreds o' pun outa that pitcher wot he marked out from we."

We all nodded in solemn agreement.

"Same as them wot tries to take yer photy," muttered Nelson. "They comes round in cars an' axes to take yer photy. Then they promises to send you one—but they never does. I reckons they puts 'em into books an' the likes, an' makes theirselves a good bit o' *vongar* outa they too."

"Ar," said Righteous. "Iffen any one. on 'em wants to take me photy now, they has to pay. I won't let no one take me photy fer less'n half a *bar*, 'ceptin' iffen 'tis on'y a child or an ole 'oman."

I could not help but feel that Righteous was fairly safe in his exceptions, as it seemed highly unlikely that anyone in those categories would have the least inclination to commit his image to celluloid.

"You're quite right too," I agreed, remembering the episode of the sixpence offered by the lady with the red fingernails. "Now we'll have to get on with our work and try to earn ourselves a penny for a crust of bread—not like you bastards that've got as many pound notes as there are stars in the sky, and can just lie round your old *yog* all day!"

They chuckled appreciatively at this sally, and we withdrew to the 'studio.'

3

By about half-past eleven Beshlie had finished several pictures, painted with quick-drying medium, and I had framed them. She was about to begin another when I heard the sound of hooves on the main road, accompanied by the faint sounds of singing and shouts of children—sporadic and uninhibited by the shackles of respectability. Our dogs started to bark excitedly and we emerged from cover and gazed over the common in the direction of the noise. A small yellow and red skylight wagon, drawn by a piebald horse, was just leaving the road and heading across the common towards us, followed by a flat trolley with what appeared to be a trap tied on behind it.

"God strike me dead if that ain't Joey an' my gal Lavinia!" shouted Righteous in some amazement.

"My bloody God! Is that me sister an' Joey—wotsever they doin' down in this country?" Nelson exclaimed.

"Whosever this a-comin'? That ain't me sister! Course it ain't!" observed Noah.

"Goo-on, you *dinilo*!" Righteous shouted, annoyed at being disbelieved. "Is you outa yer mind, boy? Think I don't know me own daughter when I sees her?"

The old white greyhound bitch had rushed out to greet the newcomers, snarling with wrath until it recognised them. Naylor, by command, stayed suspiciously by my side, hackles raised.

Very slowly we all walked out to meet them as the vehicles drew close, jolting and bumping over the rough track. The young man guided in his horse and wagon close beside Righteous's, backing the big odd-coloured horse sharply until the van was exactly where he wanted it.

"How y'gittin' on, mush?" remarked Righteous, without much show of emotion.

"All right," Joey replied briefly.

He was a thick-set young man of about twenty-six, heavy and dark-featured. His face was broad, square and Slavonic, and his small glittering eyes were constantly moving. Long black hair stuck out in a fringe from the back of his cap, which was worn jauntily far back on his head. He was wearing a brightly-patterned neckerchief, an old lounge-suit jacket, corduroy trousers and mud-caked, run-down boots. On his thick pudgy fingers were several large flashy silver rings. He was a 'fly' young man, hard and brutal, able to outdrink any other young men of his age.

Joey left his horse still harnessed in the wagon-shafts, and ran round to help Lavinia with the trolley and trap. A small bay pony was pulling them, its eyes rolling dangerously.

"Come on, you bloody foxin' bastard!" Joey shouted thickly as the pony shied at the sight of a rag flapping on a nearby bush.

"God's cuss this horse!" he muttered, as he jerked it savagely back in the shafts almost on its haunches. Having at length pushed and pulled it into the position he wanted, he set about unharnessing.

Lavinia, meanwhile, had lifted her four small girls down from the van, and was holding her fifth child, a boy, in her arms. She stood by the fire talking to her father. She was tall for a Romani woman. Her hair was fair and braided, and she wore a black 'pinna' over a bright plaid skirt.

"O my pretty father, we've a-done seventy mile in two days," she was saying in excited tones. "An' we'm on'y stoppin' yere the night. We'm goin' so fast as we can down to Bristol to some o' my Joey's people."

"Wotsever you goin' right down that country fer?" asked Righteous, somewhat taken aback at their destination.

"Why, ain't you heared about how my Joey's brother Henry's wife's a-runned off wi' another man, an' left three little children?" asked Lavinia, horrified that we had not heard.

"Ain't heared a word, gal, true as I'm yere. Whosever she runned off wi'?"

"Ain't heared? O *dordi*! Why, it's made me feel bad a-thinkin' about it. I've a-got burnation in me guts from the worry on it—you axe Joey."

177

Lest this should not be fully appreciated Lavinia shouted to Joey, who was about a hundred yards away tethering the pony.

"Joey! Joey! Ain't I bin bad wi' the burnation fer over a week?"

"Wot?" shouted Joey.

Lavinia repeated her call.

"Ar!" shouted Joey.

"An' I ain't had nothin' but dry bread an' tablets—an' still I'm bad."

Lavinia produced a bottle of tablets.

"Wot do it say on there?" she asked me, as I was the only one present who could read.

"For acute burnation take three tablets twice a day," I replied, substituting 'burnation' for 'indigestion.' Lavinia was greatly pleased at this news.

" 'Tis one o' they furrin travellers wot's runned off wi' her," she said, returning to the subject again.

"Iffen one man ain't 'nuff fer her then a hundred won't be," commented Righteous sagely.

"An' she left they dee-little *chavies*," Lavinia went on in scandalised tones.

Joey approached the fire and sat down on an old petrol tin.

"I'm sorry to hear 'bout she wot had Henry," said Righteous consolingly. " 'Tis a bad thing fer to happen to a man. Is he goin' to git her back?"

"God strike me dead, brother!" replied Joey excitedly. "Iffen me brother an' me catches up wi' 'em we'll stripe her till she'm all-coloured. An' iffen we catches *him*, why, mush, we'll beat un to death!"

"You'll be *lelled* fer it," warned Lavinia.

"I don't care if we *is lelled* fer it—nothin' won't 'suade we not to beat un iffen we catches up wi' 'em."

"Are you *jallin'* on tomorry?" asked Nelson.

"Certainly we are, man. Me brother an' me ole mother wants us to git down there so quick as we can so as to help 'em. We got their letter wot came to us at the post office four days ago, an' we bin a-travellin' ever since then."

Noah had made some tea, and we all sat drinking it from a variety of cracked and stained vessels in the sunlight, thinking over this unhappy domestic crisis.

The little girls, with the delightful names of Mary-Annie, Leander, Kizaiah and Freedom, played about round the wagons. Occasionally they quarrelled for a few minutes, cursing and hitting at each other with great ferocity. When that happened we all listened and watched with great amusement.

"They'm brazen gals," commented Lavinia.

It was midday by the time we had finished the tea. Joey went off over the common, wooding for their own *yog*, whilst Lavinia set about peeling some potatoes into an old biscuit-tin which, half-filled with water, acted as a wash basin.

"*Dordi!* I wishes my Joey'd hurry back wi' that ole wood so as I could git these vittles cooked," she moaned after twenty minutes or so had elapsed, adding alarmingly: "I'm so hungry that the worms is eatin' into me guts!"

Soon Joey returned with an enormous bundle of wood on his broad shoulders, and we went back to our work and left them to the preparation of their meal.

During most of the afternoon Lavinia, who was by

instinct a happy person, played her gramophone. She had only four records—an American cowboy ballad, an Americanised English crooner, a negro spiritual, and a highly jazzed-up variation of an old folk-song—but she made up for this shortage by playing each disc over and over again. All were songs, for travellers prefer the human voice to orchestration, and they were all easy to remember. Nearly every Romani is a good mimic, and nearly all have a good sense of rhythm. Most travellers, especially the older ones, know a large number of delightful old folk-songs and ballads, some of entirely Romani origin, others being influenced by the sentimentality of the early music-hall. Many of the songs sung in Romani are centuries old and have been handed down for generations, never being heard of outside the race. But the younger Romanies generally prefer the modern type of sentimental catchy song, and it is no uncommon thing to hear up-to-the-minute, brash new songs being sung side by side with the old in an encampment—or in a public-house on a fair day. In fairness it must be said that most of the younger Romani singers are *natural* crooners—each phrase being long-drawn out—and often produce quite effortlessly an effect that many of our most highly paid popular singers might envy. Travellers sing a lot, often quite meaningless songs, and it is not regarded as the least odd for anybody to break into song without any ostensible cause—sometimes even in the middle of a sentence—and then resume the conversation as though there had been no break in it.

But I was a little surprised when Lavinia, tiring of the gramophone, began a delightful, sad and mournful old song that I had not heard since I was a child and that I had almost forgotten:

"I'm like the flowers in the garden when the beauty's
   all gone;
Can't you see wot I'm come-to by a-lovin' that One?
You take this yellow silk handkerchief an' bind it
   round your neck,
And you'll think o' me an' me baby while we'm
   miles away.
We're like the flowers in the garden when the beauty's
   all gone;
Can't you see wot I'm come-to by lovin' that One?
When the thief he will rob you, an' he'll take all you
   got,
And after my money's gone I can go where I like.
Like the flowers in the garden when the beauty's all
   gone;
Can't you see wot I'm come-to by lovin' that One?"

Lavinia's voice was harsh and wailing, carrying far out
across the common.

"That's wot her dear mother used to sing," Righteous
said sadly, noticing that I had been listening. "I like them
old-fashioneds best."

The children played on happily. An old wreck of a
perambulator was being used as a cart, three of them
riding in it and the tiny black-haired one, harnessed with
string, pulling them about at great speed. Suddenly,
amidst screams of joy, two wheels buckled and, simultaneously, the sides collapsed outwards, ejecting the
screeching children in a kicking mass on the ground.

"O *dordi*!" shouted Lavinia. "My blessed Jesus! Why
ain't you two gals got no drawers on?"

This surprising question was directed at the two

younger girls. Among travellers' children it is not considered necessary for such garments to be worn until the 'baby' is at least three years old, and a habit so formed is often rather hard to break. The same is true of shoes, and it is not unusual for children to be seen barefoot—from choice—up to eight or ten years old, even in the hardest weather when the ground is frozen as hard as iron underfoot. Then they will come and toast their feet in the fire's heat till they turn yellow with smoke.

The little girls did not heed their mother's cry, and looked round for another game.

"Ain't they childrens brazen?" Lavinia muttered to herself.

Joey was lying by the fire on which a great holly trunk was slowly burning. We had put our work away, and I joined Joey by the fire and talked of our mutual journeyings. He was a long-distance traveller with a very big circle of country.

"Where's ole Mattie?" he inquired.

"Down at Bridgewater in Somerset, along with Daisy Black's boy and his wife," I answered; and asked, "Have you seen old Orphie, or Hard-times Smith?"

"Not Orphie I ain't, but Hard-times is Gloucester way somewheres, so I heared," Joey replied, adding: "How many *grais* you got?"

"Only two just at this moment," I replied. "You know that little bay pony I had from old Plato Coffee?"

"Yes, I knows un."

"Dead! Kicked! Leg smashed to bits!"

"There now," said Joey sympathetically. "An' that wuz a good pullin' pony. I tried to buy it afore you had un—but the man wouldn't sell un to me, fox his mother!"

"My God! Wasn't she quick, though!" I remarked.

"I'd sooner have that than I would have a lazy horse, wouldn't you, brother?"

I agreed, for the sake of avoiding argument; though in my experience an over-quick horse is more of a liability than an asset.

"Ar, I wouldn't keep a lazy horse fer ten minutes, sooner *gie* it away than keep un I w. . . . Come outa the man's face Kizzy—why you'm wusser'n a German!" He broke off indignantly to yell at the little girl who had just passed between me and the fire. Another lapse of etiquette, and one which is regarded as an omen of ill-luck, is to pass a drink to somebody 'back-handed'—and should such a thing be done inadvertently a tradition-respecting traveller will dash the cup from the giver's hand rather than accept it.

"I wants a fag, my pretty father," the child said wheedlingly. "Gie me a fag, my pretty father. O my pretty father, gie me a fag. . . ."

Joey grinned broadly at this request, and after a few complaints about his shortage of 'baccy' he rolled a very thin little cigarette from half a length of cigarette-paper and handed it to Kizzy who immediately lit it with a brand from the fire, puffing contentedly.

"Bit o' baccy don't do 'em no harm—helps kill the germs," Joey remarked, adding: "Why I bin smokin' since while I wuz still a-suckin' the titty."

I remember seeing another child almost his equal in this when I was among some Wiltshire travellers. A small boy of not more than two and a half was sitting by the fire on the roadside, a teated, milk-filled beer bottle in one hand and a seemingly enormous cigarette in the other—puffing and sucking in turns! His parents were charmed by his precocity.

Our talk reverted to horses again.

"I've a-got the prettiest little swish-tailed odd-coloured horse wot ever you seed," remarked Joey. "An' I'd *chop* un fer that ole mare o' yourn iffen you'd gie me the right money."

"I wouldn't part from that mare, not for all the money you'd like to offer me," I replied firmly.

"I means that one wot pulls me wagon," continued Joey unabashed. "Him wot's plugged-on out there."

"Uh!" I grunted.

"See, the truth is," continued Joey, "he went an' kicked one o' me *chavies*—accidental, like, but it sorta put me agin him, don't you know? Now how much would you gie me to *chop* fer your ole mare?"

"She's not for trading, poor old thing," I replied. "Why she's so old that I have to pull the wagon myself half of the time—no, I wouldn't like to suck you in with her, you know that, my Joey."

He grinned but did not give up.

"I tells you wot I'll do," he began again, with great enthusiasm. "I bet any man here fifty pun—an' the money's yere," he patted his coat pocket, "that you can put that horse in *any* wagon yere, wi' only the hames an' traces on, an' he'll pull the wagon—don't matter which it is—*wi' all four wheels locked*—up over any hill in this country, brother. Now ain't that a fair offer?"

Joey's eyes lit up as he pondered on the improbable mental picture that he had conjured up.

"It's no good," I said. "My dear man, you can sit there and talk till the black of night—but I still wouldn't part

from that mare. I know all her ways, and she knows ours
—I'd be a *dinilo* if I *chopped* her away now, when she's
just what I want."

"You oughta be like me, mush," replied Joey. "Not
married to anythin'."

"Where's Kizzy's titty-bottle?" inquired Lavinia
suddenly, as the little girl began to cry.

"Titty-bottle? I ain't a-seed un," said Joey unhelpfully,
shouting to the other children: "Go an' look fer the titty-
bottle. Quick! Go an' see iffen it's up into the wagon."

The three little girls did not move.

So Joey, with much cursing, clambered heavily up into
the van and after much noisy searching eventually discovered the bottle—an old patent medicine container
with teat affixed—on the floor under some rags. He
brought it down and gave it to Lavinia who poured some
tea into it, diluting the blackish liquid with tinned milk
and adding some sugar. She presented it to Kizzy who
quietened at once—clasping the grimy bottle and sucking
happily from the uncleaned teat. It is said of Romani
children that if they survive the first two weeks of life
then they will almost certainly grow up. More are lost
during the first few weeks than at any other time—so
probably only the strong survive. It is worth recording
that most travellers' children escape almost all the childish
ailments which the majority of the *gaujo* parents take as a
matter of course. Bronchial complaints are the most
prevalent form of illness, but tuberculosis is rare. Possibly
the fact that most Romani children (at any rate those of
wagon-dwellers) spend their days in the open air and not
cloistered in the unhealthy fug of over-crowded school-
rooms is the reason.

I myself was free from ailments until I was eight years old, but when I went to a school at that age I ran through a whole list of pestiferous complaints.

I had planned a picture-*bikinin'* safari that afternoon, but the arrival of Joey and Lavinia had rather upset those plans, so I decided to postpone that necessary outing until the next day.

Nelson and Noah drove to the village shop later in the afternoon, and just before their departure I called to them to fetch me some bread, bacon, and candles. And they repeated their own requirements parrot-like—being unable to write them—adding my goods at the end.

"An' fetch we some tin-milk, an' some baccy an' some sweets fer the *chavies*," Lavinia shouted to them as they galloped the little pony and cart off across the heath.

"Will she turn a hare, mush?" Joey asked, pointing at the greyhound under our wagon.

"Certainly she will—quietest and best working dog I've ever known," I replied, enthusiastic about my then untried dog.

"I'll gie you five shillin's for her!" Joey suggested.

"Wot? You bid me five shillings for that *jukel*? Why, man, I wouldn't take less than two pounds for her. Give me two pounds and she's yours."

But I knew that he was not seriously interested in her at any price in excess of ten shillings.

Our talk drifted erratically on. After what seemed a short space of time Noah and Nelson returned, and Righteous got up from beside his fire, where he had been lying asleep. He retrieved the frying pan from the middle of a bush—where it had been flung out of reach of the dogs—and lodged it on the fire ready to fry something for their tea. He had taken over most of their domestic duties since the death of his wife, and he still asserted that he felt ". . . too bad to do much else'n sit about all day just studyin'—or p'rhaps have a deal now an' agin when I takes it into me head."

I returned to our own fire and, rekindling it, put our kettle on its crane. Beshlie had gone across the common for a walk. While waiting for it to boil I ate a little raw oatmeal and tinned milk—a form of repast which other travellers viewed with the gravest suspicion.

"If I wuz to eat that I'd have to bide in me bed fer a week, I'd be so sickified," Righteous remarked.

Joey was rather anxious that we should look at his wagon. He wanted some 'lining-out,' and a few birds or similar decorations painted on it later in the year.

"Wot I wants doin'," he explained, "is fer yous to line him out a bit—'specially on the lock an' the wheels. Then p'rhaps you could mark out one or two *kanis* or flowers or somethin'. Do 'em straight out offen yer eye, nice an' bright, don't you know? I'll pay you—I don't 'spect you to work fer nothin'."

Some months after this encounter we did, in fact, completely repaint Joey's van for him. I did the actual paintwork and Beshlie added the decorations of birds and flowers and 'lined out' the wheels and underworks. We usually redecorate several travellers' vans during the course of each year for returns of between five and twenty pounds—depending on the amount of work involved. In Joey's case we drew a sum in excess of twenty pounds as he insisted upon a fabulous amount of decorative work being applied.

Joey always kept to skylight vans, scorning open lots,

and it was a pleasure to meet a traveller who still had pride, and taste enough, to keep his wagon gaily painted and thus make it a pleasure to look upon. His wagon at that time was a very pretty little van with a lantern roof, and made of 'penny-farthing' wood, with carved-out ribs and lintels. The body of the van was red, picked-out with yellow; and the underworks and wheels were yellow, picked-out with red. Not, perhaps, the best choice of colouring, but infinitely preferable to the many shades of green which seem to afflict so many of the wagons—the green of man's making which vies so hideously with the greens of nature.

Its interior was especially delightful, even though it was panelled with plywood for lightness. The layout was traditional: stove inside the door on the left, locker-cupboard just inside on the right, and then a built-in chest of drawers. The bed lay across the end of the van, with sliding doors, upon which were fixed cut-glass mirrors, to enclose the occupants at night if so desired. Underneath the top bunk, of course, was another floor-level bed in which the children slept. There was a sash-window in the centre at each side of the van, and a tiny hinged window near the roof at the back. Two larger cut-glass mirrors were on the side walls, their edges splintering and slightly corroded. A number of articles of clothing, shoes and other personal belongings lay about on the floor and hung on the walls—and the curious sweet sickly scent characteristic of travellers' wagons was in evidence. A single large frame filled with snapshots of relatives, horses, wagons and babies hung as a picture just inside the door. It was a pleasant little wagon, scarred by usage rather than by neglect.

"Have you seen me sister Ellen, wot's got Jabez?" Joey inquired suddenly.

"Not since Christmas," I replied, "and that was down on Honiton Common, don't you know?"

"Ar, I 'spects we shall go down that way after we gits me brother's trouble settled," he said.

"Are you *jallin'* on tomorrow?" I asked.

"Yeah—we'm goin' away in the mornin' so early as we can," he answered. "How long is you goin' to bide yere?"

"I'll bide here a day or two yet," I said.

We sat silent for a few minutes; and Noah's curious, wild-sounding, high-pitched voice rose in song, enveloping us in its hypnotising futility.

". . . an' I courted that gal fer near seven years,
  An' I sez to her: 'Little gal,' I sez. 'Little gal, ain't you
    never bin kissed?'
  An' her dear mother there she shouts at me: 'Go away,
    you h'evil young man!'
  O I courted that gal fer near seven years, an' still she
    never wuz kissed.
  I gid her fine *covels*, an' dear diamint rings, an' still
    she never wuz kissed.
  An' I courted that gal fer near seven years,
  An' I sez to her: 'Little gal,' I sez. 'Little gal, ain't you
    never bin kissed?'
  O I court. . . ."

"Pox on you, boy!" shouted Righteous in exasperation. "You don't know the meanation of a good song—why, you wants yer brains 'saminated!"

"I knows that's a good song," began Noah indignantly "He'm ole-fashioned."

"Wot!" Righteous exclaimed, horrified. "Ole-fashioned? Goo on, nose-an'-a-half! That waren't no ole-fashioned song. My dead mother, it waren't!"

To be "old-fashioned" is often the criterion of quality among travellers.

Noah relapsed into sulky silence.

"I bet there ain't no man livin' as knows more ole-fashioned songs than me Uncle Jobi," declared Joey. "Why, some of his songs is hundreds of years old!"

"I reckons the best singers you can find today is up in the hop-country agin Kent; 'specially some o' they London-travellers," Nelson announced.

"Iffen I wuz in me proper old-fashioned singin' voice today, an' not all worried grey-headed, an' wore out by movin' so far, I'd sing some songs wot me dear mother taught me, an' them's better'n any o' they London-travellers," Lavinia asserted primly.

"Ar . . ." murmured Righteous wistfully. "Me dear wife wot's dead an' buried wuz the finest singin' 'oman in this country—an' in anywhere in all o' England."

The others could scarcely refute this statement, and the conversation was changed out of respect for the dead woman's memory.

Joey remembered that part of his cob's harness needed attention, so he went and picked up a set that was lying on the ground by his van and brought it over to the fire to survey its weaknesses. It was a London set, about forty years old, I judged, and had been a very good set in its prime. But now, like so much harness of today, age and neglect had taken their toll. It was cracked and glossless, much of it mended and joined together in the traveller's way, with bent nails or string and wire. In this case the breeching had snapped and had had to be rejoined.

"I got a lovely set of harness a-hangin' up inside me wagon wot I'd sell you cheap—or you could have it fer this un iffen you'd gie me the right money to *chop*," Righteous said hopefully.

"You means that ole set you had offen Smiler Joe, wi' the red moroccy on to it?" asked Joey, one step ahead.

"Ah, that's the one, a good set," Righteous agreed.

"He'm no foxin' good to me, man," answered Joey knowingly. "An' you knows it so well as I do. Think I wuz born yestiday?"

Righteous rolled another cigarette, smiling faintly to himself.

The children began playing with the harness.

"Come out, you brazen little bastards!" shouted Joey. "Fetch me they nails wot's in the kittle-box, Mary-Annie. Quick, gal, quick!"

"Wot nails?" inquired the child.

"Wot nails?" repeated Joey in astonishment. "Why them little uns in that tin wot's got brushes in it wot's up into the kittle-box."

The little girls all ran over to the van, two of them bare-foot, all wearing multi-coloured, dirty, ill-fitting clothes which clung to them with the oddly unnatural look that cast-off clothes acquire—seeming to still hold the shape of their previous owners.

The girls eventually approached us with the nails; then two of them, without warning or apparent cause, suddenly began fighting and the third child, in an effort to quell them, hit both wildly with the tin of nails—whereupon we were all deluged with thousands of nails and tiny tacks which fell everywhere.

"O my blessed Jesus Christ A'mighty!" screamed

Lavinia. "They'm the unbelievingest *chavies* in the world!
O look wot I'm brought-to now, my father!"

"God's cuss you!" shouted Joey, not moving. "Now
look wot you've a-done. Pick up every one o' me nails
or I'll git a stick an' stripe you all!"

Laughing and crying, pleased to be temporarily the
centre of attention, the children began half-heartedly replacing the nails and tacks. The baby boy, at Lavinia's breast,
continued feeding, unperturbed by the screams and shouts.

Joey, having mended his harness to his satisfaction, dolefully remarked, "I reckons this ole harness could do wi'
a-cleanin' up—I'll do it when I gits the time."

"Is you two goin' out callin' tomorry morning?"
Righteous.

"Yeah," answered Nelson. "We'm goin' out *tattin'*—
where's the bills to?"

"They'm up in the wagon," said Righteous, referring
to the printed cards which most travelling-people leave
from door to door, calling for them again in the day.

Some of the cards are mere plain straightforward state-
ments of requirements, while others are written in
delightful verse-form. Righteous's fell into the latter
category.

Nelson, to satisfy himself, fetched them from the van.
There were about fifty of them, printed on blue card, all
very grimy.

"Is you a scholar, mush?" Righteous asked me
doubtfully.

I admitted that I could read.

"Read that un out," he urged. Really, I knew that this
was solely for the benefit of showing off his cards to Joey.

I took the card and looked at it. It was headed in large

letters with the name *Ezra Barley*, under which was
printed *Licensed Dealer*, followed by: 100 *Tons of Old
Rags Wanted*.

Then, in smaller print, came the verses:

> I beg with most respectful feeling,
> Leave to inform you what I deal in:
> I have not come your purse to try,
> Yourself shall sell and I will buy.

> So please look up that useless lumber,
> Which long you may have left to slumber.
> I'll buy old boots, old shoes, old socks,
> Jackets, trousers, and smock frocks.

> Towels, cloths, and cast-off linen,
> Cords, cashmeres, and worn-out women's
> Old gowns, caps, bonnets torn to tatters,
> If fine or coarse it never matters.

> Bed ticking, fustians, velveteens,
> Stuffs, worsted cord and bombazines,
> Old worn-out handkerchiefs and shawls,
> Umbrellas and parasols.

> Sheep netting, canvasing and carpeting,
> Whatever else you have to bring:
> And of the weight I'll soon convince you,
> For which I pay the utmost value.

> I'll purchase dirty fat, dusty bags,
> Old roping, sacking and old rags:
> Both bottles, horsehair and old glass,
> Old copper, pewter and old brass:
> Old saucepans, boilers, copper kettles,
> Pewters, spoons and other metals.

> Old coins (not silver), ancient buttons,
> Ladies' and gentlemen's left-off clothing,
> Skins whether worn by hare or rabbit,
> However small your stock, I'll have it.
>
> I'll buy old rags, however rotten,
> If made of woollen, hemp, or cotton,
> I'll buy old iron, cast or wrought,
> And pay the money when 'tis bought.
> If you have any bones to sell
> Their value in a trice I'll tell.
>
> So over your dwelling give a glance,
> You never will have a better chance.
> My price is good, my weight is just,
> And mind I never ask for trust.
> So just look up if but a handful,
> And for the same I shall be thankful.

This moving and thorough statement of requirements ended with the stern admonishment: *Do not lose this card. This notice will be called for in two hours' time and I will take away all the old lumber you may have.*

"Cah!" breathed Joey, much impressed. "How much did you have to gie to git 'em done out like that?"

"I gie the man two pun fer five hundred on 'em," answered Righteous, pleased with the effect. "They'm the best bills in this country, brother. Gits our livin' easy from 'em—ain't that right, boy?"

"Sure it is," said Nelson. "They'm much better'n they little *biti* ones wot we used to have—people likes readin' 'em."

"Some travellers come to we one day," said Righteous, "an' they wanted to have some took of them wot we've a-got there. Bid me five pun they did. But I told 'em: not fer fifty pun you wouldn't have none took of they, my brothers. That all come outa me brains wot's writ on there. And iffen you wants somethin' like it then you go an' study it out fer yourselves. 'Tis a *jinkly* ole game, this is."

I knew full well that Righteous had not composed the verses himself, and suspected that Joey knew it, too. However, we looked impressed and said nothing.

4

I got up early next morning, for I had resolved to go out 'calling' with my half-dozen pictures in order to replenish our purse. I left the dogs tied-on under the wagon and went to fetch some water from the nearest source, a cattle-trough some half a mile or so distant, taking care that I was not seen by the farmer or any of his men. This farmer disliked our people intensely—and not without reason. The horses were always *pooved* in his fields at night when the grass had been exhausted on the common during the winter months, and the travellers frequently made use of his fence-posts as firewood. But he was a thoroughly ill-natured and unlikeable man who deserved little better: a New Era farmer, with polished boots and a shining car which Righteous surprisingly described as "one o' they newtilities."

After breakfasting on oatmeal and much over-sweet tea I climbed back up into the wagon and, with Beshlie's help, packed the pictures, changed my heavy old labourer's boots for some equally old but lighter boots, put on a clean silk neckerchief and black felt hat, and jumped down again. By this time the others had their fire blazing and were arguing as to where they should go 'calling.'

I tied Naylor under the wagon near the greyhound bitch, but not near enough to reach her. I hauled the pony's set of harness out from the little gig, which we had painted black and yellow with the wheels red, and then went over the common to fetch the little pony that we had recently bought. He was only eleven hands, and had been bred to the travelling life and could, as it is said, "pick a living from a hedgerow." I harnessed him up as quickly as I could, for the housing estate, where I hoped to sell the pictures, was some four or five miles away, and I wanted to be there as early in the morning as possible so as not to spend the whole day out hawking. The little skewbald was restive. I backed him into the shafts, lifted them and slipped them in, and hitched on the traces. Then I threw the end of the reins into the gig and jumped up after them. The pony was very quick and a little nervous, and I knew that the moment he felt me up in the gig he would start off with a bound. This indeed he did and we sped out across the rough track. He was, in fact, faster than Nelson's pony, although Nelson would never have admitted it. His little hooves were sound and high-lifted, up and forward.

There is nothing that I have experienced in the way of transport which is so satisfying or thrilling as driving a really fast-trotting pony along a good road on a summer's morning. The clattering of the hooves, the wind in one's face and the scraping of the iron bonds—such simple pleasure is one which very few but the much-maligned 'gypsy' enjoys today. And enjoy it they do! Even the oldest man or woman will be excited by the rattling, splendid thrill of a ride in a light vehicle behind a fast pony.

The most exhilarating vehicle that I have ever driven was a genuine American 'buggy' which I purchased for ten shillings at a sale of old horse-drawn vehicles in Wiltshire some time ago. This well-designed gem, with its ornately upholstered seat for two slung between four large dainty wheels, each of which was fitted with hard rubber tyres, was a joy to drive. Its only fault was its American shafts, which are too wide for my liking, and in which a small pony is apt to feel lost. It was a sad sight to see those fine vehicles, all over fifty years old, mostly craftsman-made and immaculately preserved, being knocked-down for a few shillings each by the auctioneer's man, who obviously thought them a great joke.

Gigs and traps are, of course, pleasant to drive also— the riders sit high and have a fine view of the surrounding countryside. But I do not like governess and other 'tub' carts, as they are very seldom comfortable and are usually heavy. Of course, in a two-wheeled cart there is always the danger that if the horse slips and falls one is almost certain to be thrown out, whereas with the greater stability afforded by four wheels this is less likely to happen.

I was in a happy frame of mind as I sped forwards along the flat, main road towards my destination, through several hamlets and villages.

"Gyppo! Gyppo!" some children screamed derisively from the safety of a school playground as I passed.

I cursed them softly to myself, grieved that their scholarship had taken them no farther.

Soon enough I approached the council house estate. I

dismounted from the gig and tethered the pony on the grass verge, fastening the halter to a stout tree and tying his collar to the saddle to prevent its dropping forward as he grazed. White lather dripped in foamy blobs down his hind legs and flanks.

I lifted the small bundle of our framed masterpieces from the rear of the gig and walked up the incline towards the first of the blocks of terraced houses.

I knocked on a thin-sounding composition-board front door, and it was opened by a rather shapeless woman wearing a check turban over devilish-looking and wholly unattractive steel curlers. Her face shone and was blotchy in the morning sun.

"Yase?" she asked, regarding me with some suspicion.

"Good morning," I began. "I've got one or two small hand-painted pictures in oil-colours here—lovely things you know—that might interest you."

"Pitchers?" she said, somewhat taken aback. "Oo, I don't want none of them—me hubby don't like them. Says they makes patches on the walls. . . ."

"Well, they'd cover up patches, of course. Have a look," I suggested.

"No," she said, looking round in a hunted way. "No, I think I'll leave it. . . . Yes . . . I think I'll leave it. Thank-yew, thank-yew."

And the door was shut.

I moved along a few doors and tried again.

This time a thin, starved-looking little body answered my knocking.

"I've brought some nice little pictures to show you, hand-painted—and I wondered if you might be interested in buying one for your front room?"

She giggled nervously.

"He-he! You an artist? I thought you was a gypsy at first!" And she giggled even more nervously at her supposed mistake.

"Well, I don't mind 'avin' a look—if they're not too dear, that is." Her voice was squeaky and not pretty.

"Now please don't feel obliged to buy one," I murmured glibly. "No, not in any way at all. Just buy one if you like it."

I brought them forth in rapid succession. She scanned them with an attempt at professional interest.

"I quite like this one. I like . . . the shapes," she said finally, pointing to the worst flower-piece.

"Then do buy it—I always like to sell to those who appreciate pictures. I'll let you have that one at a specially reduced price—only half a guinea."

"Eh? Ten-an'-six? That's reely more than I can afford, I'm sorry. . . ."

I knew that I had turned the screw a little too tightly.

"Give me seven and sixpence and it's yours!" I said quickly.

"Oo . . . all right then," and after some scrabbling in a green plastic handbag she withdrew three half-crowns and presented them to me.

"That's today's food bought!" I thought as I pocketed the money.

I moved onwards on my depressing round, sometimes meeting curiosity, rebuffs, rudeness and sternness, and just occasionally striking the right note and making a sale.

My best 'touch' that morning was a woman in early middle-age who affected an air of false refinement. After some rather off-balance badinage I managed to obtain no less than fifteen shillings for a tiny landscape of our wagons in a woodland setting—mounted, ironically enough, in a frame that I had previously begged from that very same terrace some weeks before.

After nearly three hours my rich supply of 'hand-painted paintings' was exhausted, and I found that we were a little over three pounds the richer. It had been quite a good morning.

It was noon when I returned to the pony and cart and, having made the necessary purchases of food, began the homeward journey.

After buying some baccy and our *moro* and *mass* I found that I still had fifty shillings left. I was in good spirits as I trotted the pony homewards—occasionally letting him break into a gallop on the quiet road—and I sang "The Lily-White Hand" to myself at the top of my voice.

When I was in sight of the wagons I turned in across the common at full gallop, the little gig bouncing like a ball over the ruts, the pony steaming and lathered.

Only Righteous and the dogs were there to greet me. He was lying propped up on one elbow, smoking, and the dogs were all barking with excitement and tugging and rattling at their chains. Joey and Lavinia had gone, true to their word. Nelson and Noah had not returned from 'ragging.'

"Did you have a good day?" asked Righteous.

"Not too good," I answered, for it is traditionally regarded as inviting ill-luck to admit to having done any more than 'sell out.'

"Ar, times is bad fer the likes o' we, ain't 'em?" Righteous muttered. "Still, there's one thing," he continued, brightening. "A traveller'll always pick a livin' where others'd starve, ain't that right, mush?"

"True, but times are bloody hard nonetheless," I re-joined. Adding, "So Joey *jalled* on, then?"

"Here one minute—gone the next. Like spit in a ditch," said Righteous scornfully. "He cain't rest, mush, that's wot 'tis. Why, he don't need to go right down there to see about that trouble. Iffen his brother ain't man 'nuff to keep his 'oman, then 'tis no use to be fightin' about it, if you sees wot I means."

It is an unhappy characteristic of travellers that—with nine-tenths of the *gaujes* against them—they can never refrain from 'back-biting.' One scarcely ever hears a traveller speak *well* of another behind his back.

Righteous was interrupted at this point by Naylor, who was almost choking himself in his excitement at seeing me back again.

"Wotsever the matter wi' that *jukel*?" Righteous asked. Like most travellers he was secretly frightened of any large breed of dog other than a greyhound.

"Shouldn't be surprised to see him took by fits or some kind of badness like that," he added pessimistically.

I quietened the boisterous creature after a moment or two, tossing him a bone, and another to the greyhound, who showed somewhat less joy at the sight of me.

"I wouldn't take that bone away from he, not fer a hundred pun," Righteous said, eyeing Naylor with great mistrust.

"No, and that's how it should be!" I answered. "What good would that dog be if *anyone* could handle him, and take his bone away—or anything else? I can though, see...."

To Righteous's astonishment I staged a demonstration. Since puppyhood, I had taught Naylor to surrender his food to me on command. To have one's own dog growl at one would, in my opinion, be the greatest indignity. And in my case such an animal would be disposed of immediately.

"I don't like the look in his *yoks*," Righteous muttered, still quite rightly distrusting Naylor.

I set about preparing lunch. The embers of the morning's fire were still red hot, so I tossed a few dry twigs into them, waited for them to catch, and then added some larger sticks. I fried a piece of steak which I had rashly bought, then some potatoes and tomatoes, and then I pushed an opened can of beans into the ashes to heat. I called to Beshlie, who had been far across the common gathering flowers, and we ate the meal with great speed and enjoyment, finishing up with two bananas and some tea. I lay beside the *yog*, basking in its warmth, gazing into the mystery of the leaping flames, my hat pulled down over my eyes. The dogs dozed nearby. I rolled a small cigarette and inhaled the smoke, acrid and strong from the coarse black tobacco, and then I tossed the cigarette papers and packet of tobacco to Righteous, who rolled one for himself. Soon the cigarette was gone and I too slept through the afternoon.

I did not wake until the noise of Noah's and Nelson's return aroused me. They drove slowly over the heath, singing and whistling with unmusical abandon, the trolley laden high with rag-filled sacks.

"... an' her dear mother there she shouts at me: 'Go away, you h'evil young man!'
An' I courted that gal fer near seven years, an' still she never wuz kissed. . . ."

Noah's singing rang out above Nelson's shrill lachrymose whistling.

They had taken their vanner cob, a large-boned ugly
animal which was sweating profusely under the heavy
load she had pulled; and I guessed that she had probably
had to trot most of the way home.

"How about that fer one day's callin'?" Nelson shouted
proudly to his father.

"That ain't too bad," Righteous admitted grudgingly.

Nelson and Noah, fatigued and hungry, sat down by
their fire and began hungrily to eat the food that
Righteous had ready for them. Using only pocket knives
and their fingers, still blackened from their morning's rag-
collecting, they devoured it rapidly, much as we had done.

"You wants to git yerselves an 'oman to git yer vittles
ready fer you," complained Righteous.

"We seen the *gavmush* a-comin' back," Nelson said,
ignoring his father's suggestion. "Has he bin here?"

"No one ain't a-bin yere, my son," Righteous reassured
him.

"A man tole me he seed six wagons goin' along the
Telegraph road this morning," Noah observed.

"Six wagons? Who wuz they, boy?" asked Righteous
with great interest.

"The man said he'd never seen 'em afore," replied
Noah, adding: "He thought they wuz furrin travellers."

"Furrin travellers! Wot furrin travellers?" exclaimed
Righteous scornfully.

"I dunno, but that's wot the man said," Noah answered
defiantly.

"Huh! You cain't put no pendation in wot they *gaujes*
tells you—they don't seem to have no sensible talk!"

"Will you gie me some more '*meskie!*" urged Nelson impatiently. "You two carries on jest like a pair of *dinilos.*"

"You git yer own tea, my son," said Righteous. "Noah an' me's a-goin' to sort through these ole rags."

The sorting of rags is usually a rewarding experience, full of excitement and surprises. In this instance Righteous and Noah emptied the contents of the sacks into one large pile near the fire and tossed the sacks aside to receive the graded rags later. The classifications were 'white,' 'woollens,' and 'cottons.'

In general, the actual sorting is purely Dickensian, offering the curious spectacle of men, women and children burrowing and searching amidst mounds of multi-coloured garments and rags.

On this occasion the boys' collection was above average in its yield of wearable garments and 'usable' pieces. As the respective piles mounted under each classification so did an ever-growing separate mound of old trousers, waistcoats, jackets, shirts, pieces of silk for neckerchiefs, and odd lengths of cotton for use as towels and hand-kerchiefs. Righteous also kept back a few fragments of soft white woollens to wrap round his feet as socks—quite a common habit amongst the men.

At last the whole mound was sorted and graded and divided into separate sacks, and all but a few charac-teristic scraps were packed away. Then all the sacks were loaded back on to the trolley and the whole was covered by an old once-green sheet of canvas. The rags were now ready to be taken to the town next day to be sold accord-ing to the weight of their various categories. 'Whites,' of course, fetch a considerably higher price than 'coloureds,' and 'woollens' more than 'cottons.' Most travellers know of several ways of increasing the weight by ingenious, if not thoroughly honest, methods. It is not for me to describe them.

5

Sunday is a day that is always set aside for rest or for visiting among other travellers (many of whom regard it as ill-luck to move on that day).

Once I was stopping on a rather busy piece of common-land in Devonshire with some Lees. The woman of the family had boiled a vast tub full of washing on the Saturday morning, and as it had rained nearly all day she had left it on the bushes round the wagons all night, where it remained on Sunday morning. Before lunch a tweeded *gaujo* and his brogued wife strode past our vans, and stopped for a moment or two to admire the vast quantity of clean washing.

"How beautifully clean your washing is," the woman remarked to old Violet.

"Thank you, lady," returned Violet.

"Did you do it all this morning?" the brogued woman innocently asked.

"Wot!" Mattie exploded in horror, addressing the man. "Do you think I'd let me wife wash our clothes on a Sunday, sir? No, I wouldn't, sir! We'm Christian travellers, sir!"

One Sunday, Nelson and I decided to drive over to see his Uncle Abri, who resided in an ancient railway-carriage on his own piece of ground which was about six miles away from our stopping-place.

Before we could set off, however, Nelson discovered

that his pony had cast a shoe from a hind foot; and as another was also rather loose he decided that his father had best replace them both for him. Righteous was a fairly competent farrier, and his skill in that respect was much above that of most travellers. Nelson was anxious that we should drive *his* pony rather than mine, for he wanted to show off its capabilities to his uncle.

From his wagon Righteous brought his canvas bag, containing a number of wheel-spanners, horseshoes, a knife, nails and a hammer. Nelson brought the little pony close up to their wagon and Righteous lifted each foot in turn, removing the loose shoe and cutting back each hoof half an inch or so. Then he rasped each hoof smooth. The first shoe was just right and within a few moments he hammered home the nails and secured it firmly. The second, from which the shoe had been cast, was more difficult, and only after much hammering and more rasping could it be made to fit at all well. The pony became very fidgety and moved as Righteous was hammering home a nail, and the hammer gashed his knuckle instead.

"Waaaaaaay! Stand still, you bloody foxin' bastard!" he shouted, sucking his knuckle and spitting.

He tried again and this time succeeded in driving home the nail. But as he was about to insert another the pony shifted again, attempting to kick out at him.

"God's cuss you!" roared Righteous. "You poxy bastard! Ain't you never bin shoed afore?"

He struck the pony a thudding blow on the flank with the hammer head. It rolled its eyes but did not flinch.

"Wotsever the matter wi' the pony today?" Righteous remarked wrathfully to himself.

And still cursing to himself in indignation he drove home the other nails, bent over their exposed tips professionally, filed them slightly, and the task was completed.

Nelson soon had the pony harnessed, and we hitched him into my gig for greater speed.

For visiting his uncle Nelson had arrayed himself magnificently. He wore a black hat far back over his long watered-down hair; a vivid floral silk scarf knotted about his neck; an aged and far too large brown whipcord coat, corduroy trousers with fall-front and raised seams, similar to my own; and run-down brown boots, laced with string. Four wide silver rings adorned his fingers.

"Me Uncle Abri likes to see me dressed ole-fashioned when I goes to see un," he remarked a trifle self-consciously.

I jumped up into the gig from one side, and Nelson at the same time did likewise from the other. The pony was rearing to go.

"Hand me me *koshti*," he called to Noah, who obediently threw him his hazel switch.

"Come ooooooooooonnnnn!" Nelson shouted unnecessarily to the pony, banging the switch against the footboard and sending the pony, half in fear, bounding forward in bouncing gallops. My little gig jumped and rocked over the bumps, its red wheels spinning round.

"Come-on, come-on, come-on, come-on!" Nelson shouted again to the speeding pony, whirring his switch through the air and across the pony's flanks. He was a reckless 'mad-headed' driver, who had turned-over and broken up many a trap and trolley as a result of his wildness. He once confided to me that he would meet his death driving a horse and cart. He had foreseen it.

We reached the smooth tarmac road with a straight run ahead of us, for Abri's property lay beside the main road itself. It was early morning still and there was little traffic about. Nelson kept the pony going at a fast trot, whistling piercingly to himself and occasionally exchanging a shouted observation with me. A modern trailer caravan was drawn-up beside the road ahead of us, its owners consulting the engine of their motor-car. The pony flattened its ears as we drew closer and, lowering its head, veered across the road diagonally away from the caravan, puffing with fear and suspicion. Nelson was thoroughly annoyed at this, for no traveller likes his horse to show a fault, no matter how small, before another. He cracked the switch down sharply on the pony's flanks and, shouting the while, we shot forward even faster, at a full gallop, leaving the broken-down motor-car's owners gazing at us, white-faced, as we receded into the distance.

The pony's flanks darkened with sweat as we sped along, still with no decrease in speed. Presently, some fifty yards from the main road on our left, the tall cluster of cypresses that marked Abri's place came into sight. The small peninsula of land, less than half an acre, was reached by means of a narrow winding track running between fields. It had been acquired by old Abri some twenty-eight years earlier, in the times when one could do what one wished with one's own land—even to living on it! It was the kind of property that only a traveller would have contemplated buying. It had no water supply, no sanitation, nor any other amenities. Upon it, since the death of his wife, old Abri had lived with his daughter in a railway-carriage. But this excellent home (No

Smoking. First Class) had weathered badly over the years, and was now in the final stages of dereliction and collapse. It was patched-up with old pieces of corrugated iron, tins, and old tea-chests. Abri had been having a considerable amount of trouble with various representatives of Local Authority who had been vigorously campaigning to have the carriage and the whole property condemned. Their success had been partial. Old Abri had been ordered to vacate and board-up or destroy the carriage, and to provide himself with a better type of home. In no way senile or helpless, despite his eighty-one years, Abri had been fighting—as best a complete illiterate can—for his rights to live as he himself wanted.

Having heard of all this, it was no great surprise to see, as we trotted up the lane, the old carriage boarded-up and a new square tent and an open lot beside it. Hearing our approach, which was announced by the barking of a variety of mongrel dogs all baying and tugging at their chains by their kennels of barrels and tin lean-tos, old Abri emerged from the tent and stood motionless at its entrance. He was very dark of complexion, and the combination of pigmentation and dirt caused him to appear almost black. His aged features were lined and pitted by years of open-air living. One eye was permanently closed, the other half-open and running. He was wearing a very old-fashioned black Derby suit, with high round collar and many pockets. It was greenish now, and torn and frayed. A large silver watch-chain stretched across the waistcoat, and an old piece of blue silk was knotted about his neck. The dogs continued to bark, until old Abri shouted querulously at them and they slunk back into their shelters.

I glanced about me. Huge mounds of scrap-iron were everywhere, and two trolleys stood fully-loaded. Old cart-wheels and broken or rotted pieces of horse-drawn vehicles were scattered over the ground, some almost buried in dried mud. Some speckled bantams and an Indian Gamecock scratched daintily about in the dust and sump-oil.

In a precarious-looking two-sided shed a fire was burning on the earth in the middle of the floor, and Lydie, his daughter, was sitting by it frying some meat. Around the fire there were several dented petrol-tins to serve as seats. This was old Abri's summer daytime living-quarters, where he and his daughter ate, cooked, and rag-sorted: for, true to the habits formed in his earlier days of wagon-travelling, he did not go indoors except to sleep. At that time half the space in the lean-to shed was taken up by an enormous quantity of rags, loose and in sacks and partly covered by an old carpet.

"We'm jest a-goin' to have our vittles," old Abri muttered. "Tie on the pony an' come in an' have a warm."

We tethered the pony to an old lorry axle and walked over to the shed.

Old Abri pulled half an ancient mattress from the rag-heap and lay down on it by the fire, sighing with the effort.

"How is you, Uncle Abri?" Nelson asked politely.

"Me rheumatickses is bad still," replied the old man mournfully. "An' the *funkem* wot the *drab* gie me don't seem to do me no good neither."

"O *dordi*!" said Nelson, smiling unsympathetically.

Old Abri turned to me. "How you gittin' on, mush?" he asked. "I ain't a-seed you fer nearly a twelve-month."

Lydie handed Nelson and myself a cup of tea in rather pleasant willow-patterned cups with two handles. We sipped happily.

"My, Lydie, ain't these some nice cups?" Nelson observed ingratiatingly.

Abri was a very 'fly' but nonetheless kind and pleasing old man, far more perceptive than many. Once, when I was in great financial need, he had loaned me fifty pounds—which he had asked should be repaid only when I could afford it. It was a kindness which I have never forgotten.

Old Abri was the eldest of nineteen children, Righteous being his youngest brother. Their mother had died some three years earlier at the reputed age of a hundred and six.

He inquired interestedly into our whereabouts and about the number of horses we had in our possession.

"I've a-got three, my son," he replied to Nelson in answer to a query as to his own horses.

"I've a-still got me dear ole Darky, wot I wouldn't take a hundred pun fer—why, a man bid me seventy pun for un t'other day! I sez to him, I sez: no money in the world shouldn't buy that horse offen me, brother, an' when I goes on I wants him shot dead the same day. Then I've a-got a nice big grey mare wot I bought in the 'bloc' last month. An' I got the prettiest pony wot ever you've seed, young men. 'Tis a little odd-coloured mare, pretty-marked pony she is, an' can warranty her good an' sound if you've a mind to make me a bid for her—or I might *chop* her away fer one a bit smaller if anyone'd gie me the right money to do it." And he eyed Nelson's pony for a fleeting instant with his one good eye, mopping at it the while with an old greyish piece of rag.

" 'Tis fer yer cousin Lydie to drive out wi' that I wants

a little pony," he continued. "There ain't the grass 'bout yere fer three big hosses. How d'ye like yer cousin Nelson's dee-little pony over there?" he inquired of the greying-haired Lydie who had been sitting silently smoking while we had been talking. She was deaf and partially dumb. Her jaws moved rapidly for some moments, as though striving to get themselves into gear, and then she suddenly uttered a rush of unintelligible gabbling which none but her father understood.

"She don't talk so plain today, 'cos she've lost her mumblers," he explained, adding comfortingly: "Still, she can git some more on the market next week, I 'spects."

It is sad but true that most travellers suffer from bad teeth, and most of the women, at any rate, are compelled to wear false teeth before they are thirty. This dental decay is caused partly by the failure ever to use a tooth-brush and partly by the continual eating of cheap sugary sweets when they are young. When travellers *do* eventually visit a dentist, often after weeks or months of agony, they almost invariably insist on having the offending teeth extracted, regarding fillings with the utmost distrust and horror.

"She'd like to drive down the lane an' back in the trap to see how he goes," Abri explained. "Will you drive him up an' down, Dom?" he asked me.

"Certainly I will," I assured him. I untethered the pony and led him over to the shed to enable Lydie to climb into the gig—which she did with the agility born of long years of practice.

I trotted the pony quickly down the lane to the main road, demonstrating to Lydie the sensitivity of his mouth and the speed of his trotting. She had missed nothing, and

taking the reins from my hand, she picked up the switch
and galloped him back to her father and Nelson. She
pulled the pony up sharply to a standstill, suddenly and
hard in the manner of travellers with quick ponies, then
backed him round in a circle, all of which he performed
very well. She jumped down without a word and
beckoned her father aside for a brief whispered conversation. Nelson winked at me.

"O *dordi*!" he muttered. "Me Uncle Abri ain't half-fly,
you know, mush. I 'spects we'll have a deal, though."

After a minute old Abri shuffled back to us and,
glancing at the pony's teeth again, inquired whether we
would like to walk round the back of the shed and see his
horses; and on our agreeing he led the way.

The horses were tethered along the verge of a newly-
ploughed field. The black cob and the grey mare were in
sight, but there was no sign of the odd-coloured mare.

"I 'spects she'm led down agin that ole fuzz-bush," old
Abri said, pointing to a clump of gorse.

We walked over and there she was. She sprang quickly
to her feet when we appeared; and we saw that she was
most strikingly and finely marked, with a two-coloured
tail and mane. She was a nice thick pony, almost a cob in
fact, and could obviously pull a small wagon if necessary.

"There ain't nothin' the matter wi' this mare," said
Abri confidently, and began the old Romani salesmanship,
including that of leaning against the pony's rear and
drawing the tail over his shoulder and tugging it
vigorously, simultaneously resting his back against the
pony's rear. In this case, however, the mare—doubtless
growing a little bored—took it upon herself to move
forward a few paces to continue grazing, and old Abri,

who was not as nimble as he had once been, was left without support and toppled over backwards. He fell to the ground and lay there for a minute still in full spate of praise for the pony. Rocking to and fro on his back like an overturned tortoise, his arms and legs waving feebly, he struggled to his feet as though nothing had happened.

". . . an' I gid sixty pun fer her *an'* a white-metal set o' harness wot fits her—an' may God strike me dead this minute iffen that ain't right an' the truth," he concluded vehemently.

"Ain't a bad sorta pony," Nelson admitted. "Hard-toothed un, ain't she, Uncle Abri?"

"Certainly she is, my dear," he answered. "She'm nine year old."

"O my uncle, she'm older'n that," rejoined Nelson quickly.

"Nine year old," repeated Abri firmly, "that's wot she is. I knows the age of a pony so well as you does. An' to tell you the truth, boy, I ain't perticular to sell her—but I heered you wuz thinkin' o' goin' wi' ole Meeannie's gal, an' then you'd want a horse to pull a little wagon, ain't that right?"

"Goin' wi' ole Meeannie's gal?" exclaimed Nelson. "Which one? That one wot has fits, do you mean?"

"I don't mean that Meeannie, I means yer Aunt Meeannie's gal—yer cousin, boy," old Abri explained, blotting feebly at the discharge from his eye.

"I ain't a-gwin wi' no gal jest now," answered Nelson, finishing that trend of conversation. "Now how much is you goin' to gie me to *chop* that ole mare fer me pony, my Uncle?"

"My bloody God!" rejoined Abri vehemently. "I's old

—but I ain't *that* old, my sonner! Iffen you likes to gie *me* ten pun you can take that mare on—an' that's the best deal wot ever you've had, my son, an' 'tis on'y 'cos you'm me brother's boy."

Nelson did not answer, but ran his hand down each of the mare's legs. He lifted each hoof and scraped all round the inside 'frog,' and smelled the feet in case she was suffering from the rotting disease of the foot known as 'thrush.' He looked at her teeth again, and then brought his hand up suddenly in front of her face to see if she flinched—which she did but only a little. Then he backed and trotted her up and down. She had a lovely movement and was a nice-looking little cob. If I had had the money at that time I should have tried to buy her myself. But I knew, in any case, that Nelson had decided to have her.

"I'll gie you five pun to *chop*," he said suddenly.

"Make it eight pun ten an' you shall have her," replied Abri stolidly.

Nelson hesitated. He knew the offer was a bargain, made partly because his uncle was fond of him. But his natural instinct to fight to the last had not quite deserted him.

"I'll gie you seven pun," he fired back.

"Eight pun—an' that's me last word, an' not a penny less," Abri returned firmly.

"Gooo-on, then!" shouted Nelson, and the old man's right hand palm met his in a resounding clap—and the seal was set on the transaction in the traditional Romani manner.

Nelson thereupon turned his back upon us and fumbled energetically in the interior of his jacket in order to withdraw the necessary sum of money. Most travellers are wary of allowing anyone to see just how large the wad of notes is from which they extract the money for a deal. In a few moments he swung round and counted out the pound notes, one by one, into the black palm of the old man, who watched the slow counting carefully.

"An' yere's a bit o' silver back fer luck," he said, handing a half-crown back to Nelson with a smile.

The deal having been amicably concluded, we led the new mare back to the pony and gig and Nelson quickly unharnessed the pony, which Lydie took away and tethered by the mare's plug-chain. Luckily the pony's collar was of the adjustable buckle variety so that we had no difficulty in letting it out sufficiently to fit the mare. The rest of the harness, of course, also had to be adjusted in order to fit the stockier little cob.

"She ain't so fast as the little-un," Abri admitted, "but she'll trot on nice an' steady, an' she kin do thirty mile a day easy."

Nelson backed her into the shafts and I hooked on the trace on my side and fastened the breeching straps, while Nelson did the same on the other. The little mare stood quiet and still, patient and docile compared with Nelson's high-spirited, impatient pony.

"I hopes you ain't gid me a *bouncer*," he grinned at his uncle.

We climbed into my gig and, shouting farewells to Abri and Lydie, trotted sedately down the track to the main road.

"Think I done right in *choppin'* the pony away?" Nelson asked a little dubiously.

"Certainly you did," I reassured him. "This is a lovely pony—a pretty thing."

"She ain't so fast, though," Nelson said, experimentally bringing his switch down with a rattle on the footboard to see her reaction. She ignored it.

"Ain't she quiet?" he muttered admiringly, adding, "I don't reckon she's bin wi' travellers long, do you?"

"No, I don't," I replied. "I like her and if you've still got her in about three months and you want to sell her, then perhaps we might have a deal."

It was early afternoon by then, and we trotted homewards, the mare lifting her feet daintily and quickly, though without the essentially *forward* movement which had given Nelson's previous pony such speed.

"O *dordi*!" Noah shouted, as we approached the wagons. "They've *chopped* away the pony."

"Did you git that un offen yer Uncle Abri?" Righteous inquired, leaving his cooking pots as we drove up.

"Yeah, had a *chop* wi' me uncle," Nelson agreed proudly.

"How much did you gie un to *chop*?" asked Righteous, narrowing his eyes.

"I gie him five pun, ain't that right, mush?" replied Nelson quickly, turning to me for confirmation.

"That's right," I agreed tactfully.

"Then there's somethin' wrong wi' her somewheres," asserted Righteous, having seemingly little faith in his brother's good will.

"The ole man thinks I've had a good deal," Nelson surprisingly announced to me as we unhitched the mare and I pulled the gig over alongside our wagon.

"The vittles is ready," shouted Righteous. "Is you a-comin'?"

Two large pots were simmering over the big fire,

emitting fragrant scents, and several large floral-patterned plates, somewhat cracked, were on a low table beside the fire. The larger of the two pots contained two finely roasted pullets in rice-filled gravy; while the smaller one was three-quarters full of potatoes, swedes, onions and kale-tops. Two large white 'cottage' loaves lay on the ground nearby.

"How d'ye like they *kanis*?" asked Righteous, grinning, for we had been invited to lunch in order to sample his cooking.

Beshlie and I complimented him on their excellence and on the superiority of the meal provided for us.

"T'aint like me dear wife used to do it," he said mournfully.

The vast meal was soon served, and we all consumed it with relish, assisted by knives, fingers and large lumps of white bread!

When one cooks and eats outside in the open air during all seasons of the year and in all weather, one cannot enjoy a meal indoors—even in a wagon. Even if cooked outside on a paraffin stove, a meal is never so good as one prepared on a wood fire.

A family that I know bought a paraffin stove during one very bad spell of weather when they were stopping in a place where there was no wood. A short time later I met a member of the family who, pale and wan, explained to me that the whole family had been overcome by ". . . that ole 'flu wot the parryfin gid us."

We ate the birds and most of the vegetables. The remains were thrown to the dogs, who all stood watchfully at hand during the meal. Travelling-people rarely prepare a special meal of any sort for the dogs, simply tossing them large quantities of scraps at each of their own meal-times.

Having finished this enormous meal, we drank some tea, and lay or sat beside the embers of the fire, smoking and talking.

"I kilt two snakes this mornin'," Righteous remarked. "This place is alive wi' 'em. 'Tis wusser'n where we wuz down agin Heckfield ways."

"Ar," agreed Nelson. "I minds they had a great board up there wi' 'ware o' the varmints writ on to it."

And so the talk drifted on; and, subconsciously half-expecting visitors, we waited for any other travellers who might chance to come over to see us from another encampment.

There, in the dirt, confusion and squalor of our own making, oblivious and unburdened by a knowledge of world affairs or by a developed sense of beauty or ugliness, we rested contentedly.

Perhaps one of us could have busied himself clearing up some of the old tins, rags, and other litter about the encampment; or we could have cleaned the harness, or washed, or mended the door of the wagon, or . . . but no! For this was Sunday. The day of Rest.

The End of the Year
"Cold Old Weather"

PART FOUR

The End of the Year

1

I T was Monday morning and we were still on the piece of waste land behind the hospital, having come to retrieve Miella, old Nelson's wife, who had had an operation. Miella had been duly discharged and our wagons had been there for nearly a week, despite combined attempts by both police and Public Health officials to persuade us to leave. There were five vans in all. The police had announced their intention of having us forcibly dislodged if we were not gone by nine o'clock that morning. It was by now nearly half-past ten, but none of us had made any particular effort to get things ready for a move. However, as we were still sitting talking and smoking round the smouldering embers of the morning's fires, we suddenly became aware of the ominous chùg-chugging of a heavy tractor; and sure enough, round the corner which was screened by some smoke-wilted bushes, the great vehicle came into view, accompanied by no less than four police constables, a sergeant and a tall, bespectacled, unhealthy-looking young man wearing a cheap blue suit, who proved to be the sanitary inspector. On learning his occupation Rosina sarcastically informed him of the cleanliness of our habits in no very pretty terms, remarking at the same time: ". . . an' 'tis they ole drains wot causes the fevers—not the likes o' we!"

"Well, I'm goin' to have me a dish o' tea afore we shifts," Daniel observed calmly.

However, with quiet single-mindedness, two of the constables had already hitched Mooshie's wagon to the rear of the tractor and, before we had time to complain, had begun hauling it slowly up the steep incline towards the secondary road which ran alongside the hospital. The other constables, eyed by the sergeant, began harrying the rest of us—having taken all our names and ages—to get our horses harnessed and to be ready to move. We knew by then that argument was of no avail, although various members of our group tried both persuasion and hard-luck stories in an effort to achieve a few extra days' grace. So, with a mixture of curses, obscenities, laughter, shouts and tears from the younger children we slowly harnessed-up the *grais*, hitched them into their respective wagons and carts, and collected up all the oddments of our belongings which were still scattered about. Meanwhile Mooshie and his wife were hastening up the hill after their disappearing wagon, cursing and screaming with wrath and frustration and leading their ancient dun cob who remained placidly impervious to the noise and their gesticulations.

It was a cold morning, with Christmas only a few weeks distant. I remember that I found this particular incident strangely depressing, almost symbolical in its futility.

Eventually, when all the wagons were lined-up one behind the other on the road, and we had all climbed up without mishap, a brief but loud argument ensued as to

the direction we should take. Since we had private names
for all the places mentioned, it was doubtful whether the
police had the least idea where they were.

"We'd be best off up agin the fuzzy-break."

"Wot? You wouldn't git five minutes there afore the
gavvers come to you, man."

"I'm *jallin'* to the pits. . . ."

"Theys fenced-in now, man. . . ."

"Hows about Gulliver's tree?"

"Wot? I wouldn't go to that lonesome ole place, my
brother, not fer a hundred pun. . . ."

"Let's go down in the withy beds then. . . ."

"God's cuss that place!"

"I'm *jallin'* to the pits. . . ."

"Well we ain't—we'm goin' to spring pond, so we'd
best make two roads of it."

And 'make two roads of it' we did. Daniel and Mooshie
and their families turned in one direction, whilst Nelson,
Jesse, and Beshlie and I took the other way.

The weather, which up until then had been hard and
dry, showed every sign of change and I feared that we
were about to suffer a long wet spell. True enough, after
we had covered a mile or so the sky darkened and a
steady rain began to descend upon us. This rather upset
Nelson, who pulled his van, which was in the lead, to a
halt and a further discussion took place about our destination. It was then decided that we should make for the
Downs. The journey there would entail only one roadside night before the proposed *'atchin' tan* could be
reached. I had never myself approached the Downs
stopping-place from that direction; but I was assured by
the others that the intermediate halt, fascinatingly called

The Big Board, was pleasant and fairly free as a rule from interruption by the police.

"I've a-bid there fer a week an' more sometimes wi'out anyone comin' to us," old Nelson said comfortingly.

Jesse was a little nervous of meeting the police in that area at that moment as he had failed to answer a summons which had been issued against him for "lighting a fire within forty feet of the centre of the highway." It had been a difficult summons to answer, because on the one hand the police had ordered him to move on out of the area, and on the other they had issued a summons against him which lawfully compelled him to remain within an accessible distance from the courts. (Later I managed to help him to settle the incident by post, and he was compelled to send a pound for this minor offence.)

We had been asked to spend Christmas with old Nelson and his wife Miella and their family. Unfortunately Nelson, then in his mid-seventies, was not a long-distance traveller. In fact his territory covered only about ten or fifteen miles in all! It was, therefore, his principle to stick in his stopping-places—which, in view of the minute area of his 'country,' were not numerous—until the bitter end. Consequently, episodes in which he and his family were towed out from their encampments by the authorities were quite common. I sometimes had a suspicion that they rather enjoyed the feeling of importance that it gave them. I did not. But old Nelson, after a lifetime on the roads, was hardened to almost anything. He had, in his younger days, served a prison sentence of two years for knocking down a constable who had kicked the burning fire up and over his wife and children when they had not moved at his command. The police, farmers and indeed all who ill-treat Romanies know themselves to be quite safe in so doing, as the travellers will never complain to a higher authority. And even if they did so, who would believe a 'gypsy's' word against that of the others? As illiterates (for the most part) and as unpopular minorities at that, the travellers are an easy prey for those in authority who happen to be unpleasantly disposed.

We arrived at The Big Board soon after midday. It was an agreeable stopping-place, being a downland drove at right angles to the main road. The road was bordered by lines of splendid beech trees, and the fallen dead branches from those trees provided us with ample wood for the fires. We drew the three wagons in one beside the other—Nelson's vast skylight van dwarfing the two little open lots belonging to Jesse and ourselves. Jesse's open lot was a squat little wagon, covered by a new green canvas sheet roughly tacked on with clumsy nails. Its wooden back and front were painted orange and maroon in sections, and the spectacle of those two colours applied next to one another was somewhat unnerving. Like so many traveller-constructed wagons it was quite out of alignment wherever it could be—even its front door was not centrally placed, but had been misjudged so that, when surveyed head-on, it appeared neither in the middle nor yet to one side. It was a worrying sort of wagon however you looked at it.

Jesse's wife, Britty, and two of Nelson's daughters went out 'calling,' so we set about gathering up the wood and lighting the fires ready for their return—one for us, one for Jesse and Britty, and one for old Nelson and his wife and daughters and their younger son Jobi. The rain had ceased by the time we had unhitched the horses and had pegged them out on their plug-chains to graze in the drove. The wood was damp but we soon had the fires piled high and blazing merrily, with the black kettles hanging from their thin cranes in the flames. There was a convenient cattle trough in a nearby field so that we were relieved of the necessity of begging the *pani* from neighbouring cottagers. We were all very damp from the rain, and we sat close to our respective fires with the steam rising in clouds from our clothes. Beshlie and I were rather worried just then by the fact that our mare's collar was threatening to 'ring' her, that is to say rub the neck and shoulders so that if nothing was done the fur and outer skin tissue would ultimately come right off. The collar the mare was wearing did not really fit her, but it had been the best we had been able to find since selling our previous cob. However, the Downs was one of the few stopping-places where one could be almost sure not to be molested or interfered with for several weeks: in fact, one traveller and his family were reputed to have stayed there for four months before being forced to go. And so, if old Nelson and Miella decided to remain there for two or three weeks, as we rather suspected they might, there would be ample time for the mare's shoulders to heal, and in the meantime I might be successful in finding another collar for her.

"Iffen I had me health an' strength I'd be down there along o' you by the *yog*, my mush!" Miella shouted from the black depths of her van—for she had not stirred from her bed during the whole journey. She had been bed-ridden for two or three months since being struck down quite suddenly by a variety of maladies which she defied any doctors to cure, and since she had left hospital her demeanour had become even more mournful, and she stoutly insisted that the wrong operation had been performed upon her! Gradually her brown, beautifully weathered face paled and grew haggard and putty-like from her refusal to leave her bed in the dark van after fifty years spent in the open air; and a once happy, strong, vigorous, fine-looking woman had degenerated into a self-pitying, grey-faced, prematurely-aged crone, entirely wrapped up in the mysteries of her own ailments, with only the briefest flashes of her old self showing—usually when she pondered on those who, as she was convinced, had wished ill-fortune upon her.

"God's cuss they wots 'witched me," she would spit, her large dark, black-rimmed eyes flashing and glittering with wrath and evil intent.

"When that bloody banty cockbird flew up on to me shoulder an' crowed three times . . . then I knowed as someone'd begged a prayer on me. . . .

"I'd like to git up an' dance on me bloody ole gran'-mother's grave—'tis she wots brought this complainement on to me. . . .

"I'm a-goin' to the herbalist-man, now, my brother. Hark! He's gid me these pills. Is you a scholar? Then read me wot it sez on the box, my brother. . . .

"He sez he'll have me walkin' an' dancing in three weeks if I takes they pills.

"God's cuss that doctor . . . very nigh killed me, he did. . . .

"I'm a-goin' to live to be a hundred, my son, an' I'll dance on me gran'mother's grave wi'out me sticks an' crutches. . . .

" 'Twas that ole Mary-Jane wot begged that prayer on me. . . . She'm a witch fer sure. . . .

"Boy! Boy! Git me some baccy! Quick! Git me some. . . .

". . . oh, I don't want no gilded mansion nor no house of golt. . . .

"I knows wot made me bad! 'Twas all they bottles o' stout I bin a drinkin' all these years. God's cuss that stout!

"O my brother, wotsever brought this badness onto me? I ain't bin a h'evil 'oman like some . . . so wotsever brought this badness on me?"

Her husband and family had gradually tired of the novelty of her illness and had reached the stage at which they appeared to think of her as little more than a nuisance which had to be borne. This was, of course, largely due to her disinclination to allow any subject other than herself to be discussed within her presence or hearing.

It was a sad state of affairs, which offered little or no promise of a happy or enjoyable Christmas for us or for anybody else.

A singularly gruesome and unpleasant habit of Miella's while sitting alone in her bed in the semi-darkness of the van was the extraction of her own teeth! They were very decayed, and her method was to prize them one by one from her gums by means of an old peg-knife. These gougings would occupy her for some considerable time and would be intermittently punctuated by outbursts of lurid cursing or, whenever the gum was lacerated too much by a slip of the knife, by a sharp scream of pain. But once the tooth was finally out she would spend the rest of the day examining the gum in an old cracked looking-glass, dabbing it the while with a grubby piece of rag.

By the time we parted company I was sad to learn that she had only two teeth left. I should have liked to have been present to the last.

Britty and Nelson's two daughters, Sophie and Lily, returned in the early afternoon. Their baskets, which had been full of paper flowers when they had set off, were now filled with food: tins of condensed milk, sugar, butter, tea, cheap scraps of bacon, potatoes, and countless large white loaves comprised the bulk of their purchases. Britty had, of course, added a considerable quantity of sticky sweets to her purchases for she and Jesse had four small *chavies*—three of whom ran out at the sight of her, scrambling and shouting for the expected gifts.

I fried some bacon and a few bantam eggs which Beshlie and I enjoyed, even though we realised that we ate far too much fried food, especially in the winter months—mainly, I confess, because it was easy and quick to prepare.

Britty and Lily were somewhat distressed because a policeman had caught them hawking without licences and had threatened to see that they were 'inside' for Christmas: and a householder had turned a 'wolf-hound' (which I knew to be an Alsatian) on Sophie when she had called selling her flowers and she had narrowly escaped being bitten. This kind of behaviour cannot, surely, be too strongly deplored. Every year many travellers and their children are bitten by house-dwellers' dogs—yet these dog-owners are *never* brought to court as they would be in any other circumstances. Only recently when I called at a farmhouse to ask some directions I was forced to stun a collie dog with a thick stick which I happened to be carrying. It was deliberately incited to attack me by its owner—before I had even had time to speak! This man then threatened to sue *me* for injuring the dog! However, he received a reply of a kind which he obviously did not expect—and his threat to enter into litigation faded away with surprising speed. He even attempted to placate me with a gift of half a dozen eggs!

"I'm sorry—I thought you were a . . ." he began.

"I am!" I replied, and turned on my heel.

After we had all eaten and rested by the fires for some little time Jesse and I moved the horses to fresh grazing for the night, tethering them farther down the drove. The grass was plentiful and there was no need to *poove* them, though Jesse momentarily toyed with the idea—more from habit than for any other reason!

Jesse was a striking-looking young man with fine Red Indian features in which were set a pair of hooded, piercing black eyes. He was unshaven, the dark stubble accentuating his good jaw-line. Tufts of hair, long and matt, projected from under his cap, and his clothes hung on him in tatters, raggedly and as flapping as the clothes on a scarecrow. The ground was spongy and wet from the heavy rain and when we returned to the fire Jesse took off his aged rubber wellington boots—emptying a pint or so of dirty water from each of them. His feet, malformed from a lifetime of wearing other people's shoes, were wrapped in rags which he carefully unwound and dried in the heat of the *yog*.

"Cain't you *mong* me a pair of *choks* tomorry, gal?" he asked Britty, who had been sitting calmly observing his footwear operations without any apparent sympathy.

Few travellers bother very much about such a small thing as having wet feet, even though—as I know from too-frequent experience—it is very uncomfortable in cold weather.

Nobody 'came to us' that night and, surprisingly true to the plans we had made, we *jalled*-on the next morning before ten o'clock, hoping to reach the Downs soon after noon.

The first part of the journey was not very eventful although several of the hills were steep, and on these Jesse's small grey pony found the going very hard, being too small to manage the heavy lot it had to pull. On the ascents its tiny hooves scrabbled and slipped, making sparks fly on the tarmac in its endeavours to maintain a foothold. But being well-schooled in the hard lessons of the roads, the gradients were conquered without disaster.

The track leading from the main road to the section of the Downs where our people always stopped was deeply rutted with mud-filled pot-holes and was much over-grown from each side by hazels and hawthorns. The wagons lurched, jolted and swayed, and the vicious thorn-bushes tore at the canvas sides of the two open lots, threatening to rip the sheets to pieces. Quite unperturbed by the state of the road, old Nelson had swung his immense skylight van into the trackway, almost over-turning it as one of the great wheels sank deep into a muddy rut. Miella emitted screams and guttural cries of wrath from the interior:

"God's cuss they routs! *Dordi*, the wagon's broke-up!"

But on we went. Britty, Sophie, Beshlie and Lily were walking behind the wagons with two of Jesse's children and three of the dogs. I could faintly hear their cries of alarm as the wagons swayed and tossed like galleons in a storm.

. . . surprisingly true to the plans we had made, we *jalled*–on the next morning before ten o'clock, . . .

Matters were further complicated when Jesse's pony abruptly stopped dead, with the wagon tilting at a drunken angle, one front wheel sunk hub-deep in a pot-hole.

"Wotsever this, you mother's *minch*!" the enraged Jesse burst out on finding that his pony refused to budge.

"My bloody Saviour! Is you a dead-napskin, you bastard?" he added, delivering a cruelly-aimed kick at the pony's stomach.

This thoroughly alarmed the little grey and it gave a leap forwards, its eyes rolling. There was a staccato cracking and rending of wood, and the pony, accompanied by the shafts and the front half of the lock, shot forwards—almost crashing headlong into the rear of Nelson's van and leaving the wagon and the remainder of the shattered lock still firmly lodged in the hole.

I hastily left our mare's head, for she would stand still when told, and ran round to the front of Jesse's wagon to assist him and to inspect the damage.

"God's cuss this blood foxin' place! O *dordi*! I wouldn't have had this happen fer a hundred pun! Me wagon's all to pieces. . . . O *dordi*! God strike me an all me children dead if I ever comes up yere agin. . . ."

"Quick! We don't want to '*atch* here all day," I urged. "Fetch a plug-chain and we'll wind it round the rest of the lock and on to the shafts, and then we can mend it when we get to the stopping-place."

After some further lamentation from Britty and Jesse this course was followed. We had to take Nelson's huge black vanner out of his wagon and use her to pull the deeply-embedded wagon from the hole.

"It's a wonder he never broke up they sharpts as well,"

muttered Jesse, glaring at the pony who stood dejectedly waiting. "I shall send him on to the fust mother's son I meets," he added furiously, demanding of us: "Is I three parts *dinilo*?" We did not answer.

"Wot? Do you think I'd keep a dead-napskin? Certainly I won't, my brothers. God's cuss that pony!"

By the time all this was done and we had replaced the horse and pony in their respective wagons, it was well past midday and we were all rather tired and short-tempered.

At last, after a further jarring and bumping, we reached a corner in the lane and, rounding it, were no longer hedged-in—the downland and meadows spreading out before us. It was no difficult task to find our usual stopping-place and that of all other travelling-people who periodically stayed there. The ground was marked with the small round black scars left by countless *yogs* and the usual variety of old iron, bicycle frames and pieces of broken wheels and shafts lay everywhere. Half an old trolley lodged up-ended in a thicket, and a pile of rotted rags was decaying in a ditch. Old Nelson gazed about him, fondly eyeing the remnants of the trolley that had once been his. It was a homecoming.

There was not a great deal of available wood on the Downs so we agreed to share one *yog* between us all—a rather unusual procedure. While the men set about unharnessing the *grais*, Sophie and Lily started the fire. This did not burn to their satisfaction, so they encouraged it by the throwing on of an old bicycle tyre which they had retrieved from a bush. Pungent black smoke and choking fumes swirled about us for some minutes, but the flames were soon licking high and bright.

Towards the end of the afternoon the weather broke

again. A solid downpour began, and it seemed obvious that there would be little or no let-up that evening.

The horses were all tethered in the *lue* of a thicket; they were used to the hard weather and it would not be likely to worry them unduly.

We retired to bed quite early, the heavy rain pounding down on to the taut canvas roof of the wagon with a noise like a drum and making sleep difficult.

I emerged from the wagon next morning to find that fifteen hours of rain—which had still not abated—had reduced the trackway by which we had come to a positive morass of mud on which it would have been difficult for a horse to have kept its feet.

Nobody had collected any wood for the morning's fire, so I scrambled into the middle of a tangle of thorn-bushes, the limbs of which were heavy with rain that showered down on me; and within a matter of minutes I was completely soaked. I did not possess a raincoat and my old jacket and cord trousers were inadequate to with-stand the water. Nevertheless, I managed to gather quite an imposing amount of dead wood, all sodden, and I returned with it to the site of the previous night's fire. I took a stump of candle from my pocket and broke it in half, then I lit one half and set it upright in the watery ashes, piling some twigs and small wood round and above it. When I had placed sufficient twigs above the tiny flame I laid the other half of the candle stump in the wood directly above the flame so that the heat from below gradually rose upwards, melting the wax which then caught fire and ignited the soggy twigs. It is an old Romani trick, and a very successful one.

The actual rights of way and commonland on the

Downs were surprisingly few and small, the greater part being privately owned by two families. Of these only one was even remotely tolerant of the travelling people; the other was violently hostile, threatening to shoot any of us who trespassed on his land. We used, nevertheless, to creep across his fields at dusk in order to take water from one of his cattle troughs, but even that was a hazardous business as he was apt to prowl about his property at all hours with the express desire of catching us. If he succeeded he would invariably summon the local constable to get us moved on.

That stay on the Downs seemed, from the first, to be marred by a succession of misfortunes and happenings all of which combined to render the lives of all of us more uncomfortable than they need have been, and to reduce our spirits to a low ebb.

The women hastened through a somewhat soggy breakfast in order to be off as early as possible to make for the nearest town in which to sell the paper flowers which they had fashioned from crepe paper the night before.

"Hurry up! Quick, my sisters!" Sophie urged. "The busty goes at half-past nine an' there ain't another till 'leven."

"O *dordi*! I wishes I had some wellitens," Lily wailed as they stumbled off through the mud towards the road and the bus-stop.

"She'm a *kushti diking rackli*, ain't she?" laughed old Nelson from the fireside, looking at the retreating form of Beshlie who had gone with the other women. He added with a wink: "I reckons she an' me's a-goin' to be sweethearts."

"God's cuss that man!" shouted Miella from the van on

overhearing the remark. She added to me: "Let un go on then! An' you come up in the *verdo* 'long o' me, my mush, an' we'll make the wagon shake!"

We all laughed. It is a most delightful reflection of the fact that even the oldest man or women among the travellers is never too ancient to enjoy a 'bed joke.'

Jobi, old Nelson, two of Jesse's children and I were seated round the fire. Jesse himself had not yet made an appearance that morning.

He suddenly appeared at the door of his wagon, and lowered himself very slowly to the ground. He then made his way delicately to the fire, picking his way carefully between the pieces of harness and old tins that were scattered about the front of his wagon.

"Wot's the matter wi' that man?" Jobi inquired, having been busy cutting his fingernails with a peg-knife.

"I feels bad—I reckons I've a-caught one o' they ole germs wot's about this country," Jesse replied in a weak voice, regarding us dolefully.

"Gooooaaan! There ain't nothin' the matter wi' you," pronounced old Nelson callously, his voice as grating and rough as the edge of a saw.

"So help me my dear mother! I feels bad in the guts," Jesse stated indignantly, throwing an old piece of matting down in the mud by the fire and flopping down on to it. He was quite determined, like all travellers when they succumb to any slight complaint, to make the most of it and to demand as much sympathy as possible—even though it would surely be very little.

"Iffen you wuz as bad as I is you'd be led up in the bed still—an' not a-jumpin' about by the *yog*!" called his mother, deeply offended that any one of us should have dared to be ill in her company, thereby detracting even a little from the attention that she felt was due to her own complicated illness.

"Iffen we wuz *'atched* in a better *tan* I'd git the boy to fetch the ole *drab* up to see me," Jesse remarked, his face assuming an expression of martyred suffering.

"Wot?" screamed Miella. "An' me led up in this bed a-near *mullo* an' they won't fetch *me* no *drabby* nor no *funkem*. Why, iffen I still had that doctor from South Hafricky wot wuz treatin' me out agin the *Dinilo's* Corner, I should be h'up an' h'on me feet a-walkin' about be now 'stead of bein' led up yere. 'Why,' he sez, 'I can cure you in. . . .' "

"God's cuss you! Hold yer bloody row!" interrupted Nelson impatiently, temporarily succeeding in reducing Miella to a series of inaudible mutterings.

2

We had been up on the Downs for five days, and Jesse's illness had passed its worst, though he still lay by the fire all day, regardless of the rain which poured down on him.

He pulled up his trouser-leg, revealing spindly, dirt-streaked legs for my inspection.

"Since this badness come on me I've a-lost five stone in weight," he muttered feebly. "All me health an' strength is gone, brother. O my blessed gran'mother, I wouldn't wish this badness on anybody."

Later that morning, however, he shaved himself slowly—using a child's hairbrush and some evil-smelling washing-soap to achieve a lather. He had borrowed old

Nelson's razor and gradually scraped away much of the ten days' growth of beard, cutting his finger on the ragged edge of the milk tin which held the warm shaving-water. Despite his assurance that his health and strength were still badly impaired, I knew that the act of shaving was symbolical of the end of his illness.

Jobi arrived back at the encampment on his old rattling bicycle in the middle of the morning with news that, in spite of the 'mud and water,' his Uncle Manny, Manny's wife, Louie, and his family were on their way to the Downs from Pond Lane where they had stayed for nearly a week without being moved on.

And sure enough, shortly after Jobi's return with the news, the heads of all our tethered horses turned, their ears pricked, in the direction of the road, picking up the sound of the wagon wheels and horses' hooves—still inaudible to us.

Within ten minutes or so we could clearly hear bursts of shouting. Sporadic singing and the sounds of the wagons ploughing through the mud of the track grew closer, then the roofs became visible at intervals through the hedges of the track as they passed along.

"They'll be drownded—wi' the mud an' water up to their necks," Miella announced gloomily on being told of their approach.

There had always been a certain amount of ill-feeling between the two families, despite the fact that they were so closely related—Miella being Manny's sister and Nelson being Louie's brother. Manny's and Louie's son, Liberty, who had 'got' Miella's and Nelson's daughter Rosie, was with them, together with a considerable number of children, some being Rosie's and Liberty's and others

241

Manny's and Louie's. We all greeted each other with a mixture of suspicion and affected goodwill which was the inevitable result of years of backbiting and jealousies that were a failing with both the families.

The wagons belonging to Manny and Liberty were crudely constructed, though better than Jesse's. Their canvas sheets were torn and faded, and the paintwork of Liberty's was peeling off to reveal its previous colour—red—in streaks and patches. The rear wheels were tall, and two spokes were missing from one of them—thereby causing its collapse to be imminent.

They pulled-in some fifty yards away from our group—wisely not going so far off the track and over the soft ground as old Nelson had insisted we should.

Manny's wagon had been less neglected than his son's and was still quite reasonably painted in blue and yellow—bearing on its sides the four panels depicting game-bantam cockbirds which Beshlie had been commissioned to paint for him some years before.

Manny had a delightfully picturesque and old-fashioned air—he and Miella came from a family of Romanis which was almost untainted by *gaujo* blood. Hence he was a particularly handsome man, with huge luminous eyes and a dark complexion. He was—and indeed still is—the personification of the romantic ideal of how the Romani should look and be. Quick and lithe, he had been one of the best 'step dancers' in the south of England in his younger days, and now, though in his middle sixties, he would still perform in the public-houses at the horse-sales and fairs. Manny and his wife had had a large family, even by travellers' standards, producing fifteen sons and three daughters! Beshlie and I had not encountered the parents for over a year, but we *had* been stopping with several of their sons in different parts of the country in the south. We were thus able to impart to them various items of interest, including the news that they had two more grandchildren than they knew of. In fact, we had been stopping with one of their sons when his wife had had her confinement. I have been present at many births, which usually occur in the wagons though some of the women prefer tents. I have also attended many funerals—which are very important affairs among travellers, who flock in vast numbers to the church. To some extent a man's standing and past reputation may be gauged by the number of mourners in evidence at his burial.

Manny was wearing a pair of chestnut-coloured, almost new, fall-front " Ockford" cord trousers similar to my own, which were black. We toyed for some minutes with the idea of 'having a *chop*' before mutually deciding against it. Manny and his family were even more rain-soaked than we were, and they all sat shivering and steaming close to their fire, which had fallen rather low.

"Fetch some postees an' lay on the *yog*, boy!" Manny told one of his sons, who disappeared with some grumbling, to return after a few minutes with four or five half-rotted fencing-posts which he had uprooted from a nearby field where new ones were lying ready to be set. Manny laid all the posts on the fire at once, crosswise, and within a few minutes—after tremendous blowing by two of his small sons who acted as human bellows—the heat was intense and comforting.

Unlike most Romani men Manny had a habit of carrying immense sums of money about with him, preferring that to leaving it hidden in the wagon or in his wife's safe-keeping—for no travellers ever patronise banks. Of course, in his case, Louie may have also carried even larger sums about with her, for she was naturally so bulky that it would have been hard to detect an artificial projection. It was difficult to judge how profitable their lives had been, but it was rumoured that Manny's father had given him over a thousand pounds just before his death, and as Manny and Louie were both very 'fly' there seemed little reason to doubt their wealth.

In any event Manny's chest was invariably puffed out by an enormous bundle of notes which he kept in an oil-skin bag pinned inside his waistcoat. Once, when he had engaged in a deal in my presence, he withdrew fifty pounds from the wads of notes—and this did not seem to decrease the bag's contents to any appreciable degree. I asked him whether he did not fear being robbed, especially at fairs and horse-sales.

"That's all right, brother," he answered with pride. "The retectives knows I carries a lot o' money on me, an' they'm always lookin' out to me."

Later that evening when we were up in their wagon talking, Louie began showing Beshlie some jewellery, as they were hoping to engage in some dealings. Nothing interested Beshlie sufficiently until under the flickering candle-light she noticed a large brooch pinned to Louie's throat and asked to see it.

"Ar, I couldn't part from that, gal, not fer any money," said Louie primly, removing it and gazing upon it affectionately. "That's wot my Manny gid me."

It was a coin-like brooch, and at first sight I took it to be a five-shilling piece.

"I gid seven shillin's an' sixpence to have un silveryed an' a pin put on to un," remarked Manny expensively. "Show un to her," he ordered.

It was one of the saddest experiences of my life when the 'coin' was handed to me by Beshlie. Holding it in my hand near the candle, I saw it was a silver-covered bronze medallion—'In recognition of Long and Faithful Service in the —— County Police!' None of that family being able to read or write, the ironical significance of the brooch had been hidden from them. Needless to say we did not enlighten them.

Beshlie was so touched by this incident that she gave Louie a pair of silver threepenny-piece earrings 'for luck.'

At this point our peace was unexpectedly shattered by a heavy bump against the side of the wagon, causing it to sway from side to side like a pendulum. This was followed by much shouting and cursing and by a few lesser thumps.

On looking out we discovered the cause of the disturbance to be Manny's three youngest sons, aged between seven and twelve, who were locked together in mortal combat beside the van—having apparently come to blows whilst gambling on the turn of a card, which is a very popular pastime for young and old alike. The smallest, Pincher, had a gash on his cheek from which blood was trickling.

"O my blessed Jesus!" cried his mother. "O my dead mother! The baby's dead—O wotsever happened to the dillycate boy?"

'The dillycate boy' had not, however, suffered any serious damage, despite his cut face; and after a few minutes more of struggling, the children returned to the fireside to continue their gaming.

"So help me God, iffen that little un didn't win five shillin' offen they other two yesterday," Manny informed us with great parental pride.

After a final cup of tea we prepared to leave them for the night. But before our departure old Louie drew two large patterned cups from their food-hamper and gave them to Beshlie.

"You take on they two weepin' willies pattened dishes, gal—an' think o' we when you drinks out on 'em," she said, smiling and revealing long black teeth.

I was very fond of old Louie. She reminded me of some of my mother's people in the Midlands whom I dimly remember from my early childhood in the wagons—before I was snatched away from it all for twelve years and more of respectable *gaujo* upbringing.

At our own encampment, with Nelson and Miella and Jesse and Britty, much vicious talk ensued regarding the others—partly caused, I fear, by envy. Miella envied Louie her unimpaired health; and old Nelson envied Manny his greater youth and activity. And through it all ran a thread of bitterness and regret for the passing years, and an inability to accept old age—the bitterness of disillusionment and lack of love. So the days were marked by ill-feeling and long-standing feuds into which I had no desire to be drawn—having already enemies enough.

Five days later the atmosphere was no less tense. It culminated unexpectedly and suddenly, quite late in the morning. Louie was sitting up in the van with old Miella, who was lying in the bed. I was lying by the fireside in the mud talking to old Nelson and Jesse, and Beshlie was up in our wagon making a 'pinna,' when without warning the air was rent with shouts and curses and screams of fury from Miella.

"You God's-cussed h'evil 'oman! You'm a bloody witch—'twas you wot begged this prayer on me an' made me bad! I knows who's me friends an' who ain't—an' I knows 'twas you wot 'witched me! God's cuss you an' all yer children fer wishin' this badness on me. . . . An' me a good-livin' 'oman wot ain't never done no one no harm in all me life. God's cuss you—you'm a bloody witch, an' I hoped the dear God a-years me axin' him to cuss. . . ."

In the middle of this tirade the figure of Louie suddenly appeared clambering from the van. Sobbing with temper and distress, she hurried back along the sloshy muddy track towards her own wagon.

We were all too much taken aback to say anything to her; but as she disappeared Sophie and Lily gathered their wits together and began shouting reprimands to their mother concerning her behaviour. These were of such force that old Miella herself was reduced to loud sobbings of vexation and rage. She lay swearing and moaning in the bed—and the rain began again, falling loudly on the mud around us.

The scene had apparently struck Louie more forcibly than we had realised, for within half an hour their wagons were ready and off they went, regardless of the driving rain and the scarcely navigable mud. And with them, Beshlie and I felt, went something better than that which was left. For Manny and Louie were true travellers, in the best sense of the word, unwilling ever to allow the elements to stand in their way once they had made up their minds to *jal*-on.

When the other two wagons had pulled-out matters

247

seemed even worse than before. The rain which had been falling steadily since our arrival on the Downs showed no sign of abating and, had we but known it, was to continue during our entire stay there.

"I reckons they'm *dinilos* to move off on a day like this," pronounced old Nelson.

I could not agree with him and was saddened by the feeling of contempt that I felt for his remark.

At that particular time Beshlie and I were living on capital which we had managed to save during the summer and autumn. Somehow we did not seem able to direct our activities towards money-providing pursuits just then; and we felt ourselves being sucked downwards into a mood of dull apathy. There was something in the self-centred grumbling woman, the very old man and the lethargic Jesse, combined with the rain and muddy squalor, that drugged us. Even the rook, Amos, was thoroughly melancholy and sat hunched-up in nearby thorn-bushes or in his wicker cage.

The burden of providing the money for food for *all* the family rested almost entirely upon Sophie, who had to go out 'calling' every day, very rarely assisted by Lily —the younger daughter—who was rather lazy and disliked hawking.

Sophie was a good daughter to the old couple and was long-suffering and patient with them. Her own life was one of constant work and drudgery. Not only was she expected to make the flowers and sell them, but she was also expected to do all the cooking and washing as well! She would rise in the morning, cook the breakfast for them all, go out 'calling' (after which she would buy the food with the money she had made), and then she would come back and cook another large meal for the family. Finally she would have to spend the evening making more flowers in the candle-light to sell the next day.

Often in the evenings Beshlie helped her to fashion the flowers from brightly-coloured crepe paper, and she also made many of new design—which, to Sophie's joy, sold far more readily than the usual ones of less pleasant shapes.

When the paper flowers were cut out and wired, for attachment to the greenery, they were each dipped for an instant into a bowl of molten candle-wax which was kept simmering on the stove-top. This waxing added greatly to their effect and also, in bad weather, prevented the rain from destroying them.

Many travellers also make wooden flowers from elder. These require more skill than the paper variety and, when dipped in gay dyes, form large 'flowers' resembling chrysanthemums. They will usually find a ready market, and practised hawkers can often secure as much as half-a-crown apiece for them.

Sophie, unlike most travelling girls, had not married, and it appeared very doubtful if she ever would. She was not plain—indeed she had very good features and lovely thick dark hair. But a slight birthmark scarred one side of her face, and although it would never have been noticed by the casual observer it had been played up by the rest of the family until the girl herself had come to look on it as a major disfigurement. By then, of course, when all the other daughters except Lily had left with their own men, the parents had come to rely on her entirely, so that her chances of leading a life of her own were very remote.

3

Christmas Day dawned wet as ever. Beshlie—who can achieve real enjoyment from anything that she sets out to do, no matter how simple—had transformed the interior of our little wagon into a veritable Arabian Nights fantasy of colour and glitter by means of a few bits of material and a lot of ingenuity.

The others were astounded at her achievement.

"I reckons that gal could make a hundred pounds any day she liked," Miella commented rather optimistically.

Young Jobi was so infected with enthusiasm and artistic feeling on seeing Beshlie's work that he set to work to achieve a similar effect in their own van. Unfortunately, his talents were no match for his intentions, and the result of his drapings of crepe paper in ill-matched colours, nailed haphazardly from one side of the van's interior to the other, was rather pathetic. It was strange that of all the family's members it should have fallen on Jobi to perform such a task.

Jesse had been out the night before and had returned furtively and very late with two vast Rhode Island cockerels which he promptly plucked, casting all the feathers into the fire where they crackled and sizzled and made a most abominable stench. Britty and Sophie each boiled one of the fowls in their enormous black cooking pots, while we prepared one of our bantam pullets, roasting it over the fire on a spit. The rain did stop for a few hours in the middle of the day, for which we were all thankful, and we were able to eat our meals in peace outside by the fire.

Although we all tried to make the best of it we found, inevitably, that the weather, the ailments, the mud and the frustration had caught us in their grip. Even the older ones were becoming tired of the Downs and were restless for a move.

That evening we went and sat up inside old Miella's van. She and old Nelson were in bed, with their heads at opposite ends of the bed because they had quarrelled! She insisted that all the doors and windows should be kept tightly shut, and with the stove burning fiercely and everyone smoking coarse black tobacco the atmosphere soon became thick and hazy—almost unbearable for Beshlie whose distaste for closed-in, overheated wagons (or rooms for that matter) is intense. After a while Jesse and Britty, with two of their children, joined us up in the van and so, with the ten of us there, it became even hotter and more stifling. Travellers are far from being cold in their wagons, even in the worst weather, and usually the reverse is the case, for the wood-burning stoves are in-variably kept going at full blast so that the wagons become grossly overheated. I am convinced that this habit is all too often the cause of chills and colds—especially as the occupants think nothing of going straight out into the night air without putting on any extra clothing of any sort.

After some hours of talk, mostly of bygone Christmases that Nelson and Miella had known, the heat began to make us all feel rather drowsy. The times recalled were so far away in memory that only their pleasanter aspects remained alive. But this talk had aroused a strong desire in the old man to revisit some of the areas in which he had travelled when he was younger; so much so that he suggested we should strike 'up the country' the very next day.

I readily agreed, but I knew in my heart that it was a journey which would never be made—it was too late. And even if we were to make it there would only have been disillusionment in store.

We retired to bed thoroughly downcast and saddened.

"We'll *jal*-on tomorry iffen it's fine," old Nelson called as we left.

Once back in our own wagon, I thought of other Christmases in other places—with other people and when we had been alone.

Beshlie, too, thought of other Christmases—of parties, of presents, glitter, pretty dresses, exotic food, wines, jewellery, books, theatres, cinemas, shopping. . . . So much had gone—for what?

For although Beshlie has come to know and like a great many of the travelling-people, nevertheless it is not in her heredity to feel their compelling, drawing, fascinating attraction that is my own legacy. She could withdraw, scarcely marked, from the life, and return to a house-dwelling existence. I could not. Not that her desire to do so is ever very strong—excepting, perhaps, in moments of the greatest stress.

Alas, the illusion of a land full of quiet by-roads for us to traverse, green lanes for us to rest in and happy welcoming villagers waving to us from their cottages as we pass—or perhaps pressing gifts of food and drink into our hands—lives on only in the minds of romantic lady-authors or artists with a keen perception of what will readily sell in the greetings-card market!

The next day was as wet as ever; and a morning spent

in listening to Miella relating strongly exaggerated accounts of how they had often been washed bodily from their wagons and nearly 'drownded' in floods 'down the country' in her youth did little to raise our spirits.

"Well, we cain't *jal* today in this ole rain, can us?" said old Nelson, hopefully I thought. He added: "Still, we'll go on tomorry."

"Gooaaaannn! You don't know where you'll go, man," Jesse sneered at his father. "I tells you, you don't know the stoppin'-places any more—why you ain't bin up the country, not since I wuz on'y five year old."

"I knows the stoppin'-places all right," asserted Nelson, but his voice lacked conviction and his eyes wavered. I knew he had forgotten them.

Towards evening Jobi caused a flurry by bringing back the news that his sister Tea-Annie—who had but recently married a *gaujo* against her father's wishes—was intending to visit us that evening from a nearby town where she and her husband had a tiny house in a terrace situated in the poorest quarter.

This information particularly enraged old Nelson, who at the time of the marriage had vowed that he would never speak to his new son-in-law or to his daughter again. However, after cajolings and threats by the rest of the family he was at least persuaded to allow his daughter and the young man to come. He announced, however, that he intended to go to bed—which he proceeded to do, despite arguments against it. He also announced firmly that he would not speak to either of the couple. The impending arrival caused Sophie and Lily to engage in vigorous, though rather futile, 'housework' in the van—in an effort to give a good impression to the young man whom none of us had then met. As we had known the family for many years we were also invited up into the van to await their arrival.

When the pair did eventually appear, and were ushered up into the van by Jobi, I was quite shocked.

Tea-Annie, who in dress and appearance had always been a typical Romani, had managed to affect a change that was scarcely imaginable. Gone was her long braided hair; in its place was a hideous "permed" fuzz. Her face was covered with thickly-applied powder and rouge in the manner of a stage prostitute, and her clothes were even worse—consisting of a very severe, matronly blue serge costume and a startlingly pink blouse. What struck me even more forcibly was the colour of her skin, which was now almost white—the result of removal from the ruinous smoke of the eternal *yog* and contact with an unlimited supply of hot and cold water. It was all terribly sad.

The young man was quiet and subdued, his fair hair cut very short and his face shining and rosy. His name was Arnold.

Arnold's reception by his mother-in-law was nothing if not polite.

"Good evenin', sir," she said, in her best wheedling 'calling' voice. "So you'm my dear daughter's new husband, is you, sir?"

"Oo—ah!" said Arnold.

Old Nelson maintained a steady silence.

The others smiled, a child laughed and Arnold blushed. I remembered a sudden and urgent engagement and left the van.

I sat by the still-glowing *yog*, and after a few minutes I

was joined first by Jobi, then by Jesse, then by Britty, and then by Lily and Beshlie. Finally Tea-Annie herself came down to 'have a talk.'

Britty, as a wife and mother, began questioning her upon her appreciation of married life.

There followed one of the frankest and most delightfully unvarnished accounts of early marital experiences that it has ever been my privilege to hear. It was a natural poem, culminating—quite without warning—in Tea-Annie baring herself to the waist and exclaiming:

". . . an' I got nice little titties—look!"

"Cah! You'm brazen!" cried Britty, whilst Jesse and Jobi laughed appreciatively.

The conversation spread rapidly to other aspects of house-dwelling and its intricacies and miracles. Here was a wonderful opportunity for asking all the questions that had often been a source of puzzlement.

"Cah!" Britty exclaimed, in awe for the fifth or sixth time on receipt of yet another snippet of inside information concerning the luxuries of terrace-cottage life.

". . . an' Arnold gid me a big bar o' lovely-smellin' soap an' told me I could use it all iffen I wanted—an' I has a bath every day in a big tub downstairs in the kitchen by the fire. . . ."

Food and its preparation was another subject of great interest.

"Do you git good vittles?" Britty asked.

"Yeah—cah, we has so much as we wants—an' cabbage, an' carrots, an' bread an' meat an'. . . ."

"Do you have the cabbage an' the carrots in different dishes?" interrupted Britty breathlessly, as though this was the fulfilment of a wildest dream.

"Yeah! Wi' lids on to 'em. An' Victry—that's Arnold's sister—comes in every day an' helps me clean up an' that. Sometimes I bides on in the bed till tea-time—'cos he don't mind wot I do. . . .

"I seen me Aunt Mattie down in the town the other day, when they wuz stoppin' in the lane, an' she'd jest come outa the public. Why, she wuz so *motto* she could hardly stand up. An' when she seed me she cussed me blind an' shouted out as I wuz a whore! Me—a *lubni*! An' in front of all the people in the street too. Cah, I wuz 'shamed. . . ."

The talk flowed on and on. And suddenly I realised that until that precise moment I had never before *fully* appreciated the enormous differences that exist between the life of even the humblest house-dweller and that of the rough-and-ready free-for-all way of the traveller.

". . . an' I wouldn't never live like you does again—not fer any money—I likes it in the *kenner*, 'tis warm, an' you can have baths an'. . . ."

I marvelled to myself at the incredible feat performed by Beshlie not only in reorienting herself to fit into the life of the travelling-people, but in still managing to retain her creative impulses and in contriving to work on her drawings of fantasy and imagination in the middle of so much ugliness and squalor.

Arnold came and stood by the fire, his cheap ready-made blue suit and white open-necked shirt contrasting sharply in the fire's glow. He murmured to Tee-Annie and she rose to go, quiet and subdued again for an instant. Then she shouted farewells to her mother and father in her harsh, strident open-air voice, and after a short exchange of ribaldries with us, she left . . . with Arnold.

The following day I rose, thinking hopefully, though

without much conviction, that we should be away as old Nelson had said. But the rain was still falling as heavily as ever, and I knew that it would prevent our moving—despite anything old Nelson had said the night before. And indeed it did: that day and the next—in fact for another whole week, during which the phrase "We'll move tomorry" became almost as much a matter of course as "Good night."

On the eighth morning, however, the rain had almost stopped, and it was finally decided that we should at last attempt the hazardous pull-out.

After breakfast old Nelson and I walked out along the track, in the opposite direction from that which we had come in by, to see how conditions were on the alternative way out across the downland fields. We took some 'soundings' in the mud with sticks. These were not very reassuring, as we found the depths to be in excess of eighteen inches in many places.

"My cob'll pull *us* out—will yours?" I remarked casually, knowing that the implied insult would surely goad the old man to stick to his word that we should move. The past week and more of indecision had played on my nerves. He rose to the bait:

"Wot! My horse'll pull me out from anywheres—even wi' all the wagon wheels locked," he boasted.

We walked slowly back to the wagons and began harnessing-up the horses, all of them somewhat fresh as they had not been worked for so long. It was agreed that we should take our wagon out first, it being the lightest, and the others would follow if we got through safely. I suggested this course as we had no wish to become bogged-in behind one of the heavier wagons if they got stuck.

257

The mare was already hitched-in and Beshlie was standing in the trackway waiting, so we swung out into the gluey mud of the track, the wheels sinking and sucking ominously. For only an instant the mare paused, unwilling to face the heavy pull, then—for she was an honest cob— she heaved forwards again, muscles straining, her feet slithering uncontrollably. I thought we should never make any headway, but we managed to quicken pace and I kept her going as fast as I dared, knowing that if we slowed too much, or stopped, the wheels would sink irremediably into the soft ground. The wagon lurched and swayed precariously in and out of the muddy ruts— at one point I thought that it would topple over on its side so great was the swaying—as we splashed along the track, gradually nearing the hard ground some fifty or sixty yards ahead. Mud from the mare's hooves spattered upwards and outwards, covering my whole person. Beshlie hurried along behind the van with the dogs as best she could—keeping to the edge of the track wherever possible, as the muddy water was up to her boot-tops in many places—picking up a variety of pots and other objects that bounced off their hooks as the wagon swung in and out of the ruts. At last we reached the end of the mud without serious mishap and, having pulled-in to a halt on hard turf at the beginning of the gated right-of-way across the fields to the main road, we waited for the other two vans.

Soon the roof of Jesse's open lot came into view, far back along the track. It was worse for him than it had been for us, because his pony was so tiny and because he had not bothered to mend his wagon-lock—so that it was still held together only by the plug-chain. He had not, he asserted, had time to mend it properly during our stay on the Downs.

"He'll hold together all right, brother," he had remarked to me with great confidence.

After several stops and starts and a great deal of shouting and cursing at the pony he did eventually reach us. The pony's sides were heaving with the effort, and Jesse was plastered even more thickly with mud than I was, and his legs were soaked to well above the knee.

"My bloody God! I never knowed sich a pull-out in all me life. Look at all this foxin' mud all over me!"

He threw himself breathlessly down on the wet turf and rolled himself a cigarette.

Old Nelson fared worse than any of us on *his* journey along the muddy stretch. His great van slewed wildly from side to side on the slippery surface, and he fell head-long into a puddle. Then one of the traces broke so that he was forced to stop in the worst part of the lane to mend it with a piece of wire before he could go on, which meant that his horse had to use all its strength to restart the van—which was saved from sinking irrevocably only by its wide wheels. The forwards movement was achieved in an almost frantic rush, the great horse maintaining a crazy speed until it caught up with us, panting and with rolling eyes. The old man was almost dead from lack of breath, soaked, miserable and swearing luridly.

"I'd never come up yere agin—not fer all the money in the world. It's near enough killed me up yere. God's cuss this place! Pass me the baccy, Nelson, pass me the baccy. Quick!" Miella shouted, still in her bed.

Nevertheless we set off again ten minutes later, across the lovely rolling downland pastures, through a copse and down a rough narrow chalky lane towards the first village and the main road.

As we reached the outskirts of the village the rain began again and we halted for another conference.

"I reckons we'd best make fer Blackwater Common fer a day or two afore goin' up the country. You cain't go far in this ole weather . . ." Nelson began.

"I ain't a-goin' up no country while I've a-got this badness on me—we'll go back be the hospital agin till I'm better," Miella called from the van's interior, her voice harsh and resentful.

And I knew that my thoughts, and Jesse's words, had been right. Nelson was too old to change his 'country' now. They would maintain their small and ever-decreasing circuit till they died. And I could not face another period so soon behind the hospital—with the smell of disinfectant strong in the air, or in the Pits, or on Blackwater Common.

The break had to be made there and then, so I announced that *we* should have to leave them and go on up the country alone in order to earn our living, explaining that we could not afford to stay for so long in one small area where the scope was so limited. So, with no ill-feeling at least on the surface, we parted—making two roads of it. And in spite of the miserable time we had had together during the spell behind the hospital and on the Downs we were all deeply and truly saddened by taking our separate ways.

"Cold Old Weather"

1

IT was towards the end of February, and we were stopping near Dorchester. There had not been any snow in the new year, but the promise of falls to come was ever-present in the yellow skies. The temperature during the past few nights had been the lowest ever recorded.

We had spent the previous night beside the road under some beech trees, without much shelter from the arctic wind. I had pulled an old canvas sheet up round the wagon's wheels and underworks to provide a *lue* for the dogs, and with the wisdom of all travellers' dogs they had burrowed themselves under a pile of sacks which I had thrown down for them beneath the wagon.

In the morning when I woke and opened my eyes I saw the frost crystals glistening on the wagon ceiling a few feet above my face; and the first rays of the weak February sun shone down through the skylight-side on to one wall of the van. I sat up in the bed, still wearing my shirt, two pullovers, and the waistcoat and neckerchief in which I had slept for warmth. I quickly pulled on my thick cord trousers and after a considerable amount of painful struggling managed to lever my feet into my wellington boots which were frozen as hard as iron. Then, putting on my jacket and hat, I jumped stiffly down on to the frozen earth outside. In a matter of minutes I pulled sufficient sticks from the hedge to light the fire and hung the kettle—its contents frozen solid—on the crane. In winter one fills the kettle each evening as otherwise it is difficult to obtain water, most of the cattle troughs and outdoor taps being frozen up.

None but the Romanies, or perhaps the few remaining tramps, can know how great a comfort is afforded by a fire. Once its warming tongues lick upwards into the pile of sticks and one's tingling, numbed fingers are eased in its glow, one experiences great pleasure and satisfaction. It is a creative, æsthetic, pleasure. On countless grey winter mornings, often in company with other travellers, I have sat huddled close to an immense *yog*, my front glowing and steaming with heat and my back running with rain or heaped with snow. The fire is everything to us. With it we can cook, eat, survive and live: without it we should perish.

The two dogs, stiff as I was, came out from under the wagon, and I loosed them from their chains so that they could come and lie nearer the fire. The sun shone brighter, yellow on the white frost; and the little mauve wagon glistened and twinkled like a Christmas cake. There is a beauty about a frosty English winter morning with which no other season can compete.

My rubber boots gradually thawed out in the fire's heat and I could move more easily. I fried two eggs and two large slices of bread. I put one egg on a plate and handed it up into the wagon for Beshlie who had not yet got up, and I ate my own meal from the frying pan. The black kettle boiled grumpily and spat hot water into the fire, so I hastily made the tea. For an instant the sky was overcast and a few scattered flakes of snow drifted down.

"We'd better make for Louse Lane," I called up to Beshlie. "I think it's going to snow today or tomorrow; and we should be able to stop there for a few days."

The rough track known as 'Louse Lane' by the travelling-people was about six miles away, over fairly flat roads on which the presence of ice and frost need not unduly disturb us. It was a little-used trackway running from the edge of a hamlet to a derelict cottage, and it eventually faded out in a wood.

I quickly drank two mugs of hot tea and, pouring a drop of warm water from the kettle into a bowl, I briefly rinsed my face and hands, moving closer against the fire to dry them in its heat.

Soon Beshlie was dressed and down, and we got ready to move. The sheet was rolled up and stowed on the rack at the back of the wagon, along with the kettle-crane. I replaced the teapot and the mugs and plate in the safe at the back and hung the black kettle and frying pan on their hooks under the lock, securing them to prevent their rattling as we moved. I had not let the bantams out from their baskets under the wagon that morning so they did not have to be closed-in. I fetched the mare from where she was grazing along the road verge, some fifty yards or so from the van, and hauling the tethering pin with some difficulty from the frozen ground, led her back to the wagon and harnessed her up. Rubbing our hands and running back to the remains of the fire to warm them and renew their circulation every so often, we at last had everything ready, and hitched-in the mare. The dogs jumped to their accustomed riding-places on the foot-board, Beshlie sat inside the wagon, and we set off at a rapid walk in the icy morning air.

Fortunately we knew the way well through quiet back lanes and byways and so we made good progress.

After about an hour we approached Paradise Common, having covered half our distance. Travelling-people often stopped there, but we did not favour its bleakness and lack of cover at that time of the year. However, as we neared it we soon realised that others, less fastidious than ourselves, had pulled-in there—in the customary position beside a few sparse willows and a small swamp. Two shabby, colourless open lots stood side by side, and a yellow-wheeled, broken-bedded trolley lay at right-angles to them. Spirals of blue smoke drifted upwards from their twin *yogs*, and from the thin black chimney of one wagon. A dozen or more children, tousle-headed and ragged, crouched near the fires. One old man sat huddled and motionless among them. Their encampment was only about twenty feet from the roadside, and so they were clearly visible. A few scraggy-feathered bantams were wandering about rather miserably.

Several of the children shouted greetings as they recognised us, and a woman appeared at one of the wagon doors.

I drew our mare to a halt, jumped down, and walked across to them.

It was Plato and Molendy. The other wagon belonged to Spears and Liza.

Plato, who was sitting by the fire, struggled giddily to his feet—and then sat down again. Prematurely aged, he was slow of speech and movement. His face was lined and yellow, yet pallid despite its yellowness, suggesting something that had been confined in a dark damp place for a long period. His eyes were white-blue and hooded, thick tawny curls emerged from his cap and hung over his collar and neckerchief—and a bright red week-old stubble covered his chin. The complete immobility and the air of negation that Plato presented contrasted strongly with the activity and energy of Molendy, whose fierce black lunatic-bright eyes were never still and whose skinny, be-ringed fingers were for ever seeking the 'baccy tin' to roll herself another of his interminable thin cigarettes. Both Plato and Molendy were, by appearances, in the last stages of poverty and decay. Their ill-assorted garments hung about their persons in fascinating disarray. A louse crawled slowly across Plato's shirt-front. A mangy greyhound dog crept out from beneath a wagon and sniffed at me. One of the white-headed children threw a well-aimed stick which caught it across the ribs. It yelped and disappeared again. After a few minutes' conversation regarding our destination and concerning any of her relatives whom we had seen, Molendy gave me a cup of tea and sent one of the children out to the road with one for Beshlie. The wind swept cold and hard across the heath.

"Go an' git some wood, boy," Molendy told a large youth, her eldest son, who was sitting beside her.

"Where's ever I gonna git some wood?" he retaliated.

"Go an' git some wood, you brazen bastard!" Molendy shouted, much put out. Adding with some ferocity: "See this fist? Well, go an' git some wood afore it meets yer y'ear!"

The tall youth jerked himself ungraciously to his feet and set off jauntily across the common.

"He'm a good *racklo*," remarked Molendy surprisingly. "He'll do anythin' fer anyone, he will."

I inquired after their health.

"Better'n I have bin, my son," Molendy replied sadly.

"How about the dear ole mush?" I asked.

"Someone's a-begged a prayer on him, I reckons," exclaimed Molendy vehemently, " 'cos that man've bin bad now fer these last four year—an' yet afore that he never had a day's illness."

"Ar," agreed Plato, puffing nostalgically at his newspaper-rolled cigarette. "This badness come on me four year ago. Under three doctors, I wuz—an' they couldn't do nothin' fer me." The newspaper began to burn more quickly than the tobacco and his cigarette fell to pieces. He cursed briefly and then went on: "They said 'twas too much hard work when I wuz young wot done it, brother. An' they sez fer me not to do no more."

"O *dordi*!" exclaimed Molendy, and she and the children laughed derisively. "Makin' the wagon shake too much is wot done it, brother! An' ain't I got fourteen children to show fer it?"

We all laughed at Plato, but he continued to crouch disconsolately over the fire, his boots almost in its flames, his elbows on his knees and his long dark mottled hands hanging limply from the wrists. His face was impassive and lifeless.

Whenever we have travelled in his company I have always been overcome by this semblance of death in life, and although I like Plato, I have never felt quite at ease with him. Complete resignation can, in certain circumstances, be powerfully disturbing.

There was trouble in the family that day, as news had reached them that one of their relatives, known as 'Blackitts Whippy,' had ' 'dulterated' with another traveller's wife, a mother of nine children, and had removed her to his own wagon. Happily, a few days afterward, I found this story to be quite untrue, and I immediately acquainted the family with the good news.

We spent about an hour with Plato and Molendy—Spears and Liza being out 'calling'—before proceeding on our way. Before we left Beshlie managed to negotiate a *chop* of one of our little bantam pullets—a rather colourless one—for a fine young showy cock bird which was handed to her by one of the younger boys with the commendation: "His dee-little balls ain't a-comed through yit—but he'll be all right when they does!"

2

As we approached the entrance to Louse Lane snow began falling quite heavily, and we hurried forwards over the last few hundred yards. We decided to draw-in just in front of the old ruined cottage which was windowless, its thatched roof sagging inwards. A large clump of gorse-bushes afforded us some cover from the elements and I backed the mare and wagon into the middle of them. Plenty of rough grazing was near at hand, bordering the lane and in front of the cottage, so I quickly unharnessed the mare, my fingers numbed with cold, and tethered her close by, whereupon she began cropping hungrily. The ground was frozen too hard to drive in the steel pin for the chain, so I tied it round a thick gorse stem. We released all the bantams—sixteen of them—from their baskets under the wagon, and they fluttered down, fluffing out their feathers at the sight of the light layer of snow. I tied the dogs under the wagon and hurriedly collected some 'fuzz-tops' from the gorse—dead and dry as tinder—and lit the fire, quickly piling on a few rotted fence-posts and thick gorse stumps. With Beshlie's help I lifted the large food-basket from the rack, and within about fifteen minutes of our arrival I was frying some fat ends of bacon and slices of bread and eggs. Two of my fingers had cracked open because of exposure first to cold and then, too suddenly, to intense heat. They hurt considerably and I rubbed a little snow into the wounds to cleanse them. We ate hungrily and swiftly—a habit developed early in life by most travellers, which leaves them in later life a legacy of a ruined digestive system and an 'acidy ole stomach.' After we had eaten I decided to go and fetch some water. The nearest farm was about three-quarters of a mile away and its owners would always give our people water.

I saw the farmer's wife in the yard and stopped to talk to her. She told me that three brothers of the Eyelett family were stopping on the Wide Common half a mile away, having apparently obtained permission to stay for five weeks owing to the fact that one of the women was expecting a child at any time. They had been wise enough to make the application for her own family and for two brothers-in-law as well! It was not, however, a very good *'atchin'tan*, for the common was exceedingly damp and boggy, treacherous for man and horse alike. We ourselves had once stayed there during a wet spell of weather and the wagon had sunk in to the axles, and it had needed two horses and a tractor to move it out again.

I returned to our wagon with the water, and then walked towards the common to visit the Eyeletts. I went along the narrow cottage-bordered road, conscious of the sense of unease which is every traveller's almost constant companion—caused in part by the feeling of not belonging anywhere and of hostility on the part of the natives, and in part to a sense of guilt at the many small offences one has committed in order to stay alive—perhaps only taking a few sticks from a copse to make pegs or baskets, or trespassing in order to find wood to burn. The shiftiness, suspicion and wariness of many Romanies is the reflection of the primitive existence they lead.

Presently, some three hundred yards before turning the corner leading to the common, I became aware of the Eyeletts' presence. Shouts rent the air, children screamed, women sang, dogs barked, and wood cracked. The clink-clink, recognisable to me, of a pin being hammered in to the hard ground to secure a plug-chain carried clearly through the icy air; and the curious, brief, hoarse shouts of conversation occurred at intervals. Few travellers allow distance of speaker from listener to discourage conversation.

I rounded the corner and the wagons and *lues* became immediately visible. There were only three horses in sight: the eldest brother's black pony, Caley's large bay mare, and Job's broken-winded roundsman's cob. The wagons were across the common under some large oak trees. A great canvas *lue* had been erected by the smallest wagon and looked like a wigwam with smoke drifting from a hole in its top. Another *lue*, less expertly erected, but from which smoke was also issuing, leant unsteadily by the centre wagon. The three wagons were all open lots, Lijah's and Caley's were both brightly painted, respectively red and yellow, and blue and yellow, and their canvas tops were new and green. Job's whole wagon was battered and colourless, its sheet holed and patched and the wheels unsound and rotting.

The Eyeletts were all blonde-haired and fair-complexioned, with only their facial construction hinting at their Romani blood. They were, however, traditional in the sizes of their families, there being nineteen children between them—despite the fact that one brother was under thirty. The children of the three brothers had quite different complexions, some inheriting the fairness of their fathers' families, and others as 'black as 'Talians' from their mothers' families. The Eyeletts were renowned for their roughness and haphazard living conditions. Hard drinking was to some extent their failing. Lijah, when in his cups, had on several occasions been so violent that he had served more than one prison sentence for inflicting bodily harm on other travellers who had caused him displeasure.

Job, the youngest, would often boast that he could 'pass for a *gaujo*' and could thus obtain employment from farmers where others could not; he also insisted that he would be served in public-houses where travellers were normally barred. These boasts always struck me as being singularly depressing. Why, in this day and age, should such boasts be *needed*?

Caley was the most likeable of the three. His wife, Rose, a member of a Somerset travelling family, was also a happy, generous little woman with curious malformed features—she looked rather as though someone had once dealt her a severe blow on the head, causing her features to be squashed downwards. They had eleven children, who swarmed about the ground like puppies, their tiny wizened features stained by smoke and dirt; and most of them running barefoot on the frozen ground.

Lijah, the eldest of the brothers, was the strongest in character. Very tall and heavily built for a Romani, his face was long and lantern-jawed, his mouth was a thin line, and his hard blue eyes were set high and close together, leaving but little brow on which to lodge his cap brim. He was the eternal bruiser, with vast red fists always quick to be raised in anger or to stress a point. His voice was guttural, grating, loud, harsh and undrowned in any gathering. Georgina, his woman, was thin and small, a cynical smile often playing on her lips. She seemed fond of Lijah despite his ways.

Job, with thin oiled blonde hair brushed hard against his scalp and a collar and tie at his throat, was always ostensibly neat—yet in reality he was one of the most raggle-taggle and dirtiest of travellers. His turnout was invariably little more than a rag-bag on wheels, devoid of colour or interest. His wife was a sister of Georgina, Milly by name, and she was rather a simple woman, yet amiable withal. Job knocked her about quite frequently, and had, it was said, flung her from her bed two days after the birth of their last child.

I approached the wagons and greeted the families, all of whom had just begun their meal.

They shouted greetings and ribaldries in return.

"I'll come back when you've finished eating," I said.

"Wot, mush?" exclaimed Caley. "Ain't you goin' to sit down an' have a bite o' bread an' meat 'long wi' us? Gie him some, Rose, there's more'n we can eat."

I sat down on a tin beside Caley's fire, accepting a lump of white bread with fingerprints across it on which a lamb chop was lying, fried brown and crisp. I happily devoured the lot. I am one of those people who are able to consume any kind of food at any hour, even if I have just finished a meal.

"Where you *'atchin'*—up agin the ole *kenner*?" Lijah rasped.

I said, "Yes," and inquired generally about everyone's health.

"Better'n we have bin—we've all bin bad," pronounced Georgina mournfully, "wi' that ole 'fluenzie. We wuz *trashed* we wuz goin' to lose the baby wi' it— but he'm all right now."

And she dangled the baby, naked and minute, above the flames for my inspection before replacing it to her bosom where it clung happily feeding.

"Ain't n'arn on us bin well enough to earn a crust o' bread," said Rose, smiling nonetheless. "Why, I reckons we've a-spent the price o' two ponies since we bin yere."

Most of Caley's and Rose's ten children—the eleventh being only a few weeks old—crouched or lay round the *yog*, all munching at the lumps of bread and meat in their fingers—there being insufficient plates to go round. Rose opened a jar of yellow pickle and handed it to them. When it was returned to her it was quite empty.

"O *dordi*!" she cried. "O my Caley, see wot they *chavies* has ett!"

"Cold ole weather, ain't it?" Caley remarked to me.

I agreed that it was, and asked how he had been faring in the scrap-iron market. A large mound of mixed iron lay near his wagon, and a trolley was similarly loaded.

"The mush ain't bin over fer that bit there yet," he replied, pointing to his collection, "an' I bin too bad to do anythin' about it meself fer a while."

I am a 'brass and silver' man myself, and never collect any others forms of metal nowadays. There are so many engaged in the pursuit of 'scrap' that I am constantly amazed that enough remains to be acquired by the horse-and-trolley Romanies after the lorry-men have been round. Yet, as with sacks and rags, the demand still appears to exceed the supply. My own field of brass and silver, either for melting down or for the 'an-tick' market, is even more thoroughly scavenged.

Rose handed me a cup and I sipped it gratefully, changing my grip every few seconds on the burning sides of the handleless vessel.

Lijah's eldest daughter, a girl of about fifteen, began playing a gramophone from the wagon, and the blaring imitation-cowboy tune on the record rang out hollowly in the winter air. Some village women, pushing perambulators along the road past the common, stopped and stared for a moment.

I lay, propped on one elbow, inhaling tobacco and wood smoke simultaneously, thankful that I at least realised the futility of the term 'standard of life,' thankful that I had never finally succumbed to my childhood years spent in the narrow confines of middle-class respectability, and thankful that I had managed to slough off the effect of those years.

"You bloody foxin' little bastard!" shouted Caley's son Benny, aged three, to one of his brothers. We all laughed.

"Gooo-oooon! Goo an' suck the titty-bottle!" retaliated the other, unabashed.

"Can I borrow an old *treader*?" I requested. "I want to get some baccy."

"Certainly you can, mush," replied Caley at once. "Pick

273

up whichever one you wants—but 'tis a poxy little *hoben-ker*, mind."

"Ar, 'tain't n'arn good fer *hoben*—why, they don't even sell *moro* nar *mass*!" Rose confirmed disgustedly.

I picked up an old-fashioned tall-framed bicycle from near the fire where it had been thrown down, and set off somewhat shakily to the road and in the direction of the village stores.

"Keep that ole *treader* till you goes away. I 'spects we'll come over an' see you on Sunday an' have a talk," shouted Caley as I rode off. The gramophone played on, its repetitive notes, pierced occasionally by the scream of a child or shouts from the men, following me far up the road.

I bicycled slowly, for the condition of the machine made rapid progress unwise, and eventually reached the little shop and made my purchases under the eyes of a proprietor who obviously regarded me with some distaste.

The snow had not fallen very heavily and the temperature remained far below freezing-point. My face was stiff with the cold and my fingers were numbed by the time I returned to our wagon in its little clearing in the gorse. In mid-winter, though, when days are short, every minute of daylight seems welcome and in many ways I think this season preferable to the leafy clutch of summer.

Beshlie and I had some tea and talked of the Eyeletts and their wagons and their horses. Gradually it grew dark and I filled our tiny oil lamp with paraffin—it was our only luxury, recently acquired, and it gave out a certain amount of heat which was welcome since we had no stove in the van. Previously, like most other travellers, we had burnt only candles.

The moon rose presently, full and bright, and everything seemed brittle and clear.

3

On Sunday afternoon, soon after we had finished lunch, Lijah arrived. He had ridden over on a bicycle with one of Caley's sons to "have a talk." They stopped by the wagon and, dropping their bicycles unhesitatingly to the ground, walked over to the fire where we were sitting. I tossed a sawn-down milking stool over to Lijah.

"Sit down on that," I advised.

"Cah!" he ejaculated, seating himself almost within the flames. "Ain't this some cold ole weather, brother? 'Tis gonna git colder too, so the wireless sez. I reckons me balls is near froze off!"

"Not much good to you anyway, are they?" I inquired with mock solemnity.

"Don't you believe it, mush," he laughed.

I made some tea and we all sat noisily sipping it.

"Ain't that *grasni* fat?" he motioned towards our mare, whose weight had diminished little since the summer for she was an exceptionally 'good doer.'

"My dead mother, I ain't never seed sich a fat horse!" he marvelled.

"What's the new *gavmush* like here?" I inquired, for I had heard that a new one had recently been installed.

"He ain't too bad, brother. Better'n that long-legged bastard wot's just gone. He wuz goin' to have me *lelled*, man, 'cos I knocked him down!" Lijah's eyes narrowed at the recollection and he continued: "Well, see, I comes back from the public—around Christmas it wuz—an' he wuz there when I gits back. He sez we had to shift. So I sez: 'I ain't shiftin' today, policeman, not fer you nor twenty like you.' 'I'll shift you,' he sez, an' he kicks the fire up straight over me *juvel* an' the baby. Burnt the baby, it did. I cussed him sideways an' picks up a bit o' fire an' hits un straight over the face wi' it. Down he goes—me brothers wuz there an' they'll tell you the same. 'You've a-kilt the bastard,' shouts Caley. But h'up he gits an' off he goes. 'I'll git you twelve months fer this,' he shouts. 'Wot,' I shouts, 'you only tripped an' fell—an' I've got all these yere as'll swear the same.' So we harnessed h'up the horses an' *jals*—an' when we comed this way agin we found he'd bin moved hisself."

Temporarily exhausted after his energetic recounting of this episode which had been enlivened by much fist shaking, Lijah loosened his blue and white spotted neckerchief and swigged thirstily at his mug of tea. Then he blew his nose vigorously on his coat sleeve, spat thoughtfully into the fire, and asked whether we had seen his sister and her man recently.

"They're over in Bun's Lane—or at least they were there two days ago," I informed him, having met Sachie, the man, the day before.

Lijah nodded happily, for all travellers like to keep abreast of their relatives' movements.

The greyhound lay against the fire, singeing her paws or tail every few minutes.

Each time that occurred Lijah removed his cap and drove her off.

"That bitch'll git 'stemper fer sure iffen she bides agin the fire like that," he stated.

I argued that she had always lain like that without harm. Lijah, however, remained unconvinced.

"I've just bought another horse," he suddenly announced.

" 'Tis a big chestnut cob," he answered in reply to our queries. "I got him offen a farm. Only eight year old —I knows the cob well, I do. Have you got an ole collar you'd like to sell?"

"We haven't," I replied truthfully. "We've only got two and we need them both. But I can tell you who's got one or two that I think he'd sell you cheap." And I gave him the address of a farm, quite near, where I had noticed a few large collars hanging in a barn.

Lijah thanked me, and I placed another thick length of wood on the fire.

"Do you ever see anything of Ernie Lamb—you know, the dealer?" I asked him.

"Him wot thinks hisself so fly? Why, I ain't seed un fer a twelve-month or more. I sucked him in once, brother."

Lijah chuckled throatily at the memory, rolled a cigarette, and continued:

"I had a cob, see, mush, wot's eyes wuz goin' blind— only seven year old too. An' after a bit she got so bad that she wouldn't have the blind halter on her once she wuz put in the shafts—why, soon as you put her in the shafts she'd lie down an' kick. Broke up six pairs o' shafts an' two trolleys, she did.

"The only way as you could drive her wuz wi'out the blind halter—an' you'd like as not be *lelled* fer that. So quiet wi'out it that a baby could drive her, she wuz. Yet the minute 'twas on her head then over she'd fall an' kick everything to bits. Well, I sees that ole mush Lamb in the

277

public on a Saturday night, 'cos we wuz pulled-in near his place, an' I sez to un I sez: 'I've a-got a lovely black cob wot I'm sellin' an' I wants somethin' a bit smaller fer drivin' about. Have you got any ponies about?' I axes un. 'Yes,' he sez, 'I've a-got a lovely two-year-old pony—a pretty pony, we can have a deal.' 'All right,' I sez, 'I'll bring the cob over to your place tomorry after I've had me breakfast.' So on the Sunday I walks over wi' her— pretends I ain't a-got no trolley to drive, see—wi' the cob an' one o' me brother's young boys.

"Well, we goes in an' he shows me the pony an' I liked the looks on it, though I don't say, mind. An' he likes the cob. 'Well,' he sez, 'let's try out the cob fust.'

" 'Hold hard,' I sez. 'This is the quietest cob in the world an' if you'm man enough to have a bet wi' me I'll show you somethin' wot you've never see afore.' 'Wot's that?' he sez.

" 'I'll bet you fifty pun,' I sez, 'that she'll pull any farm h'implement—say that ole chain harrow wi' some ole tins an' iron tied on to it fer noise, h'up an' down your yard *wi'out even a blind halter on her—an' on'y that little boy a-leadin' her!* An' she'll go quiet an' steady, mind.'

" 'Wot?' he sez. 'There ain't the horse on this earth as'd do that—I'll take yer bet.' 'All right,' I sez. 'An' I've got the money yere.' An' I counts it out into me hat. So he goes into the house an' fetches some *vongar*, an' then he counts out fifty pun notes into his hat, do you see?

"So we hitches the traces on the harrow, an' we ties some ole bits o' iron and tin on to it, then off I takes the blind halter, and the boy leads her off wi' a bit o' string round her neck. Quiet as a lamb she walks—wi' the ole iron an' tin makin' so much noise as you'd have thought any horse in this world would've bolted.

" 'Well, you've a-won me money,' he sez. 'Take the pony on—an' yere's me money.'

" 'Thank you,' I sez, an' off we goes.

"So we gits back to where we wuz *'atched*—agin Lion's Lodge—an' I sez: 'We'd best be movin'.' So we hitched in the horses an' off we went—makin' two roads of it, wi' some on us goin' one way and the others goin' different ways. An' we agrees where to meet—an' not to stop afore we gits there, even though 'twas fifteen miles away.

"Well, I wuz in a public about a month after when a man tells me that ole Lamb wuz a-cussin' me up an' down. Seems like he'd a-put the cob into a bran-new cart the next day—an' over she'd rolled an' kicked it all to pieces, *an'* broke up a good set of harness as well. I laughed an' laughed, 'cos by that time I'd a-sold the pony fer near enough forty pun.

"Then one day, 'bout six months later, I wuz in Salisbury market when I sees ole Lamb a-comin'.

" 'Mornin',' he sez. 'Mornin',' I sez.

" 'Wot's all this I hears 'bout you a-cussin' me h'up an' down?' I sez." And Lijah's enormous fist rose menacingly before his face in memory of the injustice.

" 'Well, wot about that horse?' he sez.

" 'Wot?' I sez. 'Yes,' he sez. 'Wot?' I sez. 'Ain't you man enough to have a deal wi'out a-cryin' over it after you'm bitten?'

" 'Well,' he sez, 'you'm the cleverest man wot I've a-met. Now come on into the public,' he sez, 'an' you can have so much beer as you can drink.' An' we bid there till closin' time."

The cold air seemed very silent, as the reverberating tones of the story-teller ceased to fill it with his grating utterances.

Then, suddenly, with a roaring and scraping of ancient gears, a lorry—nameless and battered—drew up beside us and ejected about seven small children, the driver, and old Nelson, Jobi's wife's father, who had come over from their own places to see the Eyeletts. As rapidly as we could we made more tea and handed round all the cups we had—not enough by half to meet the influx of visitors. I did not very much like the driver, Shady—blue-suited, capped, in green suede shoes and satin necktie. However, we liked old Nelson, and energetic conversation ensued for an hour or so until the hour of their departure arrived, for their homeward journey was about twenty miles and it was further still for Shady, who had to discharge old Nelson first.

"I'll see you at the bloc!" I shouted to old Nelson as they drove away.

The day of the 'bloc' dawned frosty and bright. Beshlie did not wish to go, so I decided to drive there alone, a distance of some five miles. I borrowed an old heavy four-wheeled market cart from Caley, on the understanding that he and some of his family could ride in with me—their own horse being too large and heavy to trot.

The mare was cold and anxious to be away as we hitched her into the heavy shafts of the old cart. Caley and his wife and their baby and two or three of the elder children climbed up and sat on the floor in the back whilst I clambered up on to the narrow, unsteady driving seat. At two 'clicks' from me the mare jumped forward, trotting rapidly over the frozen ground and out on to the road.

After we had travelled a mile or so we overtook Lijah, 'bloc'-clothed in a blue suit, which was too small, wrongly-buttoned and creased. He was leading a small black pony by a halter. The pony was unbroken and wild-eyed, but Lijah's youngest daughter clung fearlessly to its back. His wife and eldest daughter, each arrayed in a mass of clashing checks, plaids, stripes and spots all worn together with complete abandon, their sparse hair watered-down and 'crimped,' walked steadily along some distance behind.

"Move on there, you foxin' *diddikais*! Move on there!" I shouted in mock severity. They laughed and I pulled the mare to a halt.

"Jump in—there's plenty of room," I advised them.

And with much smiling they climbed upon the cart with Caley and Rose, leaving Lijah and the baby to walk on with their pony.

" 'Tis better'n walkin', ain't it?" they commented.

"I'll find her a new mush 'fore you get to the bloc," I called back to Lijah as we drove past him.

"An' find me a new *juvel* as well," laughed Lijah.

On we trotted, up and down the slight inclines, until the little mare was bathed in sweat. Cars sped past us, their occupants staring out at us, dogs ran barking from the cottages, a few school-children shouted the eternal 'Gippos!' but we were impervious to everything and after what seemed a very short time we were clattering through the little market town's square and approaching the sale-ground and the public-house where all the travelling-people gathered—sometimes in large numbers, sometimes small, depending on their geographical position at the time.

'The Dragon', as the public-house was called, possessed a very large forecourt along one side of which ran a strong iron fence which was ideal for tethering our horses while we were in the tavern or watching the auctioning of the horses.

On the day of the sale the bar of 'The Dragon' would be filled to capacity—but only with travelling-people or those of travellers' ancestry. In the long room none but our people would venture, lest they should become contaminated.

Several trolleys and two traps were already standing outside when we arrived, and also three lorries—one loaded high with logs, its battered sides bulging warningly under the weight.

"Ain't this a crowd fer a winter bloc?" Caley remarked as we all dismounted from the cart. I agreed, for there did indeed seem to be a vast number of travellers present.

In spite of the cold about seven women and children were sitting on the ground leaning against the wall beside the bar's entrance. Some of the women were drinking, and several of the smaller children were sucking at 'titty-bottles,' which for the most part were filled with cold tea, though one or two of the more advanced mothers were experimenting with the introduction of a little Guinness!

As I was tethering the mare to the fence an aged woman rose and detached herself from the little group on the ground and hobbled slowly over towards me. A man's hat, over which a scarf had been tied to meet under her chin, adorned her head; and a black 'pinna' was draped about her person, hanging almost to the ground. Her gnarled, lined, brown face broke into a smile of greeting and I recognised her as dear old Tilly. A hand, each finger of which was circled by a gold or silver ring, clutched at a little grey clay pipe, and her blind eye rolled white and uncontrolled in its socket, while the other, small and black, gleamed straight at me.

"O my pretty old Tilly," I exclaimed. "I'm glad to see you here—I'd heard that you were in hospital with pneumonia."

"So I wuz, but I'm a bit better now—thank the blessed Jesus an' the God A'mighty," Tilly replied piously. "Why, I wuz put into that ole hospital afore I knowed wot wuz a-happenin' to me; an' I wuz led there in the bed for tend days an' not one o' they doctors could do anythin' fer me complainiment. God's cuss they doctors!"

"Have a drop of gin with me," I urged her.

"Ar, no, my brother, I mustn't have no more'n a small stout. Elseways I shall be bad in me head wi' me nerves. The man in the hospital sez to me as I've got to gie up smokin' an' drinkin' altogether. So I tells un as I'd sooner go wi'out me vittles than me baccy—an' still has a h'ounce a day fer me *swigler*."

The lid dropped over her sightless eye, and her thin figure swayed slightly in the breeze.

"Is little Manny here?" I asked.

"Ar, he'm in the public a-fillin' hisself h'up wi' the beer," replied Tilly mournfully.

I entered the smoke-filled bar and pushed my way through the Romanies and the 'half and half' dealers.

I returned the sporadic greetings cast in my direction

and made my way over to where Caley was standing, a
filled glass already in his hand for me.

"*Kushti bok*," I toasted him, and the black ale in the pot
diminished steadily as I drank. Then I bought a small stout
for Tilly and took it outside to her.

Old Benny Leavey and his second wife were seated in a
corner watching all that was going on. We exchanged
greetings and he bought me a drink before my glass was
even empty. His immaculate appearance contrasted
strongly with most of the others present. Clothed in
black from head to foot, he wore a velvet collar to his
tailor-made overcoat, a black and white patterned neckerchief, and a heavy silver chain across his waistcoat front.
In spite of his eighty-two years he possessed a head of un-
greyed black hair, visible when he removed his black
wide-brimmed hat, and fine curling side-whiskers down
each side of his face. Only his eyes, their brightness seeming filmy, gave any indication of his great age.

Despite appearances, however, his health was somewhat
undermined.

"I suffers terrible pains—'tis me water-troubles," he
sadly explained to me. His second wife nodded in
corroboration.

He continued: "They pains is offen so bad that I wishes
I could jest lay down an' die. 'Tain't wuth livin' wi' pains
like that, young man. Once you've a-got water-troubles
you ain't never rid on 'em."

"He bides there all day sometimes wi'out sayin' a
word," said his second wife, smiling faintly from beneath
her witch's hat.

" 'Twas jest after me fust wife—the one wot gie me
all they sons—wuz dead an' buried that me troubles

started," the old man continued, throwing a look of some contempt upon the companion of his latter years. "An' they've jest got wusser an' wusser."

I always felt rather sorry for the second Mrs. Leavey for she was constantly being compared unfavourably with her predecessor. However, she seemed to bear the burden with surprising equanimity, nodding amiably every few minutes as acquaintances caught her eye.

Lijah had arrived by this time, and his strident scraping tones could soon be heard in opposition to an old man with a voice of even greater volume and harshness.

As the clock crept forwards, the noise and clamour increased. A little dark man produced a harmonica and began to play a variety of quick-stepping jigs and 'step-dances' with extraordinary skill and tunefulness. Soon everybody's feet were tapping and one person after another took up the dancing: women, girls, men, boys, and even a child. Of the women Molendy was perhaps the most skilful, her glittering eyes flashing, her feet, encased in stout button-boots, performing a great variety of steps with astonishing noise and speed. And as she stopped amidst shouts and clapping, to flop exhausted back to her seat by the wall, so old Jobi James took up the dance, his enormous bulk swaying and gyrating—his arms hanging limp and motionless by his side like a Mexican folk-dancer as his feet carried him swiftly and gracefully in the lilting jig. Quite suddenly he stopped and was followed by a girl, then a boy, then another woman— and then the floor was taken by the man who was acknowledged as the finest step-dancer in the south: a little Irish-fairy-story-like traveller named Noah. His great black luminous eyes shone out from under his flop-hat; a gay yellow silk handkerchief was at his throat, and he wore narrow cord trousers and vast iron-studded boots. His dancing was traditional, assured, graceful, noisy, varied and perfectly in time to the music. We all recognised his superiority in the dance as his feet spun and whirled in their great boots with a dazzling variation of steps. Dust rose in clouds from the old unpainted floor-boards, which by this time were engrained with beer, cigarette-ends and spittle. The harmonica-player's brow was covered in perspiration as his pace continued. Then it was finished. Noah threw his hat to the floor in a dramatic gesture of triumph and exuberance, and the noise of applause blew up louder and louder like a storm. The pots were refilled and the children driven outside again as the serious business of drinking began anew. Meanwhile a running report on the actual horse-auction was being kept up by various younger travellers who ran between the bar and the auction rooms every few minutes.

As the clock hands drew onwards to within half an hour of closing-time the singers began their orgy of sound. First came a young man, in a snap-brimmed hat and American tie. His song was a modern popular one, of which he gave a traveller's rendering, drawing out each bar, his voice breaking on almost every note. He sang as loudly as possible, and all present listened silently and reverently. When he had finished they picked up the threads of their shattered conversations and continued as though nothing had interrupted them. After a few minutes' talking, however, another traveller, somewhat older and rougher, cap over one ear, and a spotted handkerchief at his throat, began an old Romani song, his voice thick and heavy, though not low-pitched:

"O bring me back my golt,
No golt never ties me.
Bring me back the golt
'n the little diamint ring.

And you knows I loved you once,
And you knows I dares not break my vow,
O no my chilt—you've got no poor mother now.

For I look-ed through the door . . .
Not a sound could I hear,
On'y a tiny babby on his daddy's knee."

The audience gazed with sentimental awe upon the singer, their glasses respectfully lowered, their voices silent.

"You knows I loved you once,
But you knows I dares not break my vow,
O no my chilt—you've got no poor mother now.

Happy days ago since I left my happy home,
And the playmates in the woods we've got to find. . . ."

He ran through the entire song again, hanging on to each phrase lovingly, until eventually he was quite exhausted and relapsed back on to a seat amidst much approbation.

Two lesser singers then started on two different ballads simultaneously, and the listeners, disgusted that neither's voice could successfully oust the other's, resumed their conversations, leaving the two competitors to peter out in their own time.

In its colour and drunken frivolity it was a truly

Hogarthian scene. The thin lean faces of the travellers contrasted strongly with the bloated house-dwelling dealers of part-Romani blood—yet each recognised in the other a certain blood-kinship which bound them instinctively to seek each other's company. One of the dealers, a huge purple-faced, pot-bellied man, wearing a neckerchief and pumped-up black Homburg, became so enthusiastic over the merits of a pony he was describing for sale that the pint mug he was holding in his fist smashed to pieces as he hammered it down on the bar to stress a point. He drew a greyish handkerchief from his pocket and amidst much laughter mopped the black beer from his countenance.

A very small Romani began singing in a corner, his voice high and shaky. But he was immediately ushered sharply from the premises by his wife—a large bulky woman with flashy, cheap earrings, broad features, and a peaked cap on which was pinned a gilt brooch with the legend *Mother* on it.

Little Manny, Tilly's little eldest son, had begun to feel the effects of the liquor he had been consuming. Despite his forty-one years he was but four-feet-six in height, stunted but broad. He was wearing a pair of riding breeches which served him well as trousers, and a large cap which flopped low over his eyes. When slightly intoxicated he might, when so inclined, perform several curious acrobatic feats. One of these, which he proceeded to demonstrate, was to request someone to throw a coin on to the bar floor—and he would then bend over backwards and pick it up in his mouth! This seemingly impossible accomplishment he would repeat indefinitely, providing he was allowed to pocket the coins. Another of his tricks was to 'disjoint' himself with a series of loud cracking sounds. He would normally disjoint only his legs and one hand and arm—those limbs would then become as limp as pieces of rope, pliable in any direction. On occasions, however, ill-natured individuals had been known to quickly disjoint his remaining limb, thus rendering him entirely immobile, and leaving him writhing helplessly on the ground out of both joint and temper.

I remember how on one occasion, when we were stopping in company with Tilly and some others, little Manny—much the worse for drink, one winter's evening —suffered the indignity of being dragged bodily back to the encampment by one leg, a distance of some two miles across fields, and deposited, like a sack, beneath his mother's wagon—where he was discovered cursing and 'out-jointed' the next morning. But his prestige suffered no harm, for, like artists and idiots, travellers are fascinated by the bizarre.

Once, many years before, and on several subsequent occasions, circus proprietors had offered Tilly large sums of money for her eldest son.

". . . would a-gid me five hundred pun for un," she told us, adding: "But I wouldn't sell un. No, I wouldn't tek a *thousand* pun for un."

But little Manny himself privately confided in me that he was much disappointed that he had been deprived of the glamour of the sawdust ring.

I have also met other travellers who have been offered large sums for their children—both malformed and otherwise—on the assumption that 'gypsies' will sell anything, even their own flesh and blood. That is quite incorrect, and any attempt at such trafficking is always indignantly refused.

I might add that the superstition that Romanies are apt to kidnap the children of *gaujes* is also completely unfounded. Travellers always have quite enough children of their own without wishing to be burdened by a probably delicate *gaujo* child. I have never encountered a *genuine* case where a Romani has been proved to have kidnapped a child—and I should be interested to hear if such a case has ever been proven. I feel it is a superstition born of ignorance, distrust, and fear. It is depressing to see how it still persists.

Meanwhile a young man with black hair and gaunt features had begun playing a 'cordy box' and several couples began 'swing dancing,' changing partners alternately to the music. The accordion player sat in a corner. His face was impassive and expressionless and his eyes, their burning stare sweeping over the dancers and the drinkers, never settled on his instrument for a second. The music went on without a break.

I began to feel the effects of the immense quantities of black beer I had imbibed and left the crowded bar to walk across to the 'tea-house' opposite. This minute café was also filled with travellers, mostly women and children, who were standing and sitting drinking tea from the saucers—or munching cheap cakes and buns.

I bought a cup of tea and sat down on the floor beside Bob'n Ally, old Henry and Polly.

". . . how many you got now?" old Henry was asking.

" 'leven—youngest jest three," Polly replied, her small gleaming black eyes separated by an enormous pitted nose, which hung ominously over a runaway chin.

"That's how it oughta be at your age—one out an' one in!" grinned old Henry philosophically.

Bob'n Ally puffed more energetically at his thin cigarette. Polly's rugged leathery cheeks flushed slightly, her eyes crossing for an instant.

"Wot's it like down at the sale?" old Henry asked.

"I ain't a-bin down there yet, to tell the truth," Bob'n Ally admitted, "but they sez there ain't much wuth lookin' at fer we sorta people."

"These ole blocs ain't wot they wuz," mused old Henry nostalgically. "I can mind the times," he went on, "when I've a-drove four an' five *grais* down yere an' sold 'em fer a hundred pun apiece. An' they wuz *good* horses —an' I sold 'em to the gentries an' the likes o' they. An' I wouldn't gie a hundred shillin's fer most o' them wot's down there today."

"I've a-got a lovely pony as I'd sell you cheap, Uncle Henry," began Bob'n Ally as I got up to go back to the bar.

But I was too late to obtain any further beer, for 'Time' had been called, and as I crossed the road a multi-coloured rabble was emerging from the bar, slowly, unsteadily, laughing, arguing, shouting, singing and silent. A constable stood nearby, his watchful eye upon us. His presence seemed to rouse all the pugnacious instincts of old Henry's youngest son, Jonah, who began shouting abuse at the policeman in no uncertain manner, his voice gradually mounting in a frenzy of wrath. He was hastily grasped by his father and two brothers as he was flinging off his coat in readiness for a fight.

"Let me git at that *gavver*!" he screamed. "I'm a-gonna kill that foxin' *gavmush*, so help me God. Come on, policeman, put up yer fists. . . ."

"Here, here, here—that's enough of that talk," interrupted the policeman sternly, "or I'll have you put in a place where you'll cool off."

Several other travellers, with uncommendable disloyalty, loudly urged the constable to make an immediate arrest.

"Goo on, policeman," they advised. "Take him on down wi' you to the police station."

Old Henry and his other sons were horrified.

"Wot?" they cried. "O, don't take him on, policeman. Please, sir. . . ."

"God's cuss every foxin' policeman in this country. Let me get at un—I'll kill un fer sure. The foxin' bloody bastard. I'll kill. . . ."

"O, please, sir, there ain't no harm in him, policeman. He'll be all right, sir . . ." interrupted old Henry's eldest son hurriedly.

"I'll kill the bloody foxin' bas . . ." screamed Jonah, struggling wildly with his father and brothers.

"Here, here, now . . ." began the constable, moving forward.

"Now then, my Jony!" warned old Henry. "Come on wi' us afore you gits yerself *lelled*!"

And so saying they hauled the liquor-crazed Jonah into a disused shed beside the public-house. They pushed him inside and slammed home the heavy door, bolting it on the outside and mopping their brows with relief. But the enraged Jonah, with the power lent him by his maniacal temper, pounded and kicked on the door from the inside, threatening to break out. Every few moments his pasty white face and shock of black curls appeared at a tiny window high up in the door as he bobbed up and down with rage.

"O my Jesus Christ A'mighty," breathed Henry. "My

Jony's like ten men when he's got the beer into him. Why, I reckons if he got out he'd kill that *gav* fer sure."

"Well, you settle it amongst yourselves—and make certain he doesn't do any damage," the policeman ordered, obviously not too anxious to handle Jonah alone.

The door continued to shake with the pounds and kicks it was receiving; and old Henry and his other sons shouted unavailingly for them to cease.

"Ar," said old Henry resignedly, "he'll bide quiet in a minute an' have a sleep. Then we can let un out an' take un over to the tea-house and gie him a drop o' tea, an' then he'll be so quiet as a mouse."

A little weasel-like man called Spider was demonstrating the prowess of a small pony in a black and yellow trap, which he was offering for sale to a group of mildly interested travellers.

The pony trotted, fast and slow, round and round the courtyard, lifting his feet high and well. Spider drove straight at us, pulling up sharply to a halt in front of our faces.

"Quietest pony wot anyone ever seed," he shouted in an ecstasy of salesmanship, carrying himself along on a wave of his own enthusiasm. He leapt from the trap and skipped over the shafts, placing himself between the pony's rear and the cart's front. He lay back against the pony's tail—the pony did not move. Spider jumped out again. "This pony's so quiet he'll follow me about like a dog," he asserted.

"Look now! See this!" and he walked a few paces in front of the pony, which obligingly followed him. We breathed a sigh of admiration. Spider ran under the pony's belly and crouched there.

"Why, a babby could drive un," he shouted, rushing out and lifting one of Alice's small girls into the trap and handing her the reins.

"Goo on, gal! Drive him round!" he shouted, assuring the somewhat worried Alice that all would be well. The child, not above four years old, picked up the reins, shook them up and down on the pony's back and professionally trotted the animal round before us.

"That's a quiet pony, Spider," exclaimed a man standing beside me, his weather-smashed face shining in approval.

"Now my Sam, is you gonna have a deal wi' me?" urged Spider. "You can see fer yerself I ain't offerin' you no rubbish. Yer eyes is yer guide, man."

"Have a deal wi' un, Sam," several bystanders echoed traditionally.

But Sam was not entirely happy.

"That's a pony as I can sell anywheres," Spider continued. "But I promised I'd gie you the fust chance, ain't that right?"

Sam still said nothing.

"Come on now, Sam. Gie me wot I said an' you can take un on—trap an' all." Spider's little wizened face set harder. "Come on! Quick! An' iffen you ain't got the money I'll trust you till I sees you next time. Ain't that fair?"

"That's fair," murmured the onlookers. "Go on, Sam —have a deal!"

Sam, however, who was somewhat the worse for drink, chose to become a trifle bellicose at the hint that he might not have sufficient money for the deal.

"I've a-got the money all right, my Spider," he returned

aggressively. "Fax the matter is I could show you more'n ever you could show me, brother."

He puffed hard on his cigarette, his face flushed with anger.

"Gaaaaaaaaaaoooooooooorrrrrnnnn!" the spectators exclaimed, becoming thoroughly out of sympathy with Sam owing to his not entering into the deal.

Spider's dark face set harder still, and he pulled the peak of his cap down further over his eyes, drawing in his lined cheeks with suppressed wrath. He eyed Sam for a moment.

"Go on! You foxin' hedge-mumper!" he spat. "Why, I can show you a hundred pun now this very minute—an' I'll bet that's fifty more'n you can, you bastard!"

"I've got more *vongar* than ever you seed in all yer life an' that's God's truth," Sam rejoined, still further insulted at the slur on his financial resources.

"Wot? I can show you two hundred pun now—an' if you can top that you're more of a man than I took you fer!" Spider jeered.

"Go an' hide yer face!" shouted Sam. "I've got more *vongar* than you—an' I'll knock you down to prove it."

So saying he tore off his overcoat and jacket and flung his cap down on the ground on top of them. Then he leapt out a few yards into a clear space, automatically striking a delightfully old-fashioned boxer's stance—straight from the period of the great Romani fighter Jem Mace. Thus, with forearms held vertically and fists clenched, he challenged Spider to defend himself and the honour of his exchequer. Spider, not to be outdone, also flung off his outer garments, and leaving his cap on, took up a similar pose. The two circled each other warily, aiming occasional wild blows at one another's heads. But the effect of so much circling caused the semi-intoxicated Sam to reel slightly, and Spider, quick to avail himself of the chance, grabbed him by the scarf and shook him bodily up, down and sideways, as a terrier shakes a rat. He was about to administer further and more telling punishment with his feet and fists when two con-stables appeared and demanded to know the cause of the disturbance.

"He'm a-killin' my man, policeman!" Alice shrieked wrathfully.

"Wot? A-killin' him? We wuz just havin' a talk—ain't that right, Sam?"

"I ain't a-bin kilt—we wuz jest a-havin' a talk, police-man," agreed Sam, muzzily looking round and sobering at the sight of the constables.

"That horse is loose over there. You'd better tie him up again," one of the policemen said, pointing towards a pony, harnessed in a trolley, which had walked across the forecourt of the public-house and wedged the cart between a lorry and a tree.

"We knows more about horses than you do, police-man," remarked a black-faced Romani man inconse-quently.

"I know you do, but you'd better tie him up or I shall be giving someone a paper about it," the constable re-joined severely.

"They both oughta be took, policeman," shouted old Emma, whose partial deafness had caused her to lose the trend of the conversation.

"Wot? You'll be took yerself iffen you carries on like that, mother," Spider shouted amidst much laughter.

"The dear ole 'oman wants another mush!" remarked

Orphie. "There's ole Jobi agin the tea-house—shall I
fetch un over, mother?"

"You brazen bastard!" screeched old Emma indignantly. "I don't want no ole Jobi—nor any other ole
mush neither. If one waren't nuff fer me then a hundred
wouldn't be!"

I left the dwindling group round Spider and Sam without waiting to see if they eventually did reach any
understanding over the pony. Caley and Rose came across
from the tea-house and we strolled aimlessly about for a
while, regardless of time. At a fair our people do not
consult the time. Some of the travellers, however, began
leaving—in lorries, motor-vans, ponies and carts and some
on foot for the bus stops. Benny was trying to sell an
enormous nickel watch. In a moment of drunken rashness
he agreed to toss a coin for it against the rotund and
cunning Billy. Billy was to pay five pounds if he lost the
toss—and have the watch if he won. He won.

"Ar well, I ain't the fust to lose on a bet—an' I ain't the
last neither," remarked Benny philosophically as Billy
complacently pocketed the watch, remarking smugly: "I
allus tole you I should have that watch offen you, ain't
that right, Benny?"

"If he hadn't had the beer into him he'd never a-bet
that ole watch away. Thinks the world of it he do,"
Caley said to me sadly.

Tilly, little Manny and his brother Daniel climbed into
a small governess cart, pulled by an aged bay pony—
little Manny climbing up the spokes of the wheel—and
set off at a smart trot.

"Let's go back now—are you ready?" I called to Rose
and Caley.

"Yeah, we'm ready. How about Lijah's wife an' gal? Did he sell the pony?" Rose asked.

I noticed Lijah's wife and daughter and called to them to jump in if they wished to ride back with us. They hurried over and climbed in.

"How about Lijah?" I asked.

"The man's so *motto* he ain't fit to come. Let un find his own ways back," his wife said sternly.

So with that, and with much shouting and waving of farewell to friends and relations, we set off on the homeward journey. The mare was glad to be off and trotted rapidly without needing any encouragement.

"If ever you wants to part from that mare will you let me have the first offer on her?" Caley asked.

I shouted yes as we trotted on. We passed a patchwork coloured group of travellers standing at a bus stop amongst some *gaujes*. We hastily shouted mock-abuse at them in passing, which was full-throatedly returned to the surprise and no little embarrassment of the non-Romani element in the bus queue.

"Ain't that ole Mary-Jane lookin' bad?" Rose shouted to Lijah's wife. "Why, she'm gone grey-headed, my sister, in two months. Pretty 'oman she wuz too. . . ."

The sun was setting and the night-cold returning; and I applied myself to my driving and let the shreds of conversation from the rear of the cart, partially drowned in the rattling of the horse's hooves and the grating of the iron bonds, flow over me. We passed a constable, slow-moving and dignified on his upright bicycle, going in the opposite direction.

" 'Evenin', policeman!" we shouted amiably.

His highly polished countenance swivelled in our

direction for a second as he continued coldly on his way.

"The poxy bastard!" Caley shouted.

We all laughed.

Soon enough we reached the edge of the wide common and I deposited my passengers who, shouting farewell, proceeded a trifle unsteadily towards their wagons, a dozen or more children coming running to meet them.

I drove on, singing, towards Louse Lane.

A day or two later, Beshlie and I found ourselves once more on the *drom*, heading up the country, again with a cold icy wind blowing in our faces.

As we drew near to our first stopping-place the roofs of three wagons already there came into view, and soon I was able to recognise their owners. The smoke was curling up from the *yogs* by the lane, the cries of the children and the shouts of the adults grew louder. . . . We were home again . . . for a day . . . for a week. . . . Who knows?

THE END

GLOSSARY OF ROMANI TERMS

'ATCHIN'TAN	Stopping-place
BAR	£1
BENG	Devil
BIKININ'	Hawking
BITI	Little, tiny
BOK	Luck
BORI	Great, big
CHAVIES	Children
CHOKS	Boots
CHOP	To exchange, swap
CHUR	Steal
COVELS	Things, belongings
DIDDIKAI	A half-Romani. Often incorrectly applied to *all* contemporary travellers
DIK	See, look
DIKLO	Neckerchief
DINILO	Fool, idiot
DORDI	(Oh) Dear
DRAB (ENGRO)	Doctor
DROM, TOBER	Road
FONI	Ring
FUNKEM	Medicine
GAUJO	Non-traveller, non-Romani
GAVMUSH, GAVVER	Policeman, police
GRAI, GRASNI	Horse, mare
GUSHNI	Cow
HOBEN	Food
JAL	Go
JUKEL	Dog
JUVEL	Woman
KANI	Fowl
KENNER, KER	House
KIPSI, TRUSHNI	Basket (for hawking)
KOSHTI	Sticks (usually applied to those used in peg-making)

KUSHTI	.. Good
LELLED	.. Caught, taken, arrested
LIVENA, LIVNOKER	.. Beer, public-house
LUE	.. A wind-shield of canvas sheets or blanketing stretched over hazel-rods
MASS	.. Meat
'MESKIE (corruption of *PEAMESKIE*)	.. Tea
MINCH	.. Term of abuse
MONG	.. Beg
MORO	.. Bread
MOTTO	.. Drunk
MULLO	.. Dead
MUSKERO	.. Police
OPEN LOT	.. Any living wagon with canvas roof and sides
PANI	.. Water
POOVE (the *GRAIS*)	.. To graze horses in a farmer's field at night without permission
PUKKER	.. Talk (usually meaning Romani)
RACKLO	.. Boy
RAI	.. Gentleman
ROCKER	.. Speak, talk
SWIGLER	.. Pipe
TAN	.. Tent, place
TOVER	.. Baccy
TRASHED	.. Frightened
TREADER	.. Bicycle
VASTIES	.. Fingers
VERDO (or *VARDO*)	.. Van, wagon
VESHENGRO	.. Gamekeeper
VONGAR	.. Money
VOODRUS	.. Bed
YAUKER	.. Gun
YOG	.. Fire
YOKS	.. Eyes
YOROS	.. Eggs

EPILOGUE

After the last of my three previous books was published I decided to take a break from writing in order that I could get on with life. The break was to last longer than I had envisaged: all but forty years in fact! Thus for me to peruse any of those books is, at best, like looking through the wrong end of a telescope at a world but dimly remembered and, at worst, like reading the words of a seeming stranger—neither condition to be recommended in my opinion. In all modesty the three books appear to have given honest, affectionate and heartfelt feelings of the times in which they were set. Amazing and changing times for the Travelling People, most of whom were exchanging horses and wagons for motors and trailers in ever-increasing numbers. Indeed, within a few years, by the early 'sixties, there were scarcely any horse-drawn Travellers left in southern England, Wales or the Midlands. Those who were unable to become merchandised had settled for the incongruous life of council house-dwellers.

I think that this, my first book—*Smoke in the Lanes*—will be viewed as my best achievement. Like a first marriage it possibly had about it a freshness, excitement and truth which no later experiences were likely to equal. To the best of my knowledge there are few other books in which the authors followed the paths I trod (and have continued to tread to this day!) *in the ways* I have, but for those who may have done I can only applaud them. Alas, however, most authors have tended to become bogged-down in either the realms of sheer romanticism (investing almost every aspect of behaviour, domestic or otherwise, with an esoteric mysticism of their own imagining). Or else dreaming of 'pure-blooded Romanies' and their tribal rites. Never actually earning their living on the roads (an essential requisite to being able to command a Traveller's respect) their viewpoints have not enabled them to catch the essential essences or moralities of the people with whom, on the surface, they were freely associating. One notable exception was the excellent little work entitled *The Gorse and the Briar* by Christopher and Patrick McEnvoy, published in 1939. Sadly, in one of the nasty tricks which the celestial powers have ever been wont to play against the most harmless and agreeable denizens of this planet, both the author and his brother, who provided talented pictorial embellishments to the book, were killed whilst on active service in the 1939-1945 War. Hence we were denied the pleasure of any further productions from either of them.

For me, who has known the most exacting poverty, never afforded the luxury (taken for granted these days!) of being 'signed-on', having to live in other people's cast-off clothing and eating poor quality victuals, combined with the harshest of outdoor living conditions—a stick-fire our only comfort and means of cooking. From the mid-'sixties onwards, however, our circumstances rose to comparative luxury, and I

can assure the reader that it provided a great relief.
Like malice, it is the *right amount* of possessions that
brings satisfaction. Romanies have always, through
recorded history, been conscious of the necessity of
retaining at least some resources—and rightly so.
Even George Borrow frequently recorded their
monetary dealings, in amounts far beyond his own
means, sometimes with wonder, at others with
disapproval! That bureaucracy and well-intentioned
but mis-guided do-gooders have, or soon will have,
achieved the feat or forcing the Travellers from the
roadsides and lanes of Britain cannot be denied.
Personally, and many might agree, I would prefer to
be stopping 'illegally camped' (as it is called today) on
a roadside, a car park, an old common or a piece of
wasteland, temporarily and without 'amenities', to
experiencing the trapped-feeling, fenced and walled-
in, on a miserably-situated council site (and I *have*
experienced it!)—despite the hot and cold running-
water, baths, lavatories, and 'educational facilities' and
prying health visitors. All the latter 'necessities' are as
nothing compared to the loss of the *feeling* of freedom
which is in the blood of almost all Travellers.

It is for the reader to ponder such vexatious
questions. Gypsy-people, in a never-ending, lifelong,
endeavour to keep up an independent economy, are
forever without the security which *gaujes* take for
granted. They have, of necessity, to grab at any
opportunity that presents itself. Theirs is not the life of
a kind of itinerant holidaymaker—as all too often
appears to be the conviction of the average *gaujo.*
Indeed, one may note with some rancour, that

whenever there are local press reports of an eviction of Travellers, or even of their undesired presence in their area, no credit is ever accorded to the Travellers for their abilities to actually earn a living, whilst providing themselves with decent trailer-caravans and motors, in the face of open hostility from all around them. It seems to evoke no wonder in the imaginations of outsiders that an existence can be successfully maintained in the face of almost universal condemnation by police and local authorities.

Since the year 2000 I have been producing a record of the alterations in the Travellers' lifestyle (and my own!) within these shores, from 1960 until 1999. In the course of time (not too long, I hope, as Time is My Enemy) I hope that these memoirs, which I have entitled *Over the Hills—Fragments of an Autobiography*, may appear to confront those few of my 'fans' from the past who are still extant! In the meantime, dear reader, please 'duck and dive' into this re-print of my first book: it is but one man's experience in a way of living now almost died out. Lived by people whose social expectations can never be repeated in the world of today, whose children would have been taken from them by rabid social-workers with no respect for traditions of a Separate People. I was never-failingly amazed and rewarded by their generosity and style, their disshevelled beauty and their eternal optimism.

Friendship and admiration is what this, and my other books, are supposed to be about.

Dominic Reeve—May 2002